Encounters With Archetypes

Advanced Curriculum From Vanderbilt University's Programs for Talented Youth

Encounters With Archetypes

Integrated ELA Lessons for Gifted and Advanced Learners in Grades 4–5

Tamra Stambaugh, Ph.D.,
Emily Mofield, Ed.D.,
Eric Fecht, Ed.D., & Kim Knauss

NEW YORK AND LONDON

First published in 2019 by Prufrock Press Inc.

Published in 2021 by Routledge
605 Third Avenue, New York, NY 10017
2 Park Square, Milton Park, Abingdon, Oxon OX14 4RN

Routledge is an imprint of the Taylor & Francis Group, an informa business.

Copyright © 2019 by Taylor & Francis Group.

Cover and layout design by Allegra Denbo

All rights reserved. No part of this book may be reprinted or reproduced or utilised in any form or by any electronic, mechanical, or other means, now known or hereafter invented, including photocopying and recording, or in any information storage or retrieval system, without permission in writing from the publishers.

Notice:
Product or corporate names may be trademarks or registered trademarks, and are used only for identification and explanation without intent to infringe.

ISBN: 978-1-0321-4424-5 (hbk)
ISBN: 978-1-6182-1806-3 (pbk)

DOI: 10.4324/9781003234890

Table of Contents

Acknowledgements vii
Introduction 1
Pretest 16
Pretest Rubric 21

Lesson 1	Understanding Encounters: Concept Introduction 23
Lesson 2	Understanding Archetypes and Their Origins 35
Lesson 3	Encounters With Character Archetypes 49
Lesson 4	Encounters With Our World and Ourselves 61
Lesson 5	Encounters With Situational Archetypes 79
Lesson 6	Encounters as Experiences 97
Lesson 7	Novel Study: Encounters With Archetypes 115
Lesson 8	Encounters With Symbolic Archetypes 131
Lesson 9	Encounters With Symbols, Images, and Visual Media 155
Lesson 10	Encounters With Art 167
Lesson 11	Writing Narratives With Archetypes 179
Lesson 12	Encounters With Archetypes 193

Posttest 197
Posttest Rubric 202
References 203
Appendix A: Instructions for Using the Models 205
Appendix B: Blank Models and Guides 231
Appendix C: Rubrics 243
About the Authors 247
Common Core State Standards Alignment 249

Acknowledgements

We would like to acknowledge several individuals who have been influential in the shaping of this unit. Dr. Joyce VanTassel-Baska and her Integrated Curriculum Model and inspirational work in curriculum development continue to breathe life into content in ways that provide students with opportunities to access advanced content, explore content in depth and with complexity, and examine abstract relationships through concept development. Additionally, we acknowledge the content experts in various fields who willingly shared their passions and helped us translate advanced content into student-centered lessons. We also acknowledge those students and teachers who piloted lessons and provided constructive feedback.

Introduction

Encounters With Archetypes integrates the study of archetypes with the concept of encounters. Students will read and analyze fictional and informational texts, speeches, and visual media as they learn about character, situational, and symbolic archetypes, and discuss how encounters in stories are similar to and different from encounters in their own lives. This unit, developed by Vanderbilt University's Programs for Talented Youth, is aligned to the Common Core State Standards (CCSS) for English Language Arts and features accelerated content, engaging activities, and differentiated tasks and assessments.

CONCEPTUAL FRAMEWORK

Encounters With Archetypes is designed specifically for gifted elementary school students (grades 4–5) to support the acquisition of textual analysis skills, including identifying the relationship between literary elements within a text, enhancing thinking and communication skills, and connecting conceptual generalizations from crosscurricular themes through a variety of media, including literary texts, nonfiction texts, video, and art. The Integrated Curriculum Model (ICM; VanTassel-Baska, 1986) is the conceptual framework used for the unit design. Components of the framework are embedded in each lesson: accelerated content, advanced processes of the discipline (e.g., literary analysis), and conceptual understandings. For example, the accelerated content includes English language arts (ELA) standards, aligned to the CCSS. The CCSS selected for each unit are above the grade level(s) for which the unit was intended. Additionally, higher level resources are used in a variety of lessons. Each lesson also includes videos, specific models, or activities to help students analyze a variety of texts and art in ways that develop their own expertise. The content of each lesson is connected by the overarching theme of encounters and key generalizations that connect to a variety of literary and informational texts and events, particularly in ELA and, perhaps, social studies.

INTENDED GRADE LEVEL(S)

The positive academic effects of grouping gifted students and accelerating the content they are taught are well documented (see Assouline, Colangelo, VanTassel-Baska, & Lupkowski-Shoplik, 2015; Kulik & Kulik, 1992; Steenbergen-Hu, Makel, & Olszewski-Kubilius, 2016; Rogers, 2007). Not all elementary and middle schools, however, are designed to support accelerated courses for their high-achieving students. Experienced teachers of general classrooms may use this unit with their gifted and high-achieving students as part of a deliberate differentiated approach that includes in-class flexible groupings based on student needs.

This unit is intended for gifted students in grades 4–5. The unit is aligned to CCSS standards primarily focused on grades 6–7, with some lower grade standards included as needed. The accelerated content is necessary so that gifted students have the opportunity to gain new ELA content knowledge at a pace and level that are appropriate for their learning needs. Gifted students' readiness and experience levels vary, as do their abilities. Because school contexts and content emphases are different, it is up to each teacher to determine whether the unit is best suited for their particular students and at which grade levels. Some gifted students may find this unit engaging as a fourth or fifth grader (or younger), while others may find the unit more engaging in middle school.

LESSON FORMAT AND GUIDELINES

Each lesson in this unit follows a similar format for ease of use. Teachers select from a variety of questions, activities, and differentiated products to best meet their students' needs. Table 1 provides a summary of lessons with key questions and topics. There are also opportunities for talent development and discussion of social-emotional components within the curriculum. Key features of the unit and each section of the lesson plan are outlined next.

Alignment to Standards

The unit incorporates the key pedagogical shifts highlighted as part of the CCSS. For example, students read both literary and informational texts from a variety of sources to show their understanding of key concepts and ideas. Through the examination of multiple texts, they learn domain-specific content from their readings and are required to provide text-based evidence to support their answers or ideas. The ELA-focused lessons also support opportunities for students to make or analyze an argument, defend a position, or interpret a text. Of course, part of close

Introduction

Table 1
Lesson Summaries

	Lesson	Key Question	Summary
1	*Understanding Encounters: Concept Introduction*	How do encounters shape ourselves and our world?	Students are introduced to the concept of encounters and explore how encounter generalizations are evident in the short story "Eleven" by Sandra Cisneros.
2	*Understanding Archetypes and Their Origins*	How do encounters with archetypes help us understand the human experience?	Students learn about the origins of archetypes and begin to see how archetypes are part of every culture by looking at European and Japanese versions of a similar fairy tale. Students examine archetypes in children's books, relating archetypes to encounter generalizations.
3	*Encounters With Character Archetypes*	How is our understanding of characters enhanced through our encounters with archetypes?	Students take a more in-depth look at character archetypes and the ways in which encounters shape our understanding of them. After reading "The Dog of Pompeii," students examine the interactions among literary elements and explore how characters are shaped by their encounters with situations and events.
4	*Encounters With Our World and Ourselves*	How do encounters with situations allow for reflection and change?	Students learn about encounters that make up the hero's journey and explore Joseph Campbell's ideas of the monomyth. Students examine if and how the hero's journey is evident in a short film, a poem, and short biographies of Oprah Winfrey, Mother Teresa, Jackie Robinson, Sally Ride, and Lin-Manuel Miranda.
5	*Encounters With Situational Archetypes*	How do encounters with situational archetypes shape our views?	Students learn how encounters with situational archetypes, such as unhealable wounds, tasks, and good vs. evil, shape perspectives. After reading through an excerpt from President Reagan's First Inaugural Address, students complete a rhetorical analysis and examine the situational encounters within the speech. Students also compare Reagan's speech to an excerpt from Maya Angelou's poem "On the Pulse of Morning."

Table 1, *continued*

	Lesson	Key Question	Summary
6	*Encounters as Experiences*	Do our experiences shape us, or do we shape our experiences?	Students examine how encounters between situational archetypes and character archetypes determine perspectives about experiences. This is examined by reading two texts, "The Emperor's New Clothes" and "The King and the Poisoned Well," followed by linking these ideas to texts and video clips from previous lessons.
7	*Novel Study: Encounters With Archetypes*	How do encounters with literature and archetypes allow for reflection and change?	Students select one novel, *Counting by 7s* or *Wonder*, as a vehicle for them to examine the different ways that literary elements interact and to determine how encounters are used to reveal character, situational, and symbolic archetypes to provide meaning.
8	*Encounters With Symbolic Archetypes*	How do symbols in texts allow for a deeper understanding of the author's message?	Students read "Rikki-Tikki-Tavi" and analyze how symbols interact with other literary elements to provide a deeper understanding of the story's message.
9	*Encounters With Symbols, Images, and Visual Media*	How are messages conveyed through encounters with images and symbols?	Using a variety of commercials, students explore ways in which symbolic archetypes are used by companies to sell products or experiences. Students complete a rhetorical analysis of the commercial "Built to Serve" and hypothesize why the everyday person archetype is used.
10	*Encounters With Art*	How do artists use their work to convey messages?	Using the painting *Landscape With the Fall of Icarus* by Pieter Bruegel the Elder and *Invisible Homeless* by Luke Jerram, students complete a visual analysis and examine the ways that artists use their work to tell a story or send a message to those who encounter it.

Table 1, continued

	Lesson	Key Question	Summary
11	*Writing Narratives With Archetypes*	How do authors use encounters with archetypes to convey meaning?	Students watch a video of an author explaining how stories are developed. They then analyze a short video and discuss how story elements interact in ways that have relevance and meaning by applying archetypes as a way of communicating their own experiences and feelings. Students write their own narratives, shaping character archetypes through situations, symbols, and encounters.
12	*Encounters With Archetypes*	How do encounters with archetypes in real life and fiction allow for a deeper understanding of ourselves and our world?	Students are provided various options to demonstrate their understanding of content, advanced process, and concept connections throughout the unit through a project of their choice.

reading and understanding of a text includes the use of domain-specific vocabulary. The readings selected throughout the unit build upon specific concepts and showcase a variety of texts and media.

The beginning of each lesson includes a list of the overarching goals and objectives as well as CCSS specific to each lesson. The end of the unit includes a CCSS alignment chart. This unit was not designed to meet every CCSS ELA standard for a particular grade level but focuses in depth on advanced skills. Supplemental information may be necessary to complement a full literature course and ensure that all required content for a specific grade level is taught.

Materials

When differentiating for the gifted, it is important for the materials and readings to be at a level commensurate with the student's ability. The readings and resources in this unit have been carefully selected and include either sophisticated concepts or reading selections at or above the indicated grade level. The materials section includes a list of resources needed for the lesson. Some of the listed materials are optional, and many of the selected texts, visuals, or videos are readily available online as a free download. When possible, reliable sites and specific links, available at the time of this unit's printing, are provided.

A word of caution: Some of the readings or some concepts may be controversial or contain advanced or sensitive concepts and content. It is up to the teacher and school administration to understand the context of his or her district and to determine whether or not a reading or discussion is appropriate or whether a different text or question should be used.

Introductory Activities

The introductory activities provide a real-world connection or "hook" that sets the tone for the remainder of the lesson and enhances student engagement. Sample options include quick debates about an issue or dilemma, illustrations to convey a key concept or idea, or key discussion questions that help students better understand the relevance of a lesson's text, art, or content-based concepts. Often these introductory debate topics or discussion questions are revisited at the close of the lesson, allowing students to review their initial answer or stances given newly learned content.

In-Class Activities to Deepen Learning

The activities included here provide hands-on or thought-provoking ideas that support or solidify student learning. These tasks are considered to be the core of the lesson content. Tasks incorporate hands-on activities, real-world connections, and opportunities to construct explanations through the development and use of analysis models. The activities in this section are intended to be modeled and discussed and to allow for more practice of new or previously learned information.

Choice-Based Differentiated Products

Several choice-based differentiated products are also part of each lesson. Students may select one of the choice products to showcase their strengths and individual understanding of a particular content area, or, if pressed for time, teachers may require two or three choice-based products from various lessons for students to complete during the course of the unit. The options listed allow students an opportunity to pursue their interests and to gain a deeper understanding of a learning objective as they present their understanding in a creative way. Differentiated products vary by lesson and may include investigating a real-world problem, designing visuals to represent abstract ideas or conceptual understanding, applying an advanced model to other related sources, writing essays, and developing products or presentations for an audience. Rubrics are provided in Appendix C to guide product creation and teacher feedback. The rubrics may also be used for peer and self-evaluations.

Opportunities for Talent Development

Students need opportunities to build upon their interests, strengths, and curiosity in ways that expose them to new ideas and allow them to extend their learning. This section provides students with ideas and opportunities to go beyond the unit or lesson principles in a variety of ways that are connected to the lesson content but expanded to engage students in in-depth study or to help them learn new information that is not part of a key standard or objective.

Social-Emotional Connections

Social-emotional connections are an important part of processing and understanding oneself in addition to relating to events in a story. The social-emotional connections are meant to encourage students to identify with story characters, biographies, and lives of others; learn about career trajectories; and create meaning from the lesson content to their own personal lives, understanding the real-world implications and relevance for them as part of self-reflection.

ELA Tasks

Designed with the CCSS assessments in mind, the ELA tasks support the writing and argument analysis items typically tested as part of a state assessment. The ELA tasks incorporate multiple standards and require complex thinking. Students are asked to respond to a prompt by creating a well-developed essay in which they create or analyze arguments, critique texts, explain an issue from multiple perspectives, or explain the development of key concepts presented in an informational or fictional text. It is at the teacher's discretion to determine how many practice tasks students should write throughout the course of the unit. Although not explicitly instructed in each lesson, teachers are encouraged to model the writing and literary analysis process, help students analyze exemplars and inappropriate responses, and provide individual feedback.

Concept Connections

The concept connections section focuses on the third component of the ICM. The purpose of this section is to help students see the relationships between different texts and perspectives as they relate to key generalizations about encounters. A graphic organizer comprised of the conceptual generalizations and key unit read-

Encounters With Archetypes

ings is provided in the unit to help students organize their ideas and determine connections among the various readings. It is important to refer to the concept generalizations in each lesson, even if the concept chart is not completed for every lesson. It is also recommended that teachers create a concept map-working wall that students can continue to build upon throughout the unit. Teachers may post the specific concept generalizations on a wall or bulletin board and ask students to add relevant content understanding and connections between concepts and newly learned content to the wall after a lesson. This can be used as an informal assessment and way to help students continue to reflect upon and process their learning.

Assessment

The assessment section focuses on assessing a student's understanding of a single-faceted objective, such as making inferences or determining how an author used a literary element to convey an idea or theme. The assessments may be used to determine the extent to which students understand the meaning of a text or content and can provide supporting evidence and target instruction based on individual needs. Teachers may require students to complete an assessment, a variety of different formative assessment tasks throughout the lesson (e.g., responses to questions, concept connections), or differentiated product tasks so that students' thinking and understanding can be measured in a variety of ways. Additionally, exit tickets are included in this section to check for understanding of various lesson concepts and content. They may be used to guide whether or not teachers need to reteach portions of a lesson or concept.

Handouts

Following each lesson, all necessary handouts for lesson completion are included (e.g., readings, visuals, organizers, blank analysis models, and other resources not readily available online). As previously stated in the materials section, sometimes teachers are led to specific web-based links or it is recommended that popular sources be found online. This is especially important for featured art or graphs (which may not copy well). Also know that if picture books are recommended, teachers may be able to find read alouds in their classroom, school library, or through general web-based searches.

Other Unit Features

This unit includes a culminating lesson that synthesizes many of the learning objectives into a comprehensive project so that students may showcase their learning in a creative way. These options may include the application of the advanced content learned throughout the unit, real-world problem solving, and the development of authentic products. Additionally, the culminating lesson includes opportunities for students to focus on in-depth self-reflections that relate concept-themes to real-world connections. Rubrics are provided so that students understand the expectations of a task and teachers can easily analyze student products given set criteria. The rubrics are also useful for peer and self-evaluations.

Teacher background information is another feature found in some lessons. Although some background information is provided, teachers are encouraged to study specific literary analysis critiques for a particular reading and seek varied interpretations of the text or visual. When needed, lessons include a section on background knowledge, primarily as videos teachers can watch or suggested articles. We encourage teachers to view this information well in advance of lesson implementation.

Sample responses are also included for some of the more complex questions and analysis models. It is important to understand that the answers provided are a guide and should not be construed as the only correct response. Student answers will vary, and many unanticipated responses may be correct. Teachers are encouraged to use the provided answers to better understand the intent of the question, to model how to arrive at an appropriate response, to demonstrate how to use a specific analysis model, and to familiarize themselves with the intent of a particular passage.

Finally, this unit features instructions for using models, sample lessons, blank model handouts, and guides to support students' thinking about each element of a given analysis model. Rubrics are also provided to assess student products and responses. Specifically, Appendix A highlights instructions, handouts, and examples for each analysis model. Appendix B includes blank models and guides for thinking about each element of a particular model, and Appendix C includes rubrics for assessing student progress.

Time Allotment

Most lessons can be taught within 90–120 minutes, although some lessons may take longer. The length of the lesson also depends upon how many models and activities are employed, how interested students are in a particular issue or text, the length of the text, and time needed for fully working through steps in analysis or writing processes. The length may also depend on how many times a text needs to be read or analyzed or a lesson needs to be discussed or retaught for students to gain understanding. In general, it is anticipated that this unit can be taught with approximately 30–40 hours of instruction time if teachers follow the recommended guidelines as reported in this section.

The unit is designed so that the introductory activities and the in-class activities to deepen learning be taught for each lesson. Depending upon the time available, teachers may vary each lesson conclusion with an additional activity from one or more of the following sections, varying the selected section throughout the unit so that students have equitable exposure to each—choice-based activities, concept connection activities, and social-emotional needs activities. For students who need extensions or want to dig deeper into a particular topic, teachers can encourage students to embark on another choice-based activity not presented as part of the lesson or activities from the talent development section. The ELA tasks and exit ticket assessments can be used to measure progress and student understanding along with products created from the social-emotional, choice-based, or concept connection sections.

Evidence Support for the Unit

Besides the use of an evidence-supported conceptual framework (ICM), the models used in the unit are vetted by content experts and designed to develop expertise in ELA. Data collected from previous unit pilots in this series that applied the same models implemented in this unit but with different content yielded statistically significant and important pre-/post-results (*d ranging from* .5 to 1.4). This unit was piloted with rising fourth and fifth graders ($N = 9$) in an accelerated summer program with positive pre-post gains using a concept map focused on archetypes and making inferences with text. Additionally, the unit was piloted with gifted sixth graders in a local school district using open-ended questions as found in this unit. Students ($N = 62$) made statistically significant pretest ($M = 4.23$, $SD = 2.1$) to posttest ($M = 8.24$, $SD = 2.4$) gains [t (-10.78), $p < .000$)] with important academic effects ($d = 1.37$) after correcting for dependence (see Morris & DeShon, 2002). After instruction, students were able to provide more meaningful and accurate examples of archetypes, make connections among various archetypes and their features, and provide in-depth information about archetypes.

Differentiation

Gifted students are a heterogeneous group and their ability levels, pace of learning, interests, and depth of understanding vary. Although this unit was written with gifted elementary school students in mind, differentiation is still necessary. A variety of differentiated opportunities are embedded in the unit, such as choice-based product options, open-ended questions, and more simple and complex ways to adapt the analysis models and adjust instruction based on students' readiness and interest.

Introduction

In addition to the individual lesson activities and differentiated product options found in each lesson, the final lesson synthesizes unit goals and provides opportunities for students to select a project of their own choosing to explore in depth. The close reading questions can also be differentiated. Teachers may assign specific questions or tasks to individual students or groups of students based on their responses from formative assessments, concept maps, content specific lessons, or ELA tasks.

The ELA process model (e.g., literary analysis) is easily differentiated as well. For example, the Literary Analysis Wheel automatically provides a framework for teachers to ask simple questions using only one element, or more complex questions by emphasizing relationships among various elements (e.g., how setting influences conflict, how figurative language contributes to characterization). Examples of simple and complex questions are included in selected lessons and also in Appendix A. The teacher may also differentiate the in-class activities by assigning different groups of students to specific tasks. Of course, not all students would complete work at every station, but would be assigned a station based on their readiness. After the complexity of the task is established, activities, questions, or product choices are then incorporated to accommodate various learning needs. The process is similar for writing and the use of the rhetorical and visual analysis wheel (also in Appendix A).

Assessment and Grading

Formative, diagnostic-prescriptive, and summative performance-based assessments are an essential part of the unit. Assessment data come from a variety of sources and are used to monitor student growth, provide student feedback, allow for student self-reflection, or differentiate content or instruction. Descriptions of the assessments used in this unit are as follows:

- **Diagnostic-prescriptive assessment:** The unit pretest provides a first glimpse of a student's current level of performance. Each question focuses on a different key understanding. For example, Question 1 focuses on the relationship between different literary elements, Question 2 focuses on making inferences and providing evidence, and Question 3 focuses on concepts or themes. Responses for each question can be used to differentiate questions for different groups of students and to assign specific tasks that support student learning in a key area. Prior to Lesson 1, administer the pretest and use the rubric to score responses, and use this data and other information gathered throughout the unit for ongoing differentiation.
- **Formative assessment:** There are many opportunities throughout the unit for teachers to check for student understanding. Teachers may occasionally ask students to expand, in writing, upon their answer to an assigned ques-

tion from the text-dependent questions. The ELA tasks may also be assigned and graded to determine the level of student understanding, as well as misconceptions about specific sources or texts that may need reteaching or further exploration. It is not recommended that every lesson's assessment task be assigned or graded, although teachers may select two or three of each throughout the course of the unit to use for this purpose. Informally, teachers may gather formative assessment data by listening to student discussions to ensure that students are learning the information presented and mastering or exceeding the goals. Differentiated choice products may also be used as a formative assessment and graded using the provided rubric. Teachers should encourage students to engage in self-reflection as they receive feedback from a variety of assessments. Additionally, it is recommended that students continue to build and develop a concept map-working wall to show their understanding of encounters, including the overlap of encounters with archetypes.

- **Summative assessment:** There are two different summative assessments in the unit. The final lesson (Lesson 12) includes culminating choice-based products for students to showcase their understanding of key unit content, processes, and concepts through selected product-creations. In addition, the postassessment of the unit can be used as a summative assessment and also to measure student growth, when compared with the preassessment.

MAKING THE MOST OUT OF THE UNIT

The following ideas are important to consider before teaching the unit:
- Provide professional development about the units that includes both content and pedagogy. Some of the unit content is complex, and background knowledge may be needed. Read the instructions and examples for using the analysis models in Appendix A before teaching the unit. Practice completing the models on your own using specific texts before asking the students to do so.
- For those students who need more scaffolding in ELA, consider teaching the models, expectations, and processes separately first with easier texts to get students accustomed to different ways of thinking before adding complex resources, issues, and concepts.
- You may need to teach the individual elements of each analysis model before combining them. Still, it isn't necessary to teach an entire unit on characterization or setting, for example, before using the literary analysis model, although students may need explanations and practice applying the

Introduction

individual elements first if they haven't been exposed to those ideas prior to this unit. This can be done in context and not separately. Because gifted students learn at a faster pace, teaching individual elements can be done more quickly so that you can focus on depth and complexity through the relationships between the different elements.
- Read the texts and prompts ahead of time to make sure the selections are appropriate for your district context. Substitute readings and visuals as appropriate. Similarly, in non-ELA content lessons, read the background knowledge information or follow the URLs provided to learn more, prior to teaching the lesson—especially if the content is unfamiliar. Attempt the assignments prior to teaching each lesson, so that you can predict potential outcomes, better support student learning, and provide tips or predict potential issues students may encounter. For all lessons, make sure the online resources and videos are still available before teaching a particular lesson. All URLs were active at the time of this printing.
- Follow your students. Sometimes a lesson or reading may prompt important discussions that continue beyond the allotted time period.
- Know the intent of the models and the lesson outcomes so that you can best guide students toward important process, content, and concept goals. Otherwise, the issues discussed may supersede the objectives, especially with passionate gifted students. Don't assign text-dependent questions as in-depth writing activities or homework as the norm. Discussion and teacher feedback are important, and most of the questions in the unit are intended to be part of a small- or whole-group discussion. By engaging students through group discussions, you can correct misconceptions right away and solicit multiple perspectives and ideas that can enhance student learning. Similarly, know that differentiated tasks and talent development sections are not intended to be assigned for every lesson or as homework for each student. Instead these talent development opportunities and assignment tasks are options that may be used in some lessons to further extend student learning. Teachers may require that students complete at least two differentiated tasks or talent development assignments for the entire unit.
- Be sure to emphasize the use of supporting evidence and the complex relationships among various elements of a model when facilitating student discussions.
- Have fun! We hope these units not only show academic gains in your students similar to what we have observed and quantified, but also encourage them to become citizens who can critically analyze situations and enact positive change while learning something new about themselves and their world.

UNIT GENERALIZATIONS

- Encounters allow for reflection and change.
- Encounters allow for prediction.
- Encounters can result in positive or negative outcomes.
- Encounters may result in threats and opportunities.

UNIT GOALS AND OBJECTIVES

Content

To analyze and interpret fiction, nonfiction, and art, students will be able to:
- compare and contrast how literary, visual, informational, and/or primary source texts reveal patterns and themes;
- analyze characters' conflicts, motives, values, thoughts and actions;
- compare and contrast the use of specific techniques various authors use to approach and develop similar ideas;
- identify and analyze archetypal patterns in stories, speeches, and real-world contexts and discuss how they are shaped by the author or real-world individuals or events; and
- analyze how multiple literary elements interact over the course of the text to develop the theme.

Process

To develop interpretation, analysis, and communication skills in the language arts, students will be able to:
- justify inferences with evidence from the text;
- elaborate in discussion or in writing on how authors use language and literary elements to create meaning;
- apply evidence to support explanations and opinions relative to a question, text, or issue;
- respond to an analysis of literature, nonfiction, media, or art by developing arguments and elaborating on explanations through writing a variety of texts (e.g., essays, paragraphs), including relevant and sufficient evidence to support claims; and
- develop character archetypes through encounters with other characters, situations, and symbols.

Introduction

Concept

To develop conceptual thinking about encounters in language arts and additional content areas, students will be able to:
- explain with evidence how encounters may lead to positive or negative outcomes in literature, media, and real-world examples;
- explain how encounters allow for reflection and change using literature, media, and real-world examples;
- explain how encounters may allow for opportunities and threats using evidence from a variety of texts and real-world examples;
- explain how encounters allow for prediction within literature and real-world examples;
- relate encounter generalizations to real-life situations; and
- examine the relationship between encounters and other concepts in multiple contexts.

Name: _____ Date: _____

Pretest

"Cinderella; or The Little Glass Slipper" *by Charles Perrault*

Directions: Read the passage and respond to the following questions, citing evidence from the text. Complete the questions within 35 minutes, using a separate sheet of paper if necessary.

Once there was a gentleman who married, for his second wife, the proudest and most haughty woman that was ever seen. She had, by a former husband, two daughters of her own, who were, indeed, exactly like her in all things. He had likewise, by another wife, a young daughter, but of unparalleled goodness and sweetness of temper, which she took from her mother, who was the best creature in the world.

No sooner were the ceremonies of the wedding over but the stepmother began to show herself in her true colors. She could not bear the good qualities of this pretty girl, and the less because they made her own daughters appear the more odious. She employed her in the meanest work of the house. She scoured the dishes, tables, etc., and cleaned madam's chamber, and those of misses, her daughters. She slept in a sorry garret, on a wretched straw bed, while her sisters slept in fine rooms, with floors all inlaid, on beds of the very newest fashion, and where they had looking glasses so large that they could see themselves at their full length from head to foot.

The poor girl bore it all patiently, and dared not tell her father, who would have scolded her; for his wife governed him entirely. When she had done her work, she used to go to the chimney corner, and sit down there in the cinders and ashes, which caused her to be called Cinderwench. Only the younger sister, who was not so rude and uncivil as the older one, called her Cinderella. However, Cinderella, notwithstanding her coarse apparel, was a hundred times more beautiful than her sisters, although they were always dressed very richly.

It happened that the king's son gave a ball, and invited all persons of fashion to it. Our young misses were also invited, for they cut a very grand figure among those of quality. They were mightily delighted at this invitation, and wonderfully busy in selecting the gowns, petticoats, and hair dressing that would best become them. This was a new difficulty for Cinderella; for it was she who ironed her sister's linen and pleated their ruffles. They talked all day long of nothing but how they should be dressed.

"For my part," said the eldest, "I will wear my red velvet suit with French trimming." "And I," said the youngest, "shall have my usual petticoat; but then, to make amends for that, I will put on my gold-flowered cloak, and my diamond stomacher, which is far from being the most ordinary one in the world."

They sent for the best hairdresser they could get to make up their headpieces and adjust their hairdos, and they had their red brushes and patches from Mademoiselle de la Poche. They also consulted Cinderella in all these matters, for she had excellent ideas, and her advice was always good. Indeed, she even offered her services to fix their hair, which they

Pretest, continued

very willingly accepted. As she was doing this, they said to her, "Cinderella, would you not like to go to the ball?"

"Alas!" said she, "you only jeer me; it is not for such as I am to go to such a place." "You are quite right," they replied. "It would make the people laugh to see a Cinderwench at a ball."

Anyone but Cinderella would have fixed their hair awry, but she was very good, and dressed them perfectly well. They were so excited that they hadn't eaten a thing for almost two days. Then they broke more than a dozen laces trying to have themselves laced up tightly enough to give them a fine slender shape. They were continually in front of their looking glass. At last the happy day came. They went to court, and Cinderella followed them with her eyes as long as she could. When she lost sight of them, she started to cry.

Her godmother, who saw her all in tears, asked her what was the matter. "I wish I could. I wish I could." She was not able to speak the rest, being interrupted by her tears and sobbing. This godmother of hers, who was a fairy, said to her, "You wish that you could go to the ball; is it not so?"

"Yes," cried Cinderella, with a great sigh. "Well," said her godmother, "be but a good girl, and I will contrive that you shall go." Then she took her into her chamber, and said to her, "Run into the garden, and bring me a pumpkin." Cinderella went immediately to gather the finest she could get, and brought it to her godmother, not being able to imagine how this pumpkin could help her go to the ball. Her godmother scooped out all the inside of it, leaving nothing but the rind. Having done this, she struck the pumpkin with her wand, and it was instantly turned into a fine coach, gilded all over with gold.

She then went to look into her mousetrap, where she found six mice, all alive, and ordered Cinderella to lift up a little the trapdoor. She gave each mouse, as it went out, a little tap with her wand, and the mouse was that moment turned into a fine horse, which altogether made a very fine set of six horses of a beautiful mouse colored dapple gray. Being at a loss for a coachman, Cinderella said, "I will go and see if there is not a rat in the rat trap that we can turn into a coachman."

"You are right," replied her godmother, "Go and look." Cinderella brought the trap to her, and in it there were three huge rats. The fairy chose the one which had the largest beard, touched him with her wand, and turned him into a fat, jolly coachman, who had the smartest whiskers that eyes ever beheld. After that, she said to her, "Go again into the garden, and you will find six lizards behind the watering pot. Bring them to me." She had no sooner done so but her godmother turned them into six footmen, who skipped up immediately behind the coach, with their liveries all bedaubed with gold and silver, and clung as close behind each other as if they had done nothing else their whole lives. The fairy then said to Cinderella, "Well, you see here an equipage fit to go to the ball with; are you not pleased with it?"

"Oh, yes," she cried; "but must I go in these nasty rags?" Her godmother then touched her with her wand, and, at the same instant, her clothes turned into cloth of gold and silver, all beset with jewels. This done, she gave her a pair of glass slippers, the prettiest in the whole world. Being thus decked out, she got up into her coach; but her godmother, above all things, commanded her not to stay past midnight, telling her, at the same time, that if she stayed one moment longer, the coach would be a pumpkin again, her horses mice, her

Pretest, continued

coachman a rat, her footmen lizards, and that her clothes would become just as they were before.

She promised her godmother to leave the ball before midnight; and then drove away, scarcely able to contain herself for joy. The king's son, who was told that a great princess, whom nobody knew, had arrived, ran out to receive her. He gave her his hand as she alighted from the coach, and led her into the hall, among all the company. There was immediately a profound silence. Everyone stopped dancing, and the violins ceased to play, so entranced was everyone with the singular beauties of the unknown newcomer. Nothing was then heard but a confused noise of, "How beautiful she is! How beautiful she is!" The king himself, old as he was, could not help watching her, and telling the queen softly that it was a long time since he had seen so beautiful and lovely a creature. All the ladies were busied in considering her clothes and headdress, hoping to have some made next day after the same pattern, provided they could find such fine materials and as able hands to make them.

The king's son led her to the most honorable seat, and afterwards took her out to dance with him. She danced so very gracefully that they all more and more admired her. A fine meal was served up, but the young prince ate not a morsel, so intently was he busied in gazing on her.

She went and sat down by her sisters, showing them a thousand civilities, giving them part of the oranges and citrons which the prince had presented her with, which very much surprised them, for they did not know her. While Cinderella was thus amusing her sisters, she heard the clock strike eleven and three-quarters, whereupon she immediately made a courtesy to the company and hurried away as fast as she could.

Arriving home, she ran to seek out her godmother, and, after having thanked her, she said she could not but heartily wish she might go to the ball the next day as well, because the king's son had invited her. As she was eagerly telling her godmother everything that had happened at the ball, her two sisters knocked at the door, which Cinderella ran and opened. "You stayed such a long time!" she cried, gaping, rubbing her eyes and stretching herself as if she had been sleeping; she had not, however, had any manner of inclination to sleep while they were away from home.

"If you had been at the ball," said one of her sisters, "you would not have been tired with it. The finest princess was there, the most beautiful that mortal eyes have ever seen. She showed us a thousand civilities, and gave us oranges and citrons." Cinderella seemed very indifferent in the matter. Indeed, she asked them the name of that princess; but they told her they did not know it, and that the king's son was very uneasy on her account and would give all the world to know who she was. At this Cinderella, smiling, replied, "She must, then, be very beautiful indeed; how happy you have been! Could not I see her? Ah, dear Charlotte, do lend me your yellow dress which you wear every day."

"Yes, to be sure!" cried Charlotte; "lend my clothes to such a dirty Cinderwench as you are! I should be such a fool." Cinderella, indeed, well expected such an answer, and was very glad of the refusal; for she would have been sadly put to it, if her sister had lent her what she asked for jestingly. The next day the two sisters were at the ball, and so was Cinderella, but dressed even more magnificently than before. The king's son was always by her, and never ceased his compliments and kind speeches to her. All this was so far from being tiresome to

Name: _____ Date: _____

Pretest, continued

her, and, indeed, she quite forgot what her godmother had told her. She thought that it was no later than eleven when she counted the clock striking twelve. She jumped up and fled, as nimble as a deer. The prince followed, but could not overtake her. She left behind one of her glass slippers, which the prince picked up most carefully. She reached home, but quite out of breath, and in her nasty old clothes, having nothing left of all her finery but one of the little slippers, the mate to the one that she had dropped.

The guards at the palace gate were asked if they had not seen a princess go out. They replied that they had seen nobody leave but a young girl, very shabbily dressed, and who had more the air of a poor country wench than a gentlewoman. When the two sisters returned from the ball Cinderella asked them if they had been well entertained, and if the fine lady had been there.

They told her, yes, but that she hurried away immediately when it struck twelve, and with so much haste that she dropped one of her little glass slippers, the prettiest in the world, which the king's son had picked up; that he had done nothing but look at her all the time at the ball, and that most certainly he was very much in love with the beautiful person who owned the glass slipper. What they said was very true; for a few days later, the king's son had it proclaimed, by sound of trumpet, that he would marry her whose foot this slipper would just fit. They began to try it on the princesses, then the duchesses and all the court, but in vain; it was brought to the two sisters, who did all they possibly could to force their foot into the slipper, but they did not succeed.

Cinderella, who saw all this, and knew that it was her slipper, said to them, laughing, "Let me see if it will not fit me." Her sisters burst out laughing, and began to banter with her. The gentleman who was sent to try the slipper looked earnestly at Cinderella, and, finding her very handsome, said that it was only just that she should try as well, and that he had orders to let everyone try.

He had Cinderella sit down, and, putting the slipper to her foot, he found that it went on very easily, fitting her as if it had been made of wax. Her two sisters were greatly astonished, but then even more so, when Cinderella pulled out of her pocket the other slipper, and put it on her other foot. Then in came her godmother and touched her wand to Cinderella's clothes, making them richer and more magnificent than any of those she had worn before. And now her two sisters found her to be that fine, beautiful lady whom they had seen at the ball. They threw themselves at her feet to beg pardon for all the ill treatment they had made her undergo. Cinderella took them up, and, as she embraced them, said that she forgave them with all her heart, and wanted them always to love her.

She was taken to the young prince, dressed as she was. He thought she was more charming than before, and, a few days after, married her. Cinderella, who was no less good than beautiful, gave her two sisters lodgings in the palace, and that very same day matched them with two great lords of the court.

Name: _____ Date: _____

Pretest, *continued*

QUESTIONS

1. Explain how the different elements of the story (e.g., use of words, point of view, setting, characters, ideas, plot/conflict, images/symbols, etc.) interact to contribute to the overall meaning of the text.

2. What archetypes are present in the story? How did the encounters reveal those archetypes? Cite evidence to support your answer.

3. What does this story suggest about encounters? Write at least two true statements about encounters in the story with evidence to support your ideas.

Name: _____ Date: _____

Pretest Rubric
"Cinderella; or The Little Glass Slipper" *by Charles Perrault*

	0	1	2	3	4
Question 1: Content: Literary Analysis	Provides no response.	Response is limited and vague. There is no connection to how literary elements contribute to the meaning, main idea, or theme. A literary element is merely named.	Response is accurate with 1–2 literary techniques described with vague or no connection to a main idea or theme. Response includes limited or no evidence from text.	Response is appropriate and accurate, describing at least two literary elements and a main idea or theme. Response is literal and includes some evidence from the text.	Response is insightful and well-supported describing, at least two literary elements and how they enhance the theme. Response includes abstract connections and adequate evidence from the text.
Question 2: Process: Inference From Evidence	Provides no response.	Response is limited, vague, and/or inaccurate. There is no justification for answers given.	Response is accurate, but lacks adequate explanation. Response includes some justification about how encounters revealed archetypes.	Response is accurate and makes sense. Response includes some justification about how encounters revealed archetypes.	Response is accurate, insightful, interpretive, and well-written. Response includes thoughtful justification about how encounters revealed archetypes.
Question 3: Concept/Theme Applied to Literature	Provides no response.	Response is limited, vague, and/or inaccurate.	Response lacks adequate explanation. Response does not relate or create a generalization about encounters. Little or no evidence from text.	Response is accurate and makes sense. Response relates to or creates an idea about encounters with some relation to the text.	Response is accurate, insightful, and well-written. Response relates to or creates two generalizations about encounters with evidence from the text.

Note: Adapted with permission from Stambaugh & VanTassel-Baska, 2001.

Lesson 1

Understanding Encounters: Concept Introduction

Key Question

How do encounters shape ourselves and our world?

Objectives

Content: To analyze and interpret fiction, nonfiction, and art, students will be able to:
- compare and contrast the use of specific techniques various authors use to approach and develop similar ideas; and
- analyze how multiple literary elements interact over the course of the text to develop the theme.

Process: To develop interpretation, analysis, and communication skills in the language arts, students will be able to:
- justify inferences with evidence from the text;
- elaborate in discussion or in writing on how authors use language and literary elements to create meaning;
- apply evidence to support explanations and opinions relative to a question, text, or issue; and
- respond to an analysis of literature, nonfiction, media, or art by developing arguments and elaborating on explanations through writing a variety of texts (e.g., essays, paragraphs), including relevant and sufficient evidence to support claims.

Concept: To develop conceptual thinking about encounters in language arts and additional content areas, students will be able to:
- explain with evidence how encounters may lead to positive or negative outcomes in literature, media, and real-world examples;
- explain how encounters allow for reflection and change using literature, media, and real-world examples;

Encounters With Archetypes

- explain how encounters may allow for opportunities and threats using evidence from a variety of texts and real-world examples;
- explain how encounters allow for prediction within literature and real-world examples;
- relate encounter generalizations to real-life situations; and
- examine the relationship between encounters and other concepts in multiple contexts.

Accelerated CCSS for ELA

- RL.6.6
- RL.7.1
- RL.7.3
- RL.8.2
- RL.8.3
- W.7.10
- SL.6.1
- SL.7.2

Materials

- Video: "Pay It Forward Video Clip" (available at https://www.youtube.com/watch?v=KxB43PxasGA)
- Video: "The Paradox of Theseus's Ship (90 Second Philosophy)" (available at https://www.youtube.com/watch?v=kVAHXiKjgRo)
- Student copies of "Eleven" by Sandra Cisneros (or video of author read aloud available online) (both)
- Chart paper and markers (for small groups of students)
- Handout 1.1: Blank Literary Analysis Wheel
- Handout 1.2: Concept Organizer
- Rubric 1: Product Rubric (Appendix C)

Introductory Activities

1. Introduce the term *encounter*. Ask: *What is an encounter?* Allow for discussion.
2. Explain the etymology behind the word *encounter*: En (in front of) contra (against). The English word *encounter* is derived from the Old French word *encortre*: a meeting, a fight, or an opportunity. The word *encounter* has come to be used in a more neutral way, without positive or negative connotations.
3. Guide students to understand that the word *encounter* in this unit refers to an unplanned experience or meeting—when a person or character meets another person, character, circumstance, emotion, or idea—that brings about a small or big change.
4. Tell students: *Write down the names of 7–8 important people in your life that you "encounter." What kind of relationship do you have with these individu-*

Lesson 1

[Margin notes: Graphic Organizer; model]

als? Label these relationships (friend, family, school, work relationship). Then, add a plus sign, your name, and an equals sign (teacher + Brittany = ____). Think about what happens when you encounter each person. How does he or *she enhance your life?* Students can share their responses within a small group and identify patterns. Ask: *Are there types of people that were mentioned a lot? What roles do these individuals play (e.g., friends are supporters, parents are caregivers, teachers are guides in learning, etc.)?*

[Margin notes: Challenging! Need modeling — people and experiences]

5. Then, tell students to think about the types of negative and positive experiences they encountered within the past week. Ask: *How do these encounters affect you? How do they change you? What do these encounters help you realize about yourself? What do they help you realize about the world or others?*

[Margin note: surprising/unexpected]

6. Share the clip from the film *Pay It Forward* (see Materials list). Tell students to look for different types of encounters that are mentioned or inferred in the video clip. Afterward, discuss the types of encounters students noticed. Ask: *What effects might encounters have on the individual, others, or society?*

[Margin note: internal/external experiences — need to model what each of these are]

7. Ask students to quickly debate or respond in agreement or disagreement to the following:
   - Encounters and interactions are the same thing.
   - Encounters involve risk.
   - Encounters can be planned.
   - Encounters require action or change.
   - Encounters only involve people.

[Margin note: Prepare to record these]

8. Afterward, ask students to create a generalization about encounters. A generalization is a statement that might be true of all encounters, whether <u>personal</u>, situational, or in <u>stories</u>. You may wish to provide sentence starters, such as:
   - Encounters may lead to . . .
   - Encounters cause . . .
   - Encounters allow for . . .
   - Encounters can be . . .

9. After students share their own ideas, share the following generalizations (that will be used throughout the unit) and ask how their responses relate to them:
   - Encounters allow for reflection and <u>change</u> (internal and external).
   - Encounters allow for prediction. *(Stories especially)*
   - Encounters can result in <u>positive</u> or <u>negative</u> outcomes.
   - Encounters may lead to <u>threats</u> and <u>opportunities</u>.

Encounters With Archetypes

[margin note: may need to pre-teach how to create a concept map]

[margin note: Model: Challenging]

10. Distribute chart paper to small groups of students. Assign each group a different generalization to write in the middle of its chart paper. Ask groups to create a mini concept map that shows at least five different examples that represent their generalization in another subject area or in their lives. Afterward, conduct a gallery walk for students to view and ask questions about each other's posters.

[margin note: Prep a Working Chart]

11. Explain that students will explore encounters throughout the unit as they look at stories, art, videos, and speeches, as well as applications in their own lives. (*Note*: Display the generalizations, as they will be referred to throughout the unit. Consider creating a concept map-working wall so students can add their connections between the content and the concepts they learn in each lesson. Note that some students may have a difficulty with the generalization "Encounters allow for prediction." Make sure they understand that although we cannot predict encounter outcomes, we can determine patterns based on what we know, which allows us to make decisions about encounters from past experiences and predict outcomes.)

In-Class Activities to Deepen Learning

[margin note: must model this!!]

1. Ask students to discuss in small groups: *How do encounters help you learn more about you?* *[margin note: Graphic Organizer]*

2. Have students read the short story "Eleven" by Sandra Cisneros, or show a video of the story being read aloud. Ask students to look for encounters—both internal and external. *[margin note: needs to be explained before!]*

[margin note: confusing "encounters"]

3. Afterward, select from the following text-dependent questions for discussion:
   - What were the encounters that took place within the story? (Sample response: Examples include Rachel's encounters with Mrs. Price's remarks, the sweater, Rachel's humiliation, her ruined birthday, her intense disappointment, her thoughts about her birthday as a day of small change, etc.)
   - Compare the two settings (home vs. school). How are they described differently? What might these two settings represent? (Sample response: Home represents safety and security with family, while school represents growing up in the real world, away from the safety and security of family.)
   - *[margin note: HOTs]* Was Mrs. Price making an honest mistake, or was she treating Rachel unfairly? (Answers will vary; ensure students defend their responses with evidence.)
   - What does the sweater symbolize? (Sample response: The sweater may symbolize encountering a problem one faces while growing up and not really knowing how to handle it.)

[margin note: may need to scaffold]

Lesson 1

- How does the encounter with Mrs. Price lead to positive and negative outcomes? (Sample response: The encounter leads to negative feelings, shame.)
- What does Rachel learn about herself based on her encounter with Mrs. Price? (Sample response: Rachel realizes she is still very much like a child because she does not know how to respond in the embarrassing situation, but this realization is a step toward maturing.)

[handwritten note: unlikely to make this connection independently →]

- Throughout the story, Rachel thinks of her family. How does her encounter with these thoughts affect her? (Sample response: It presents a sense of relief compared to the present uncomfortable situation.)
- Rachel says that 11 is like an onion or rings in a tree trunk. What does she mean by this? (Sample response: She means that 11 is just a layer away from the previous year, and it includes the emotions and experiences of all the other years. It is an addition to your identity, not a separate, new, "older" identity.)
- What is the author's message about growing up? (Sample response: Growing up is hard and requires being able to advocate for yourself; there is responsibility with growing up.)
- How does this story make you feel? How have you changed after encountering the story? (Students may explain that they have a new perspective on the difficulties that come with growing up. Growing up happens incrementally, not overnight, and through these difficult experiences, a person takes small steps toward maturity.)
- In what ways do external encounters often lead to internal encounters, or vice versa? How is this evident in the story? (Sample response: Rachel's external encounter with Mrs. Price not really seeing, understanding, or valuing her led Rachel to the internal encounter of intense embarrassment and realizing that the real world is hard.)

Literary Analysis

Distribute Handout 1.1: Blank Literary Analysis Wheel for groups to complete. Explain that students will examine different ways in which various story elements interact (arrows on the wheel indicate interactions), including how encounters within a story can shape the message. Guide students through the following questions using the wheel. If this is the first time using the wheel, you may need to explain some of the categories to students. Begin with individual portions of the wheel (e.g., setting, characters, mood), and then add complexity by combining different elements on the wheel to help students see how elements interact to create a message. Additional information and examples can be found in Appendix A.

Encounters With Archetypes

> *What would have happened if this took place at home → Venn diagram*

1. **Setting + Characters:** How does the setting influence Rachel? (Sample response: The classroom sets the stage for Mrs. Price to "ruin" Rachel's birthday with the red sweater; Rachel is not at home with those who love and understand her the most.)
2. **Symbols + Plot/Conflict:** How does the introduction of the red sweater propel the plot? (Sample response: The red sweater represents a problem with an authority figure and the struggles of growing up that Rachel does not know how to handle. The sweater incites internal emotional turmoil in Rachel; it spurs the conflict that she has with Mrs. Price.)
3. **Language/Structure/Style + Point of View:** How does the author reveal a reliable 11-year-old narrator through the use language and style? (Sample response: The stream of consciousness style [e.g., "Not mine, not mine, not mine, but Mrs. Price is already turning to page thirty-two..."] shows Rachel's reaction to what an outsider may view as no big deal. Phrases such as "there aren't any more tears left in my eyes, and it's just my body shaking like when you have the hiccups, and my whole head hurts like when you drink milk too fast" and "pennies in a tin Band-Aid box" reveal details of an 11-year-old who does 11-year-old things, such as scraping her knees; these phrases indicate that she is still a child.)
4. **Characters + Language/Structure/Style:** How does the author's use of figurative language convey Rachel's feelings about growing up? (Sample response: The simile of 11 being like an onion or like rings on a tree shows Rachel's realization that 11 is just an additional part of who she has been.)
5. **Symbol + Characters:** What does her 11th birthday symbolize for Rachel? Why do you think the story was about her 11th birthday and not her 10th, 12th, or 13th? (Students may notice that 11 is a prime number and consists of two of the same digit. The number 11 may symbolize that the child and adult are both number 1, or the idea of a prime and odd number as being an unusual birthday but also the same as any other.)
6. **Language/Structure/Style + Symbol:** At the end of the narrative, Rachel talks about a runaway tiny balloon in the sky. What does the balloon symbolize, and why is this at the end of the narrative? (Sample response: The balloon symbolizes her realization that today is a step toward maturity. As an 11-year-old, the balloon might represent her comfort of childhood and security of family being let go as she makes an incremental step toward being an adult.)

Ask students: *If you have a ship made up of several wooden pieces and you change each piece to a metal piece over time, is it still the same ship? Does it still have its same identity, or is it an entirely new ship?* Explain the paradox of the Ship of Theseus (or show a video clip; see Materials list):

> *This should be an anticipatory set!!* (handwritten note)

The ship wherein Theseus and the youth of Athens returned had thirty oars, and was preserved by the Athenians down even to the time of Demetrius Phalereus, for they took away the old planks as they decayed, putting in new and stronger timber in their place, insomuch that this ship became a standing example among the philosophers, for the logical question of things that grow; one side holding that the ship remained the same, and the other contending that it was not the same. (Plutarch, 75 A.D.)

Ask: *This paradox begs the question: Are we still the same person after we incrementally change over time? How does this relate to growing up as described by Rachel?* (Sample response: The change happens so incrementally that we don't realize it; the essence of who we are is really the same; 11 is 10, 9, 8 etc., all at once, yet it is different.)

Choice-Based Differentiated Products

Students may choose one of the following to complete (*Note*: Use Rubric 1: Product Rubric in Appendix C to assess student responses):

- Read another coming-of-age story, such as "Scout's Honor" by Avi, and complete a Blank Literary Analysis Wheel (Appendix B). Consider the interactions that occur between story elements. What patterns do you notice between the themes and literary elements used in "Eleven" and your selected story? Why do you think the patterns emerged? Create a Venn diagram to show your comparisons.
- If an encounter is an unexpected event or opportunity that may lead to change, and an interaction is an action between different people, places, or things, consider the following question: Do encounters lead to interactions, or do interactions lead to encounters? Using "Eleven" as an example, explain the interactions and encounters and which one led to the other.
- Write a personal narrative about your age that shows an encounter related to the idea of growing up. Include figurative language to develop a positive or negative tone, as well as common internal and external encounters to convey your emotions about the encounter.

Opportunities for Talent Development

- Ask students to research the life of Sandra Cisneros. She has several author talks on YouTube discussing her background and motivation for writing: *Design a book cover that shows how her life story influences the themes of her*

Encounters With Archetypes

stories and books. What might the title be? How do the colors, images, and title for your book cover represent her life influences?
- Have students consider how the *Pay It Forward* video inspired them: *Think about your own strengths, talents, and daily encounters. How might you use your strengths and opportunities to promote a ripple effect of positive internal and external encounters? Create a plan of action.*

Social-Emotional Connections

- Lead a class discussion: *How do unexpected encounters with our emotions allow for reflection and change? In "Eleven," Rachel encounters a situation that brings intense disappointment. How did this disappointment bring about change? Was the change an internal or external one?*
- Disappointments are a part of growing up. Have students discuss and complete with a partner: *What are healthy ways to deal with disappointment? What advice might you give Rachel (from "Eleven") or others for handling disappointing situations? Write a "Dear Rachel" letter to share your thoughts and advice.*

ELA Task

Assign the following task as a performance-based assessment for this lesson: *How does a person's expectation impact his or her interpretation of an encounter? In a paragraph, respond to this from Rachel's perspective and include a specific generalization related to encounters.*

Concept Connections

1. Have students reflect in writing or discussion: *How does the story "Eleven" relate to one of the encounters generalizations?*
2. Distribute Handout 1.2: Concept Organizer. Ask students to complete the organizer by applying encounter generalizations to the story they read. Sample responses include:
    - Encounters allow for reflection and change: The encounter between Rachel and Mrs. Price allowed Rachel to reflect on how difficult growing up and handling situations with authority are. The encounter brings Rachel frustration as she reflects that she is not yet grown up enough to know how to assert herself in the situation. The encounter between Rachel and herself [internal reflection] allows for personal growth and awareness.

- Encounters allow for prediction: The encounter with the memories of home allows the reader to predict that Rachel longs for the security of home—a sharp contrast to the harsh reality of the classroom where Rachel is not "seen."
- Encounters can result in positive or negative outcomes: The external encounter with Mrs. Price led to Rachel's birthday being ruined and her realization [internal encounter] that even her family is not able to help in this situation; the real world is hard.
- Encounters may result in threats and opportunities: The encounter with humiliation leads to an opportunity for Rachel to realize that growing up is difficult.
- Encounters and _____ : Students may select any concept to link to encounters. For example: Encounters + Awareness: The encounter between Rachel and Mrs. Price allowed for a greater awareness of how transitioning from childhood to adulthood is hard.

Note: It is not necessary for students to make the connection to every generalization.

Assessment

- Examine choice-based differentiated products and rubric criteria, ELA Task responses, and/or Concept Connections. Use Rubric 1: Product Rubric to review the products.
- Have students complete an exit ticket: *What new insight do you have about the encounters you experience on a day-to-day basis? How do those encounters allow for opportunities?*

Name: _____   Date: _____

Handout 1.1
Blank Literary Analysis Wheel

Directions: Draw arrows across elements to show connections.

Text: _____

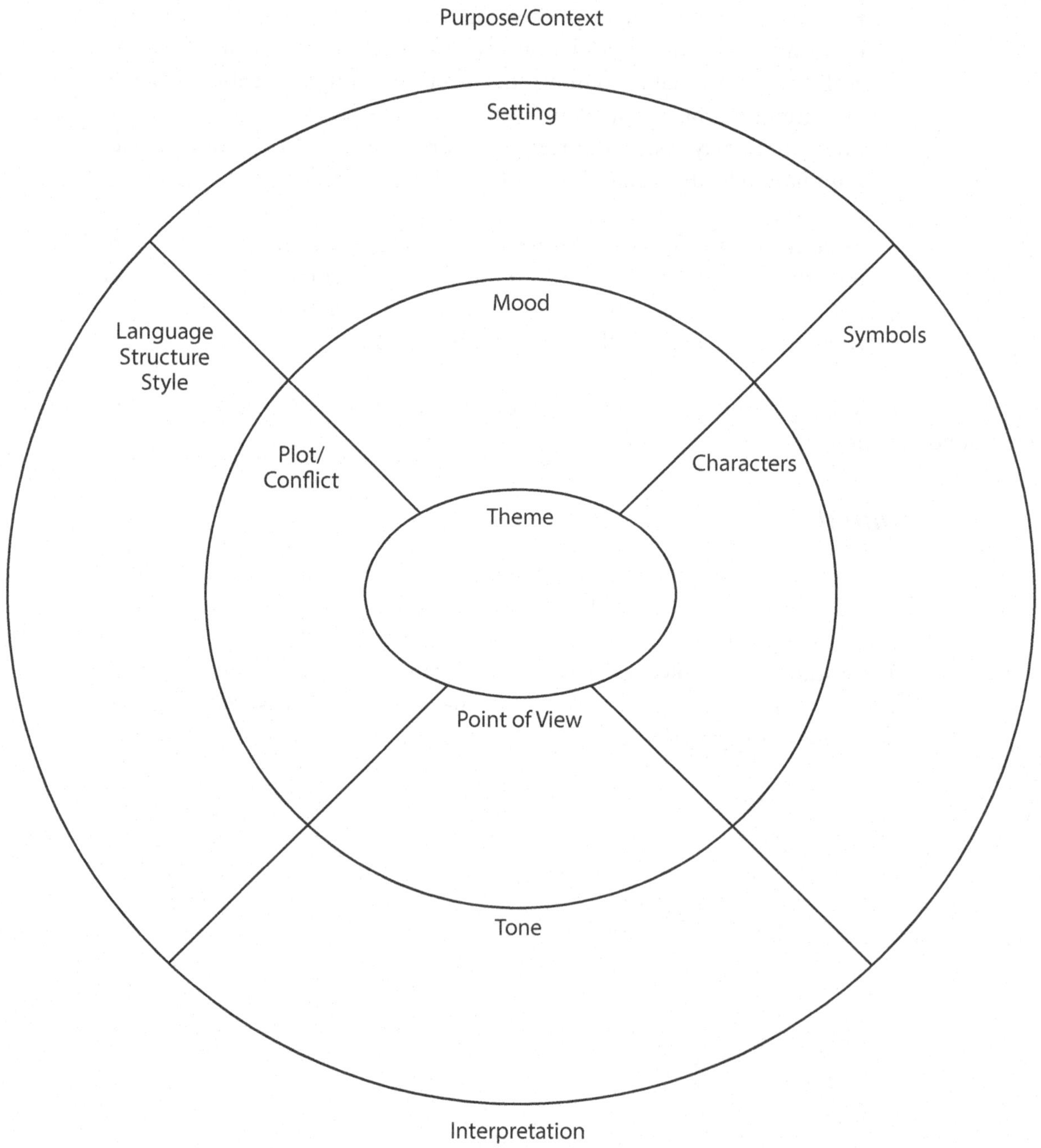

Purpose/Context

- Setting
- Mood
- Symbols
- Language Structure Style
- Plot/Conflict
- Characters
- Theme
- Point of View
- Tone

Interpretation

Created by Tamra Stambaugh, Ph.D., & Emily Mofeld, Ed.D., 2015.

Name: _____ Date: _____

Handout 1.2
Concept Organizer

Directions: How does each topic exemplify each generalization? What new generalization can you make?

1. Encounters allow for reflection and change.
2. Encounters allow for prediction.
3. Encounters can result in positive or negative outcomes.
4. Encounters may result in threats and opportunities.

	Connection to Other Concept	
Connection to Encounters Generalizations (1, 2, 3, 4)		
Lesson Topic		

Encounters With Archetypes © Taylor & Francis

Lesson 2

Understanding Archetypes and Their Origins

Key Question

How do encounters with archetypes help us understand the human experience?

Objectives

Content: To analyze and interpret fiction, nonfiction, and art, students will be able to:
- compare and contrast how literary, visual, informational, and/or primary source texts reveal patterns and themes;
- analyze characters' conflicts, motives, values, thoughts, and actions;
- compare and contrast the use of specific techniques various authors use to approach and develop similar ideas;
- identify and analyze archetypal patterns in stories, speeches, and real-world contexts and discuss how they are shaped by the author or real-world individuals or events; and
- analyze how multiple literary elements interact over the course of the text to develop the theme.

Process: To develop interpretation, analysis, and communication skills in the language arts, students will be able to:
- justify inferences with evidence from the text;
- elaborate in discussion or in writing on how authors use language and literary elements to create meaning; and
- apply evidence to support explanations and opinions relative to a question, text, or issue.

Concept: To develop conceptual thinking about encounters in language arts and additional content areas, students will be able to:
- explain with evidence how encounters may lead to positive or negative outcomes in literature, media, and real-world examples;

- explain how encounters allow for reflection and change using literature, media, and real-world examples;
- explain how encounters may allow for opportunities and threats using evidence from a variety of texts and real-world examples;
- explain how encounters allow for prediction within literature and real-world examples;
- relate encounter generalizations to real-life situations; and
- examine the relationship between encounters and other concepts in multiple contexts.

Accelerated CCSS for ELA

- RL.7.1
- RL.8.9
- RI.6.9
- W.7.10
- SL.6.1

Materials

- Student copies of or access to a personality test, such as "The 5-Minute Personality Test" (available at http://decal.ga.gov/documents/attachments/5minutepersonalitytest.pdf)
- Teacher's copy of *Corduroy* by Don Freeman (or video of read aloud available online)
- Teacher's access to "The Grandmother Tiger" (available at http://leverettfolktales.blogspot.com/2012/06/grandmother-tiger.html) or another culture's version of "Little Red Riding Hood"
- Three pieces of chart paper and markers (per group of 3–4)
- 15 sticky notes (per group of 3–4)
- Five pieces of chart paper (to display; one labeled "Character Archetypes," one labeled "Situational Archetypes," one labeled "Symbolic Archetypes," and two labeled "Encounters Generalizations")
- Copies of various children's books (e.g., *The Little Engine That Could* by Watty Piper, *Scuffy the Tugboat* by Gertrude Crampton, *The Mixed-Up Chameleon* by Eric Carle, *Strega Nona: Her Story* by Tomie dePaola, *Stand Tall, Molly Lou Melon* by Patty Lovell, *John Philip Duck* by Patricia Polacco, *Stellaluna* by Janell Cannon, *The Patchwork Quilt* by Valerie Flournoy, *Jumanji* by Chris Van Allsburg, *Thank You, Mr. Falker* by Patricia Polacco, *Mrs. Katz and Tush* by Patricia Polacco, *This Is Not My Hat* by Jon Klassen, *The Noisy Paint Box* by Barb Rosenstock)
- Handout 1.2: Concept Organizer
- Handout 2.1: Archetype Quick Reference Guide
- (Optional) Handout 8.2: Encounters With Archetypes

- Rubric 1: Product Rubric (Appendix C)

Introductory Activities

1. Ask students: *What is a personality*? (A personality is a combination of characteristics that make someone who he or she is as an individual.)
2. Have students take a personality test (see Materials list). Afterward, allow students a few minutes to discuss their personality type with a partner. Then, ask:
   - Does the personality test fully explain who you are? (Students should realize that personality traits might allow for categorization but individuals are unique; people may resemble combinations of several types of personality traits, and they may even act differently in different situations even though they may have strong preferences toward one category.)
   - Find someone with a similar personality type as you. How are you alike and different? Why do you think that is? (Guide students to understand that there is still individuality within the different personality patterns, and no person fully represents a personality pattern.)
   - How do you think the test developers know which questions to ask and which personality types or categories to use? (Even though each person is an individual, there are known patterns in human characteristics or behaviors.)

3. Explain to students that just as there are patterns in personalities, there are patterns in stories. Ask: *What does each of the following pairs have in common?* (You may choose to show each pair as part of a presentation.)
   - **"Jack and the Beanstalk" and "Little Red Riding Hood"**: Help students realize that they are similar stories in which a young person goes out into the world and encounters danger.
   - **Olaf in *Frozen* and Donkey in *Shrek***: Both are sidekicks who support main characters and provide comic relief.
   - **Harry Potter and The Incredibles**: Both are reluctant heroes who help save the day against evil.
   - **Real life and fictional stories**: Stories may resemble real life and teach us something about ourselves; stories reveal the human condition.

4. Ask students if they have ever heard of the word *archetype*. Solicit a variety of responses. Explain what the word *archetype* means (arche means primitive or first, type means model = first model). Therefore, an archetype is "an original pattern or model."

Encounters With Archetypes

5. Tell students: *The idea of archetypes is rooted in psychology and was popularized by psychologist Carl Jung (Adamski, 2011). Archetypes are models that are collectively understood by everyone. For example, if you see a devil and angel, you may immediately think of good versus evil. If you see a child, you may immediately think of innocence or youth. If you see someone taking care of someone else, you may immediately think of a caregiver or companion. Jung said that archetypes are patterns that originate in our "collective subconscious" as memories shared by the human race. He argued that people are born with a set of known information all humans can relate to, such as love, good versus evil, fear, or hope. Jung said that these patterns or modeled images and roles are archetypes that we subconsciously recognize and use to help us make sense of and explain our world. In literature, archetypes are commonly used to develop characters and situations faced by humanity. Archetypes make stories relatable because humans recognize them and understand them as part of being human. An author doesn't have to go through every detail to explain caregiving as a universal idea or say a character is a caregiver if the character embodies a caregiver archetype. Personality tests (e.g., Myers-Briggs) have been designed based on Jung's (and other psychologists') conceptions of common human behavior. Archetypes are an abstract model of behaviors, actions, situations and symbols, not people or places. Jung emphasized that archetypes are not good or bad. Archetypes just exist.*

Note: Consider researching more about Jung's conception before discussing the concept and origins. Many videos and articles are available online. The explanation provided here is quite simplistic. In general, students need to know that archetypes are patterns of an ideal concept or set character behaviors that can be used to build individual stories and characters, and that allow for relating to the human condition. Archetypes are different than stereotypes; archetypes reveal patterns or original models that embody behaviors, whereas stereotypes are narrow or limited views of an individual or group. Archetypes are not gender- or race-specific. The caregiver as an archetype may be a female, but labeling all females as caregivers is a stereotype. Additionally, someone who takes care of someone else may not be a caregiver archetype unless his or her motive is intentionally about caregiving instead of manipulation. Motives and context matter. A villain may provide care in an effort to get what he or she wants or may be loyal to family, but still be evil. Distinctions are also made between archetypes, prototypes (how the archetype is manifested in real life), and stereotypes. Prototypes are quite similar to archetypes and may embody an example of an archetype. Using the archetype of the sage, a fairy godmother may represent the prototype of the sage, whereas a stereotype would be that all godmothers are sages.

In-Class Activities to Deepen Learning

1. Tell students that they are going to examine a variety of archetypes throughout this unit and discuss how they can apply their knowledge of archetypes to real-world encounters, as well as stories.
2. Distribute Handout 2.1: Archetype Reference Guide for students to review in small groups. Encourage groups to document as many examples or archetypes that they can think of from books and movies they know. Discuss responses (Figure 1 illustrates some common examples). Students may wish to explore more on their own and continue adding to the handout. Students will refer to this handout throughout the unit.
3. Reinforce the idea that, like personality styles, archetypes do not represent the entirety of an individual's behaviors, situations, or symbols. Likewise, not all character representations or symbols are archetypes. For example, rain does not automatically mean "renewal" unless it fits the context of the story. Black is not always representative of evil, red does not always mean violence, white does not always mean purity, etc. However, within the context of the story, the interpretation of a particular color could serve as another layer or clue that deepens the understanding of the story. Archetypes must be interpreted in context. The character behaviors, encounters, situations, and symbols work together to help us make an accurate interpretation.
4. Explain: *We are going to practice identifying archetypes in stories. First, let's consider "Little Red Riding Hood." What are the character archetypes? What are the situations? Do you notice any symbols?* (Red may not mean passion/determination in this context.) List responses in a chart (see the first column of Figure 2).
5. Ask: *What's the difference between an archetype and a stereotype? Is the wolf in "Little Red Riding Hood" an archetype or a stereotype?* Explain that archetypes are about character behaviors/motives, common situations, and/or symbols, whereas stereotypes are narrow or limiting statements about people or groups (i.e., the wolf is a prototype that represents an archetype of the villain, but assuming all wolves are evil or bad is a stereotype). (See note at the beginning of this lesson.)
6. Ask: *Do you think archetypes are revealed in the same ways regardless of the culture? Do individuals in Japan, Africa, or the Middle East, for example, have similar archetypes in their stories?*
7. Read aloud a variant of "Little Red Riding Hood," such as Japan's version ("The Grandmother Tiger" or "The Grand-aunt Tiger;" see Materials list). Compare the similar archetypes (use Figure 2 as a guide). Ask: *What are the similarities and differences in the two stories?* (Sample response: The innocent is "reborn," an allusion to Christian faith prominent in Europe during

Encounters With Archetypes

Character	Situation	Symbol/Image
■ **Hero:** Link from *Legend of Zelda*; Spider-Man ■ **Sage:** Splinter from *Teenage Mutant Ninja Turtles*; Fi from *Legend of Zelda*; Yoda from *Star Wars* ■ **Caregiver:** April from *Teenage Mutant Ninja Turtles*; Sina from *Moana* ■ **Leader:** Chief Tui from *Moana* ■ **Innocent:** Judy Hopps from *Zootopia*	■ **Good vs. Evil:** Darth Vader vs. Luke Skywalker; Mario vs. Evil Mario ■ **Unhealable Wound:** Nemo's "lucky fin" (as a result of a cracked egg), Dory's memory; Harry Potter's scar ■ **Quest:** Dorothy on the Yellow Brick Road in *The Wizard of Oz*	■ **Black:** Darth Vader's cloak and hood ■ **White:** Princess Leia's white tunic; Snow White's name ■ **Red:** Mario wears a red shirt and hat; ruby slippers in *The Wizard of Oz* ■ **Water:** *Moana* (sets stage for her renewal) ■ **Darkness:** *Legend of Zelda* woods

Figure 1. Example archetypes.

Elements	Little Red Riding Hood (Grimm)	The Grandmother Tiger (Japan)
Character Archetypes	Villain (Wolf); innocent (Little Red Riding Hood)	Villain (Tiger); innocent (child); person in need of rescue (second child)
Situational Archetypes	Quest (to deliver cookies); good vs. evil; initiation	Good vs. evil; initiation
Symbolic Archetypes	Darkness (through the woods)	Tree
Encounters	Little Red Riding Hood encounters the wolf (danger), which results in a threat	The child encounters the tiger (danger), which results in a threat
Message	Be careful who you trust; listen to parents (go straight to Grandmother's house)	Be careful; listen to parent (don't talk to strangers)

Figure 2. Archetype comparisons.

Grimm's time; the message to obey your parents is a universal idea across cultures.)

8. After discussion, make sure that students recognize the similarities regardless of the culture. Jung said that archetypes are universal (as cited in Adamski, 2011). All cultures unconsciously recognize, experience, and attempt to explain similar behaviors and situations they encounter. It is their way of making sense of the world. Even though the context or culture may be different, the archetypes follow similar patterns, regardless of who is telling the story and where it originated. Many of Jung's conceptions of archetypes came from his study of mythology and patterns of stories he noted regardless of the culture.

9. In small groups of 3–4, have students conduct a scavenger hunt, investigating archetypes in various children's books and how archetypal traits emerge. Use *Corduroy* by Don Freeman as an example of how students should investigate:
    - What archetypes do you notice in the book? (Sample response: Corduroy is an explorer/person in need of rescue; Lisa is a companion/caregiver; Lisa's mom is a villain-type/antagonist; situational archetypes include a quest and unhealable wound; symbolic archetypes include a mountain, darkness, circle.)
    - What do these archetypes show about the human experience? What "idea" is captured in *Corduroy*? (Sample response: *Corduroy* represents the idea that humans have a hurt/flaw and desire acceptance.) What idea does Lisa represent? (Sample response: Caregiver.) What idea is represented in Corduroy's quest? (Sample response: Humans seek out ways to fix their hurts, to be accepted, and encounter challenges along the way.)
    - How do different perspectives in the human experience reveal different archetype traits? (Students will need to think about how characters view the main problem in the story through different lenses and how the lenses reveal characters' traits. Consider using two sets of sunglasses, one labeled "opportunity" and one labeled "threat" to illustrate the idea. Which pair of sunglasses do the characters wear?)
    - What is the main problem in *Corduroy*? (Sample response: Corduroy lost his button.)
    - How does Corduroy respond to his problem? How does this reveal his archetypal traits? (Sample response: He seeks to be fixed; he is in need of rescue and seeks to be loved and accepted, so much so that he explores the unknown in a quest.)
    - How does Lisa respond to Corduroy's lost button? Does she encounter this problem as an opportunity or a threat? How does her response reveal her archetypal traits? (Sample response: Corduroy's problem

shows Lisa's desire to nurture him physically—to make him more comfortable and also fully love and accept him.)
- How does Lisa's mom respond to Corduroy's lost button? Does she encounter this problem as an opportunity or a threat? (Sample response: Lisa's mom sees Corduroy differently; her motives reveal her to be against Lisa's goals; although not evil in this story, she could be considered a villain type.)
- How does *Corduroy* illustrate encounter generalizations? Be specific.
- How does *Corduroy* help us understand the human experience? (Sample response: We all desire to be loved and accepted. We all need others to help us in our lives.)

10. Provide each group with a set of sticky notes and 2–3 children's books. As time allows, rotate books among the groups. As students read their books, ask them to record specific examples of character archetypes, symbolic archetypes, situational archetypes, and specific examples of encounter generalizations that they find in each book on separate sticky notes. They will post their sticky notes on chart paper to illustrate the specific archetype and encounter examples they have found. Remind students that in order to accurately determine a character's archetype, they may need to consider the character's motivation and how he or she handles problems or encounters. Situational archetypes may be determined based on plot maps and the different encounters throughout the story. You may need to provide an example of what students should write on their sticky notes (e.g., if they are reading *Corduroy*, they may write "Corduroy is in need of saving. He lost his button and needs someone to help him and accept him."). (Note. You may choose to create your own version of Handout 8.2: Encounters With Archetypes as another way for students to organize their ideas.)

11. Display the five sheets of chart paper (see Materials list). On the "Encounters Generalizations" sheets, list each generalization, with enough space between for students to add sticky notes under each. Include an opportunity for students to add another concept to the generalizations as appropriate (e.g., encounter + truth = the character X had to deal with the truth that he is not invincible, which led to reflection and change). As students complete reading their books, they should place their sticky notes with specific examples on the appropriate chart paper. Afterward, ask them to rotate to each sheet of chart paper to consider how the archetypes shape stories. Ask: *What relationships did you notice across the books? In what ways were characters, situations, symbols, and encounters related?* Close the discussion by asking: *How do archetypes help us understand and explain the human condition?*

Choice-Based Differentiated Products

Students may choose one of the following to complete (*Note*: Use Rubric 1: Product Rubric in Appendix C to assess student responses):
- Create a mini-lesson or game to teach young students about archetypes. Beyond fact-based understanding, make sure students understand that encounters with other people, places, emotions, situations, or things help reveal archetypes.
- Are archetypes revealed in the same way in different cultures? Examine several stories from different cultures that tell a similar story (e.g., Cinderella). What patterns do you notice? Do you agree or disagree with Jung and his idea that there are behavioral and situational patterns common to humanity, regardless of the culture? Design and deliver a mini-presentation to the class to share your conclusions.

Opportunities for Talent Development

- To what extent can a person's personality be measured and predicted? Ask students to research more about personality theories and how they guide what is known about human behavior: *Create an infographic for the class that answers the question and applies multiple theories and perspectives about personality patterns.*
- Have students revisit their personality tests from the beginning of the lesson: *If your personality were an archetype, what would it be and why? Use your personality test results and your knowledge of archetypes to explain which archetype best resembles who you are as your true self and why. Identify a character archetype, situational archetype, and symbolic archetype as part of your explanation. Create a collage or symbol that represents your archetype personality. Discuss your collage or symbol with your family members and ask if they agree or disagree with your assessment and why.*

Social-Emotional Connection

Ask students to respond in a written reflection: *How do your personal encounters with archetypes allow for reflection? Select a specific archetype discussed in this lesson and explain how it helps you make sense of your world. What is it about the archetype that relates to you and your life?*

ELA Task

Assign the following task as a performance-based assessment for this lesson: *In an essay, compare and contrast two children's books on their use of character, situational, and symbolic archetypes, and message. How do these archetypes help us understand the human experience?*

Concept Connections

1. Revisit the encounter generalizations and ask students to make connections. Develop a large concept map-working wall for students to link ideas between Lesson 1 and Lesson 2. Write out explanations for how ideas are related between lessons. Students may use index cards or sticky notes to list words, facts, and ideas they learn throughout the unit. Students can use string or painter's tape and other sticky notes and index cards to make connections to the map throughout the unit as they deepen their understanding of encounters with archetypes.
2. Have students complete Handout 1.2, using specific information they know about archetypes: *How do archetypes and encounters interact?* (Sample Response: Encounters allow for reflection and change: Knowing about archetypes allows us to reflect on our own lives and those of others.)

Name: _____ Date: _____

Handout 2.1
Archetypes Quick Reference Guide

Directions: An *archetype* is a character, situation, or symbol that has universal meaning. You will refer to this handout throughout the unit. Keep in mind: There are many character, situational, and symbolic archetypes beyond those listed in this guide. Also, archetypes are contextual and may not always hold true.

Character Archetypes	
Characters behave in an expected pattern.	
Caregiver	Seeks to nurture the emotional and physical well-being of others.
Companion	Seeks to support and encourage another character. A devoted, faithful friend.
Explorer	Seeks something lying beyond the boundaries of the mind or a physical location.
Everyday Person	Wants to belong. One who has no superhuman abilities or gifts but through choices and actions brings about change.
Hero/Heroine	Seeks to define self. Performs acts of courage. Represents the best of society.
Innocent	Seeks to mature emotionally. One who is young and naive. Sees good in the world and has hope. Needs guidance.
Jester	Seeks to enjoy life and have fun. Brings humor to a situation.
Leader	Seeks to create structure and order and is dedicated wholly to the process.
Magician/Creator	Seeks to make things using available resources and/or the supernatural.
Rebel	Seeks freedom to be an individual. Stands against established rule in an effort to find freedom and/or bring about change.
Sidekick	Supports the main character; serves as a voice of reason, guide, rescuer, or loyal companion; is helpful.
Person in Need of Saving	Someone in distress who has a problem that needs solved, or someone who needs to be saved or helped from a bad situation or circumstance.
Sage/Mentor	Seeks to impart knowledge and understanding to someone who the sage feels deserves or needs this information. Generally considered wise with book/world and emotional knowledge, and often serves as a moral compass or guide for other characters.
Villain	May be evil but not always. Generally acts in opposition to the hero, serving as a contrast to the beliefs, goals, and actions of the hero. May show what the hero can become if he or she goes down a wrong path.

Name: _____ Date: _____

Handout 2.1, *continued*

Situational Archetypes	
Circumstances that occur within a story and follow a distinct pattern.	
Fall	A situation in which one loses the respect, love, power, possession, and/or authority once held, often resulting in exile from the group for a period of time. Generally linked to a rise, in which someone rises to a better place in life; sometimes there is a rise and then a fall; other times the story may start with a fall and then focus on the rise back to power.
Battle Between Good and Evil	A situation in which obvious good overcomes the odds to defeat obvious evil.
Death and Rebirth	A situation in which a character's original self dies and the character is reborn with a new outlook or purpose having abandoned his or her old thoughts and views.
Initiation	The moment when a character develops awareness that the world is not what it seems (there are problems in the world).
Unhealable Wound	A physical or psychological injury that is painful and does not mend and cannot be eased. It is often associated with a loss of innocence.
Rags to Riches	Someone goes from being poor to being wealthy (not always in a monetary way; someone may have monetary wealth but seeks personal wealth through quality of life, giving up money for happiness).
Quest	The search for something (tangible or intangible), such as knowledge, a person, answers, treasure, etc., in order to restore the land or restore/renew the "kingdom." A quest usually takes a long time and is very difficult with physical and mental challenges that must be solved. Often results in self-knowledge.
Humans Versus Technology	When machines are used instead of human ingenuity.
Experience Versus Education	A person not in authority or a person who is less educated is wiser than those in charge or higher educational attainment.
Task	The individual challenges (mental and physical) that must be completed to accomplish the task. The task usually demands something close to superhuman strength or extremely challenging.

Name: _____ Date: _____

Handout 2.1, *continued*

Symbolic Archetypes	
Symbols, images, and colors that convey a universal meaning.	
Light	Enlightenment, wisdom.
Darkness	Danger, lack of knowledge.
Desert/Wilderness	Hopelessness, isolation.
Garden	Paradise, order, safety.
Tree	Growth, life, cycles.
Glass	Fragility, transparency, brokenness (if shattered).
Water	Life, purification, renewal.
Mountains/Peaks	Gain insight, wisdom.
Fire	Energy, power, passion, destruction.
Ice	Isolation, loss.
Circle	Unity, wholeness, cycles.
Key	Answer or solution.
Red	Violence, passion, determination.
Blue	Truth, moral purity.
Green	Growth, hope, life.
Purple	Royalty.
Black	Chaos, death, evil.
White	Purity, innocence
Gold	Energy, wealth
Clock	Life and death.
Orange	Strength, endurance, determination, happiness (orange tree = love).

Note. Adapted from Archetypes, n.d.; Booth & Mays, n.d.; Guerin, Labor, Morgan, Reesman, & Willingham, 1992; Jonas, n.d.; Literary Terms, n.d.; Protas, Brown, Smith, & Jaffe, 2001.

Lesson

Encounters With Character Archetypes

Key Question

How is our understanding of characters enhanced through our encounters with archetypes?

Objectives

Content: To analyze and interpret fiction, nonfiction, and art, students will be able to:
- compare and contrast how literary, visual, informational, and/or primary source texts reveal patterns and themes;
- analyze characters' conflicts, motives, values, thoughts, and actions;
- compare and contrast the use of specific techniques various authors use to approach and develop similar ideas;
- identify and analyze archetypal patterns in stories, speeches, and real-world contexts and discuss how they are shaped by the author or real-world individuals or events; and
- analyze how multiple literary elements interact over the course of the text to develop the theme.

Process: To develop interpretation, analysis, and communication skills in the language arts, students will be able to:
- justify inferences with evidence from the text;
- elaborate in discussion or in writing on how authors use language and literary elements to create meaning;
- apply evidence to support explanations and opinions relative to a question, text, or issue;
- respond to an analysis of literature, nonfiction, media, or art by developing arguments and elaborating on explanations through writing a variety of texts (e.g., essays, paragraphs), including relevant and sufficient evidence to support claims; and

Encounters With Archetypes

- develop character archetypes through encounters with other characters, situations, and symbols.

Concept: To develop conceptual thinking about encounters in language arts and additional content areas, students will be able to:
- explain with evidence how encounters may lead to positive or negative outcomes in literature, media, and real-world examples;
- explain how encounters allow for prediction within literature and real-world examples;
- relate encounter generalizations to real-life situations; and
- examine the relationship between encounters and other concepts in multiple contexts.

Accelerated CCSS ELA Standards

- RL.6.6
- RL.7.1
- RL.7.3
- RL.8.2
- RL.8.3
- W.6.1
- W.7.10
- SL.6.1

Materials

- Optical Illusion: "Old Lady or Young Woman?" (available at https://hubpages.com/art/Two-Faces-or-a-Vase-10-Simple-but-Wonderful-Optical-Illusions)
- Select short films and movie clips, such as Pixar's *Boundin'* and *Piper* (available online), and/or "Let It Grow" from *The Lorax* (available at https://www.wingclips.com/movie-clips/the-lorax/let-it-grow)
- Image of "The Dog of Pompeii" to display (available at https://i.imgur.com/egtQ6A1.jpg)
- Student copies of "The Dog of Pompeii" by Louis Untermeyer
- Handout 1.2: Concept Organizer
- Handout 2.1: Archetype Quick Reference Guide
- Handout 3.1: Blank Literary Analysis Wheel
- Rubric 1: Product Rubric (Appendix C)

Introductory Activities

1. **Engage students in a quick debate:** Ask students to stand on different sides of the room based on whether they agree or disagree with the following statement: *Our strengths are our weaknesses.*

2. Show the famous optical illusion of the old woman/young lady (see Materials list).
3. Ask: *Is this a young girl or an old woman?* Quickly, students will exclaim, "Both! It depends on how you look at it." Respond by asking: *How might this photo relate to character archetypes? How might character archetypes (e.g., the hero, the leader, the sage) have strengths and weaknesses? How might a character archetype have both negative and positive qualities at the same time?*

In-Class Activities to Deepen Learning

1. Explain that students will examine a variety of character archetypes. Ask: *Is it possible for a character archetype to be revealed without conflict or a challenge?* Elicit responses and encourage students to think about this throughout the lesson.
2. Show a few short films and movie clips (see Materials list) that display archetypes (e.g., in *Boundin'* Jackalope is the sage; the sheep being sheared is in need of saving). Guide discussion of each video. Ask:
   - What character archetypes are in the video?
   - What is the main challenge/problem encountered? How does the challenge reveal strengths and weaknesses of the character archetype?
   - What are the motivations of the character(s)?
   - What types of encounters provide opportunities for the characters' archetypes to thrive? What types of encounters would be threats to the archetypes?
   - How do the characters' encounters allow for prediction? How would a different character archetype react differently to a problem?
3. Discuss how characters' encounters with problems can lead to positive and/or negative outcomes. Draw visuals on the board (e.g., Character archetype + problem = _____ ; see Figure 3). Explain: *When an explorer encounters a problem (explorer + problem), he or she is motivated to cross boundaries into the unknown and take a risk. How might this encounter show character strengths and weaknesses? How might it lead to positive or negative outcomes? How can a strength also be a weakness?* Students may discuss popular examples (e.g., Ariel in *The Little Mermaid* or *Corduroy*).
4. Explain that it is important to think about a character's motivations: Sometimes a character may appear to be kind or helpful, but the character's true motivations are different (e.g., the queen in *Snow White* appears to be kind to Snow White, but her actions are motivated by malice, not compassion; she is a villain, not a companion). Ask: *What are some other exam-*

Encounters With Archetypes

Archetype + Problem	Positives	Negatives	Examples
Explorer + Problem	Encounters new things	May experience hardship through the risk	Ariel in *The Little Mermaid*, Corduroy
Leader + Problem	Provides order to the situation	Could turn into self-serving control	Ted in *The Lorax*
Innocent + problem	Sees the good; honest	Might be immature; could be afraid, made fun of	Rachel in "Eleven," sheep in *Boundin'*, Piper
Everyday person + problem	Brings positive change	Might blend in with the crowd	Sy in *The Lorax*
Companion + problem	Provides care	Ignores self, needs	Lisa in *Corduroy*
Hero + problem	Develops courage through failure and success	Deals with weakness	Piper
Sage + problem	Guidance is valuable	Advice may not be practical	Jackalope in *Boundin'*
Person in need of saving + problem	Ready to accept help	May feel hopeless	Sheep in *Boundin'*

Figure 3. Archetypes, problems, and outcomes examples.

ples of stories that illustrate when it is important to understand a character's motives in order to understand the archetype? (Sample response: The Wolf in "Little Red Riding Hood" appears helpful in the beginning of the story, as does the Old Lady in "Hansel and Gretel." However, by the end we see their true motives.)

Read Text

Show a picture of "The Dog of Pompeii." Ask students: *What do you think this is, and what do you think happened to this dog?* Explain that, in 79 A.D., Mount Vesuvius erupted, covering the city of Pompeii in volcanic ash and killing more than 2,000 people. The city was discovered in 1748 by explorers who found much of the city to be still in tact. This immobilized dog was one discovery. Have students read "The Dog of Pompeii" by Louis Untermeyer.

Text-Dependent Questions

Select from the following prompts to lead small- or whole-group discussion.
1. How do the encounters experienced throughout the story enhance Bimbo and Tito's relationship? What textual evidence supports your description? (Sample response: Bimbo and Tito encounter opportunities to get food at the party, going to the theater, the smoke of the volcano, etc. These encounters show how Tito relies on Bimbo.)
2. How do both Bimbo and Tito rely on their senses? Why is this important to the story's plot? (Sample response: Tito relies on his sense of touch; Bimbo relies on smell; they use their strengths to rely on each other.)
3. What can you infer about the city of Pompeii, based on the author's descriptions? How does this setting serve to enhance elements of surprise for both the characters and the reader? (Sample response: Because Pompeii is described as festive and lively with a holiday mood, the volcanic eruption comes as a surprise to the people.)
4. List all of the foreshadowing or direct warnings about the volcanic eruption in the story. Did the encounters with these warnings affect Bimbo and Tito's actions? Why or why not? What role do these warnings play in the story? (Sample response: The foreshadowing helps shift the mood from festive to more cautious; it establishes a conflict between those who believe the volcano will erupt and those who don't; it establishes the rising action toward the story's climax. Some of the warnings allow readers to understand how Tito and Bimbo use their senses and depend on each other.)
5. Is the encounter with Rufus an opportunity or a threat? What about the encounter with the man with a strange voice? (Sample response: These encounters serve as warnings, which are threats, but opportunities to know more.)
6. How did Bimbo's encounter with adversity lead to positive and negative outcomes for Tito? (Sample response: Bimbo's encounter with the volcano led to Tito's life being saved, but his best friend dying.)
7. Which character archetypes are revealed in the story? (Sample response: Bimbo is protrayed as a companion; Tito has an unhealable wound.)

Literary Analysis

Guide students through an understanding of how various literary elements interact to create meaning in the story. Use Handout 3.1: Blank Literary Analysis Wheel. Help students synthesize their understanding of how the character interacts with each element on the wheel (see Appendix A for additional explanation and basic explanation of literary elements).

Encounters With Archetypes

1. **Characters + Setting:** How does the setting of Pompeii affect Bimbo, both before and after the volcanic eruption? (Sample response: The festive atmosphere allows Bimbo and Tito to rely on each other for getting food; the eruption is a major threat to Tito, but an opportunity for Bimbo to rescue his friend.)
2. **Characters + Plot/Conflict:** How does Bimbo respond to the volcanic eruption? How does this reveal his character archetype? (Sample response: His loyalty and care for Tito motivates his self-sacrifice.) What if the story did not end 1,800 years later? What would readers not know? (Sample response: Readers gain a deeper insight into Bimbo's sacrifice for Tito. This also enhances readers' understanding of the theme: Companionship involves sacrifice.)
3. **Characters + Language/Structure/Style:** How does the contrasting language in the sentence, "Tito would curl up in the corner (almost like a dog) to fall asleep, while Bimbo, looking quite important (almost like a boy), would disappear again," reveal Bimbo's loyalty? (Sample response: Bimbo, although a dog, is like a "mother and father" to Tito.)
4. **Characters + Symbol:** Why is the symbolism of dark and black important to the story, especially in developing Bimbo's character? How is the idea of an "unhealable wound" related to the companion archetype? (Sample response: The darkness conveys the problem and need for Bimbo; Tito's blindness requires that he depend on Bimbo, as a father, mother, and comrade-companion to help him on his quest for day-to-day survival.)
5. **Characters + Point of View:** Is the narrator reliable in the portrayal of Bimbo? (Students may note the examples of Bimbo doing what a loyal dog would do.)
6. **Characters + Theme:** How does the companion archetype help us understand the theme? What is the author's message about companionship? (Sample response: Companionship requires sacrifice.)
7. **Characters + Mood:** When does the mood shift in the story, and what does this show about Bimbo's thoughts, values, and motives? (Sample response: The mood begins with a light, festive feel, but changes when warnings are given and the volcano erupts; yet, when encountering both everyday and major obstacles, Bimbo is Tito's faithful companion.)
8. **Characters + Tone:** What is the author's attitude toward Bimbo, and how is it revealed? (Sample response: The author provides numerous examples of how Bimbo helps Tito through positive word choice, portraying him as a courageous companion).

Note: Complex "Characters" + questions can also be used to study Tito's character in more depth.

After reflecting on the videos in this lesson and Bimbo's character development, ask students:

- Do character archetypes change in response to encounters? (Sample response: Character archetypes may display strengths and weaknesses and show growth or change in a story; multiple archetypes may be present in one person—caregiver turned hero, innocent turned hero, as in Piper).
- Do characters consistently remain the character archetypes across multiple encounters within a story? (Sample response: Although characters may change, their core archetype identity will likely remain the same throughout the story. Bimbo was a companion before and after the volcano.)
- What were the strengths and weaknesses of the character archetypes in this story? How are they one and the same? (Sample response: Through self-sacrifice, Tito denied his own needs in order to care for someone else.)
- In what ways are character archetypes like the "Ship of Theseus"? Refer to the discussion in Lesson 1, and ask students to respond with examples from texts in this and previous lessons. (Sample response: Character archetypes, such as the sheep in *Boundin'*, experience change in their perspective on life; this may happen throughout multiple encounters within a story, such as plank-by-plank for the ship of Theseus, but overall, the core motivation remains the same for the character.)

Choice-Based Differentiated Products

Students may choose one of the following to complete (*Note*: Use Rubric 1: Product Rubric in Appendix C to assess student responses):

- Choose a character archetype and create a mindmap of related words, phrases, quotes, and examples from books, movies, or real-life people that portray this archetype. What are the major threats for this archetype? What would this archetypal character view as opportunities? Include these answers within your mindmap.
- Create a short comic to show the encounter of one character archetype with another character archetype (from one story or two different stories). Be sure that the dialogue reflects how this encounter reveals the motivations of each character and how these encounters lead to reflection and change.
- Watch your local news program or read the newspaper and make a list of all of the character archetypes you notice reported in the news. Create a chart that includes the people, their character archetypes, encounters, and motivations from three news stories. Also explain how the encounters led to positive and negative outcomes.

Opportunities for Talent Development

- Characters and real-life people are driven by their motivations, or their "why," as they encounter others and situations. Understanding a personal mission is an important part of persevering toward a long-term goal. Have students ask a role model to discuss his or her personal mission: *How does this inspire you as you consider your own personal strengths, talents, and career interests?*
- "The Dog of Pompeii" by Louis Untermeyer revealed the development of the companion character archetype: *In what ways can the companion archetype be applied to real-world problems? Think about how issues or areas in your community need a companion champion. Consider nursing homes, bullying, bystander effects, students feeling left out at school, or any other issue. Develop an action plan to address the issue (who will do what and how it will work), noting how your plan uses ideas of the companion archetype to address the cause.*

Social-Emotional Connection

Have students think about the stories/videos they explored in this lesson: *How did the characters' encounters with emotions influence their actions? How did emotions affect how they responded in encounters with others and various situations? How do your own emotions influence your relationships with others and how you handle various situations? When are emotions an appropriate guide, and when do we need to use logic instead? Create an infographic or image to illustrate how our internal encounters with emotions show external results.*

ELA Task

Assign the following task: *Choose a story from today's lesson. How is the character archetype developed from encounters within the story? How do these encounters allow for reflection and change? Write a paragraph response to explain your answer.*

Concept Connections

1. Ask students: *How do encounters with a particular archetype bring opportunities or threats to other characters?* Students may continue to add to the concept map wall to support this generalization from evidence in today's lesson.
2. Students may use Handout 1.2: Concept Organizer (from Lesson 1 or see Appendix B) to record how encounter generalizations are applied to a spe-

cific story from today's lesson (Sample response: Encounters may lead to threats and opportunities: The encounter with the volcanic eruption led to a threat to both Tito and Bimbo's lives, but it was an opportunity for Bimbo to display his companionship to Tito. In the last box, students should relate the idea of encounter to the concept of loyalty.)

Assessment

- Examine choice-based differentiated products and rubric criteria, ELA Task responses, and/or Concept Connections. Use Rubric 1: Product Rubric to review the products.
- As an exit ticket, have students create a motto for three character archetypes that reveals each character's major motivation or lesson learned.

Name: _____ Date: _____

Handout 3.1
Blank Literary Analysis Wheel

Directions: Draw arrows across elements to show connections.

Text: _____

Purpose/Context

- Setting
- Mood
- Language Structure Style
- Symbols
- Plot/Conflict
- Characters
- Theme
- Point of View
- Tone

Interpretation

Created by Tamra Stambaugh, Ph.D., & Emily Mofield, Ed.D., 2015.

Lesson 4

Encounters With Our World and Ourselves

Key Question

How do encounters with situations allow for reflection and change?

Objectives

Content: To analyze and interpret fiction, nonfiction, and art, students will be able to:
- compare and contrast how literary, visual, informational, and/or primary source texts reveal patterns and themes;
- analyze characters' conflicts, motives, values, thoughts, and actions;
- compare and contrast the use of specific techniques various authors use to approach and develop similar ideas;
- identify and analyze archetypal patterns in stories, speeches, and real-world contexts and discuss how they are shaped by the author or real-world individuals or events; and
- analyze how multiple literary elements interact over the course of the text to develop the theme.

Process: To develop interpretation, analysis, and communication skills in the language arts, students will be able to:
- justify inferences with evidence from the text;
- elaborate in discussion or in writing on how authors use language and literary elements to create meaning;
- apply evidence to support explanations and opinions relative to a question, text, or issue; and
- respond to an analysis of literature, nonfiction, media, or art by developing arguments and elaborating on explanations through writing a variety of texts (e.g., essays, paragraphs), including relevant and sufficient evidence to support claims.

Encounters With Archetypes

Concept: To develop conceptual thinking about encounters in language arts and additional content areas, students will be able to:
- explain with evidence how encounters may lead to positive or negative outcomes in literature, media, and real-world examples;
- explain how encounters allow for prediction within literature and real-world examples;
- relate encounter generalizations to real-life situations; and
- examine the relationship between encounters and other concepts in multiple contexts.

Accelerated CCSS for ELA

- RL.6.6
- RL.7.1
- RL.7.3
- RL.8.2
- RI.5.3
- W.6.1
- SL.6.1

Materials

- Video: "CGI Animated Short Film HD 'The Controller' by Bob Yong, Kang Yung Ho, Ian Ie | CGMeetup" (available at https://www.youtube.com/watch?v=2cBZrr2ZUsg)
- Video: "What Makes a Hero? – Matthew Winkler" (available at https://www.youtube.com/watch?v=Hhk4N9A0oCA)
- Handout 1.2: Concept Organizer
- Handout 2.1: Archetypes Quick Reference Guide
- Handout 4.1: Biographies
- Handout 4.2: "We never know how high we are" by Emily Dickinson
- Handout 4.3: Reasoning About a Situation or Event
- Rubric 1: Product Rubric (Appendix C)

Introductory Activities

1. Show the short film *The Controller* (see Materials list). As students watch the video, ask them to identify the character and situational archetypes involved (i.e., Is the lady in the video a hero archetype? Why or why not? Are there other character archetypes she resembles?), and design a plot map of the events in the video (i.e., What encounters are evident in the video?).
2. Ask: *How did the situation encountered in the video by the mom allow for reflection or change? Were the changes internal or external?*

3. Explain that students are going to examine how encounters with different situations and people allow for reflection and change through a common situational pattern called the hero's journey.
4. Divide students into groups. Ask them to respond to and agree upon responses to the following questions:
   - Define the term *hero*.
   - Can any character archetype be a hero? Why or why not?
   - How does one become a hero? Can someone choose to be a hero?
   - What are common characteristics of a hero?
   - If someone fails, can he or she still be a hero?
   - What approach do heroes have when encountering risk? What does this say about them?
   - Does someone have to encounter conflict to become a hero?

In-Class Activities to Deepen Learning

1. Explain that for fictional and real-life heroes, there is often an encounter that forces them into action (e.g., Bruce Wayne transforming himself into Batman because of the crime in Gotham City, or Professor McGonagall heroically defending Hogwarts while it was under attack).
2. Show the video "What Makes a Hero?" (see Materials list). As students watch, tell them to take notes and be prepared to discuss the following:
   - What are the steps of the hero's journey? (Sample response: Ordinary world, call to adventure, refusal, meeting with mentor, crossing threshold, tests and trials, reward, road back, resurrection, return.)
   - What other stories can you think of that resemble the hero's journey? (Guide students to understand that many books and movies follow this pattern.)
   - What makes the hero's journey an archetype or something that may mimic a real-life situation that is evidenced in all cultures? (Students may discuss how many individuals may leave their comfort zone and encounter some quest or problem and reach a new place emotionally or physically; sometimes they have mentors to help them along the way; sometimes they are resistant to move out of their comfort zone.)

3. Explain that stories may qualify as a hero's journey without meeting all of the criteria (e.g., refusal). The journey may be abbreviated as follows (list the steps on the board, and note that this version will be used in this lesson):
   - Call or departure from known to unknown
   - Encounter/quest (generally with trials or problems to overcome and a mentor or individual to support the hero along the way)
   - Return (generally with new knowledge of oneself, the world, and others)

4. Tell students to revisit their plot maps and recall the discussion about *The Controller*. Ask:
   - How was the mom's journey in *The Controller* a hero's journey?
   - What is the call to action or event that moves the mom unexpectedly from the known to the unknown?
   - Why was she being pulled to a new place? Was this an internal or external purpose or both?
   - What unanticipated encounters, people, or situations does the she face? How does she react? What does that action reveal about her?
   - What help did she have along the way? Who else did she encounter along the way?
   - To what extent did the mom learn something about herself or the world while on the journey? To what extent did her encounters shape her views?

5. Divide students into pairs. Ask them to discuss the following: *What other examples of a hero's journey can you recall from the books you have read?* (Refer students to the picture book activity from Lesson 2 or other stories they have read. Allow students time to share examples in pairs and with the whole class. Make sure they cite examples.)

6. Pose the following question and ask students to represent their thinking by standing in one corner of the room based on their thinking: *Is the hero's journey best represented as a circle (corner 1), a line or graph (corner 2), a corkscrew/spiral (corner 3), or another shape (corner 4)?* Discuss. (Students may say a circle because the journey is cyclic and never-ending, a line graph as there are ups and downs in the journey, a spiral because they end in a higher place than where they started, etc. Other ideas should include a link to their understanding of the journey as a process or situation.)

Biography Study

1. Ask students: *How is the hero's journey also evident in the lives of everyday people?* Allow time for discussion. Ask: *Is your life a hero's journey? Why or why not?*
2. Distribute Handout 4.1: Biographies, and ask students to read through at least three of the five biographies. (Each student in a small group could read one biography and then share his or her findings with others in the group.) After students have completed their initial reading, lead a discussion:
   - How did each individual deal with his or her unexpected encounters?
   - What features made each person successful when he or she encountered difficulty?

- What patterns do you notice across the lives of the individuals? To what extent do their lives represent a hero's journey?
- How did their encounters allow for threats and opportunities?
- How did encounters with mentors or education help them on their quests?
- What lessons can be applied to our own lives based on what we have learned by studying encounters in their lives?
- To what extent might the Ship of Theseus meaning (see Lesson 1) compare to a hero's journey or someone's personal journey?
- Jung argued that archetypes are consistent across cultures and time. Based on the biographies, is this true?

Poetry Reading

1. Divide students into small groups. Distribute Handout 4.2: "We never know how high we are" by Emily Dickinson for students to read, looking at another way individuals encounter their situations. As a class, define unknown words such as *statures* (our height or attainment/reputation) and *cubits* (measurement that is approximately the length of a forearm). With their groups, ask students to discuss the following questions (modeled from the Literary Analysis Wheel) and be prepared to discuss their ideas as an entire class (alternatively you may use the Literary Analysis Wheel to analyze the poem if students need the visual):
    - What does the poem say about fear? (Sample response: We should not let fear get in the way of our greatness; if we were not afraid to rise and take risks even in our successes, we could be heroes.)
    - How do the words *statures* and *cubits* help the reader visualize the difference between meeting our goals and fear? (Sample response: These words provide imagery for how fear warps/bends our potential heights of success.)
    - How does Dickinson suggest people should respond when encountering circumstances that call them into action? (Sample response: People should take risks and be bold, as their heroic acts may have positive consequences.)
    - How does the poem's structure reveal a hero's journey? (Sample response: There is a call to rise, a possible refusal because of fear, and a daily quest to succeed or meet our goals even though we may encounter our own fear along the way that we have to overcome.)
    - Is there a sage or helper in poem—like in the hero's journey? (Students may say that individuals must help themselves—they must become their own sage to overcome their fear.)

Encounters With Archetypes

- What, according to the poem, motivates individuals on their journey? (Sample response: Individuals are motivated by their desires and goals ["true to plan, our statures touch the skies"] and emotions ["the cubits warp; for fear to be a king"].)
- What does the poem suggest about encounters within ourselves? (Sample response: We have the power to rise and be heroes, leaders.)
- Does the poem refer to an everyday journey or a longer journey? (Student responses will vary.)
- What situational, symbolic, and character archetypes does Dickinson use to convey her message? (Sample response: "For fear to be a king" refers to the leader archetype by listing the position of power someone is in; "til we are called to rise" suggests a quest or a call to action.)

2. Complete Handout 4.3: Reasoning About a Situation or Event with students, posing the question: *What motivates a hero?* Explore the point of view, assumptions, and the implications/consequences for each stakeholder (see Figure 4). Discuss the positive and negative implications of different motives and the impact of these motivations on others in the short and long term. You may also discuss whether or not heroes plan to become heroes based on the evidence.

Choice-Based Differentiated Products

Students may choose one of the following to complete (*Note*: Use Rubric 1: Product Rubric in Appendix C to assess student responses):

- Do all heroes' and heroines' journeys have a villain? Explain using evidence from stories, poems, and your own life as well as how the generalization "Encounters may lead to threats or opportunities" applies.
- How does a person's internal or external conflict affect his or her response to a problem or challenge? Write a poem similar to Dickinson's to convey your response. Be sure to answer the question and use encounter generalizations.
- Can any character archetype be a hero and a _____ (companion, villain, person in need of saving, etc.)? Select a character other than a hero, and create an annotated plot map of the hero's journey that outlines how that particular archetype follows a hero's journey (or not). Then, write a paragraph that explains whether or not the archetypal pattern of a particular character impacts how the character encounters his or her journey. How is the character's perceived journey similar to or different from another archetype's response?

	What Motivates a Hero?			
Stakeholders	**Mom From** *The Controller*	**Audience of "We never know how high we are"**	**Mother Teresa**	**My Life**
Point of View	Motivated by fear, love, and protection of a loved one.	Potential heroes are motivated by their emotions and fears of success or failure.	Motivated by internal drive to help others.	
Assumptions	She will do anything to protect a loved one; she assumes that she can protect her son; she also assumes that her son's video games are pointless. When she steps into that world and embarks on the hero's journey, her mind is changed.	Fear of success or failure may cause some people to not reach hero status.	We are called to serve others and make the world a better place.	
Implications	She becomes closer with her son; being motivated by fear or protection of a loved one makes you do things that you would not have otherwise done.	Heroism is a daily thing that we are called to, and we should not let fear get in the way of it.	We all have choices and passions; we can all be heroes in the eyes of others. This everyday heroism is part of a lifelong journey that requires sacrifice.	

Figure 4. Sample responses to Handout 4.3. Adapted from "Reasoning About a Situation or Event" by Center for Gifted Education, n.d., retrieved from http://education.wm.edu/centers/cfge/curriculum/teachingmodels. Copyright 2015 by William & Mary, Center for Gifted Education.

Opportunities for Talent Development

- Ask students to think of someone in their lives or community who encountered a challenge: *How did he or she respond to that challenge, and how did that individual and/or your community change as a result? Write a letter to that individual explaining how you see the hero's journey, as well as specific encounter generalizations, evident in his or her life.*
- What would a modern-day hero look like? What would his or her hero's journey be? What characteristics would he or she have? Have students create a wanted poster for a modern-day hero that outlines a combination of multiple character and situational archetypes into a new prototype. Students may use symbols from Handout 2.1: Archetypes Quick Reference Guide as part of their designs.

Social-Emotional Connection

One of the hidden elements within the hero's journey is the element of risk. Risk can be defined as an encounter with the potential for danger. Sometimes the character, when faced with an encounter, has to decide whether the risk is worth the reward. Ask students: *Has there ever been a time in your life when you have made a calculated risk? What was the risk, and what was the possible reward? What does responsible risk-taking look like? Create a list of criteria for someone to consider before taking a calculated risk.*

ELA Task

Assign the following task as a performance-based assessment for this lesson: *After reading one of the biographies on Handout 4.1, explain how encounters led to threats and opportunities for the individual. Did those threats and opportunities align with part of the hero's journey? Are they necessary for change and growth? Cite relevant and sufficient evidence to support your response.*

Concept Connections

1. Lead a class discussion: *How do people who encounter everyday problems change our world? How is their world changed through their encounters?*
2. Continue to add to the concept map-working wall or have students use Handout 1.2: Concept Organizer (from Lesson 1 or see Appendix B) to record how encounter generalizations are applied to a specific story from today's lesson. (Sample response: Encounters allow for prediction: When a hero encounters a problem, we can predict the hero will face his or her fear

and move forward in courage. In the last box, students should relate the idea of encounter to the concept of *growth*. The trials and obstacles within the hero's journey allow the character to grow.)

Assessment

- Examine choice-based differentiated products and rubric criteria, ELA Task responses, and/or Concept Connections. Use Rubric 1: Product Rubric to review the products.
- Have students complete an exit ticket: *Select a story that you know and analyze it, discussing whether or not it follows the hero's journey.*

Name: _____ Date: _____

Handout 4.1
Biographies

JACKIE ROBINSON

Life is not a spectator sport. If you're going to spend your whole life in the grandstand just watching what goes on, in my opinion you're wasting your life.

Born in Georgia in 1919, Jackie Robinson would one day become one of the most recognized and notable baseball players in history. Growing up in Southern California, Jackie idolized his older brother, who encouraged him to pursue his growing interest in athletics. Excelling in baseball, track, football, and basketball, Jackie was seen as a quadruple threat when he entered college at University of California, Los Angeles (UCLA). Unfortunately, due to financial difficulties, Jackie was forced to drop out of college during his senior year. Following a short stint playing football in Hawaii, he went go on to serve in the U.S. Army in World War II, where he was honorably discharged following his refusal to give up his seat on a bus in Texas. In 1946 Jackie married his fellow UCLA classmate Rachel Isum. For the next few years, Jackie played baseball at the professional level in a segregated league.

After showing promise in the African American league, Jackie was signed to a farm league in Florida, where he was eventually signed by Branch Rickey (1881–1965) of the Brooklyn Dodgers. In 1947 he became the first African American to play major league baseball. Branch, the general manager of the Dodgers, knew that not everyone was a fan of the integration of an African American baseball player. He encouraged Jackie to ignore the racist outcries and focus on proving himself as an athlete. Before starting a game one day in Cincinnati, Jackie found himself on the receiving end of some harsh, racist words. Devastated and distracted, he struck out with the bases loaded and then later made a fielding error. As the story goes, the crowd's obscenities grew louder and harsher.

Pee Wee Reese, Jackie's teammate, called a time-out. Pee Wee, a White baseball player who was originally from Kentucky, approached Jackie and said, "Jackie, let me tell you something. I believe in you. You are the greatest ballplayer I have ever seen. You can do it. I know that. And I know something else: One of these days you are going into the Hall of Fame. So, hold your head up high and play ball like only you can do it." Encouraged by the words of his teammate and friend, Jackie ignored the continued slurs from the crowd and went on to help his team win the game. At his induction into the Baseball Hall of Fame in 1962, Robinson recalled his conversation with Pee Wee: "He saved my life and my career that day. I had lost my confidence, and Pee Wee picked me up with his words of encouragement. He gave me hope when all hope was gone." Jackie, remembered for his jersey number 42, continues to be one of the most celebrated and remembered baseball players of the 20th century, both for his baseball abilities and his resiliency in the face of racism.

Name: _____ Date: _____

Handout 4.1, *continued*

References

Biography.com. (2018). *Jackie Robinson biography.* Retrieved from https://www.biography.com/people/jackie-robinson-9460813

Cronin, B. (2013). *Did Reese really embrace Robinson in 1947?* Retrieved from http://www.espn.com/blog/playbook/fandom/post/_/id/20917/did-reese-really-embrace-robinson-in-47

Name: _____ Date: _____

Handout 4.1, *continued*

LIN-MANUEL MIRANDA

> Anytime you write something, you go through so many phases. You go through the "I'm a Fraud" phase. You go through the "I'll Never Finish" phase. And every once in a while you think, "What if I actually have created what I set out to create, and it's received as such?"

Lin-Manuel Miranda is an actor, performer, composer, writer, and lyricist known for his work on the Broadway musicals *Hamilton* and *In the Heights,* as well as his work in television and movies, including the animated film *Moana*. His stage productions blend elements of contemporary music, like hip-hop and rap, with more traditional musical theater, while also allowing a space for minority actors and artists to shine. His productive and celebrated career serves as an example of what young people can accomplish when they add value and cultivate their passions from an early age.

Born to parents of Puerto Rican descent in 1980, Lin-Manuel grew up in a home where a love for music and theater was embraced and encouraged. As a young adult, he took piano lessons and acted in stage productions at his high school. While attending college at Wesleyan University, Lin-Manuel laid the foundation for his first musical, *Into the Heights*. From there, as they say, the rest is history. To date, his work has been recognized with a Pulitzer, three Tony Awards, three Grammys, and a Kennedy Center Honors.

Lin-Manuel had the chance to interview one of his own idols, Broadway's historical icon Stephen Sondheim. During their conversation, Lin-Manuel learned about the different ways another composer approached the creative and collaborative processes. Lin-Manuel wrote an article about their interview, stating, "The days of competition with other musical theater songwriters are done: We now talk about his work the way we talk about Shakespeare or Dickens or Picasso—a master of his form, both invisible within his work and everywhere at once." Earlier in Lin-Manuel's career, he showed Sondheim his ideas for the hit musical *Hamilton*. The positive feedback from Sondheim kept Lin-Manuel going, even through difficult times. His admiration for Sondheim's work and their relationship continue to impact the stage of modern musical theater.

References

Biography.com. (2018). *Lin-Manuel Miranda biography.* Retrieved from https://www.biography.com/people/lin-manuel-miranda-041416

Miranda, L. M. (2017). Stephen Sondheim, theater's greatest lyricist. *The New York Times Style Magazine.* Retrieved from https://www.nytimes.com/2017/10/16/t-magazine/lin-manuel-miranda-stephen-sondheim.html

Name: _____ Date: _____

Handout 4.1, *continued*

MOTHER TERESA

Kind words can be short and easy to speak, but their echoes are truly endless.

Mother Teresa (1910–1997) devoted her life to worldwide charity and service. Originally from Macedonia, Mother Teresa began her call to service as a young girl of 12 years old. She felt the call of God early in her youth—a call that would lead her to impact the world. At 18, Mother Teresa joined a group of Irish nuns, the Sisters of Loreto, and journeyed to India. It was in India in 1931 when Mother Teresa officially took her vows as a nun, and where she spent 17 years teaching at a Catholic convent school in Calcutta, India. However, her social awareness of the suffering and poverty surrounding her spurred her transition from the convent to the slums of Calcutta. Making the move from the Catholic convent to teaching in the slums had large implications for what she could accomplish in terms of funding. Being on her own meant that Mother Teresa relied on charitable donations, volunteers, and her own faith in her calling. Her personal and spiritual convictions led her causes even further; they opened the world up to the relief and vision that Mother Teresa wanted to fulfill.

In 1950, Mother Teresa started her own order, "The Missionaries of Charity." Since then, her missions have been devoted to love and care for the poorest of the poor, providing relief after catastrophes and housing the unsheltered or marginalized. These efforts reached across the globe, as the order established in 1950 became an International Religious Family, decreed by Pope Paul VI. Mother Teresa is a name recognized internationally—her work and philosophy are embedded in societies and cultures around the world. Millions of missionaries, churches, orders, and civilians try to follow Mother Teresa's faithful charity. It might be hard to imagine Mother Teresa as a normal human being; Pope Francis declared Mother Teresa a saint in 2016. However, she faced trails and sought help from people, which kept her own faith and spirits up throughout her life.

One influence that Mother Teresa relied on, to keep her relationship with her faith and her work strong, was Father Michael Van der Peet. Mother Teresa and Father Van der Peet's meeting was a chance encounter that impacted both of their lives and legacies. In October 1975, Father Van der Peet recognized Mother Teresa as she waited at a bus stop in Rome. What initially began as a priest in awe of Mother Teresa turned into a mutually beneficial relationship. Mother Teresa asked Father Van der Peet for spiritual help, not only for the missionaries and charities, but also for prayers for her own soul. Their meeting, although short, lasted a lifetime through letters exchanged, services fulfilled, and spiritual guidance. Mother Teresa and Father Van der Peet were mutually impacted by their encounter.

References

Biography.com. (2018). *Mother Teresa biography*. Retrieved from https://www.biography.com/people/mother-teresa-9504160

NobelPrize.org. (2018). *Mother Teresa biographical*. Retrieved from https://www.nobelprize.org/prizes/peace/1979/teresa/biographical

Name: _____ Date: _____

Handout 4.1, *continued*

SALLY RIDE

The stars don't look bigger, but they do look brighter.

Sally Ride (1951–2012) was an astronaut, physicist, and educator, who changed the fields of science and space exploration. In 1983, Sally became the first American woman to go into space. She devoted the rest of her life to research, education, and inspiring young girls to pursue science. Breaking records required discipline, confidence, and perseverance for when the odds seemed against her. Sally Ride was one of thousands of individuals who applied for a spot in the National Aeronautics and Space Administration's (NASA) astronaut program. She persisted despite the fact that no other American woman had made it to that position yet. Additionally, some people were not ready to have a woman in such a powerful position.

However, Ride was not alone in her journey to success; she had support and coaching along the way. Her biggest support entered her life when she began her Ph.D. at Stanford University, where she also completed her bachelor's degree and master's degree. There, Sally met Arthur Walker, the man who mentored her and inspired her confidence to reach her goals. Arthur was no stranger to needing perseverance. As an African American man, he fought hard to make his dream of studying and teaching science at Stanford University come true. When he met Sally, their collaboration was a good fit, as he had a passion for mentoring students who were traditionally underrepresented in the sciences (namely women and African Americans), and Sally had dreams to overcome her own obstacles. After Sally's successes, she wanted to help other young people in the sciences, just as Arthur Walker had mentored Sally. She went on to focus on her educational program called Sally Ride Science to inspire young women and girls to follow their interests in science and math. Her legacy mirrors her own experiences with mentorship, goal setting, and perseverance.

References

Bergelson, M. (2014). The mentor who launched Sally Ride into orbit. *Modern Workforce.* Retrieved from https://www.geteverwise.com/mentoring/the-mentor-who-launched-sally-ride-into-orbit

Biography.com. (2018). *Sally Ride biography.* Retrieved from https://www.biography.com/people/sally-ride-9458284

Name: _____ Date: _____

Handout 4.1, *continued*

OPRAH WINFREY

> Do the one thing you think you cannot do. Fail at it. Try again. Do better the second time. The only people who never tumble are those who never mount the high wire.

Oprah Winfrey is a beloved and iconic American TV host, actress, producer, and philanthropist. Oprah was born in Mississippi and spent her childhood and adolescence moving between the small farming village with her mother and Nashville, TN, with her father. Life for Oprah was not easy. During her time in Mississippi, she was abused. A series of moves and difficult transitions led her to live with her father in Tennessee. Life in Nashville was safer, and Oprah's talent and passions were able to flourish. She gave speeches, participated in drama club, and competed for honors as a scholar and performer. Perhaps most importantly, while living with her father, Oprah learned to value education and reading. Her father set high and strict expectations for Oprah to read, speak, and continue learning every day. Oprah recognized the opportunity that reading books offered her: they opened the world to her, even as a young girl in Mississippi or Tennessee. Oprah professed that "books were my path to personal freedom," inspiring her to dream beyond her own backyard.

Oprah has honored this commitment her whole life, funding and designing ways to get people reading good books. Today, the Oprah Winfrey book club prioritizes literacy among children, adults, and every age in between. Oprah's passion for books connected her to a prominent influence in her life—author Maya Angelou. Oprah and Maya Angelou had an immediate connection, Oprah has even called Angelou her "mother-sister-friend," as she could comfort, support, and celebrate with her. Oprah could see her own life mirrored in so much of Angelou's writing. Oprah felt validated through reading Angelou's work; the writing validated her own experiences as a young African American girl growing up in the South. Oprah valued this relationship deeply, feeling comforted by Angelou's words in moments of pain or loneliness.

References

Oprah.com. (2000). *Oprah talks to Maya Angelou.* Retrieved from https://www.oprah.com/omagazine/oprah-interviews-maya-angelou

Biography.com. (2018). *Oprah Winfrey biography.* Retrieved from https://www.biography.com/people/oprah-winfrey-9534419

Notablebiographies.com. (2018). *Oprah Winfrey.* Retrieved from https://www.notablebiographies.com/We-Z/Winfrey-Oprah.html

Name: _____ Date: _____

Handout 4.2
"We never know how high we are" *by Emily Dickinson*

We never know how high we are
Till we are asked to rise
And then if we are true to plan
Our statures touch the skies —

The Heroism we recite
Would be a normal thing
Did not ourselves the Cubits warp
For fear to be a King —

Name: _____ Date: _____

Handout 4.3
Reasoning About a Situation or Event

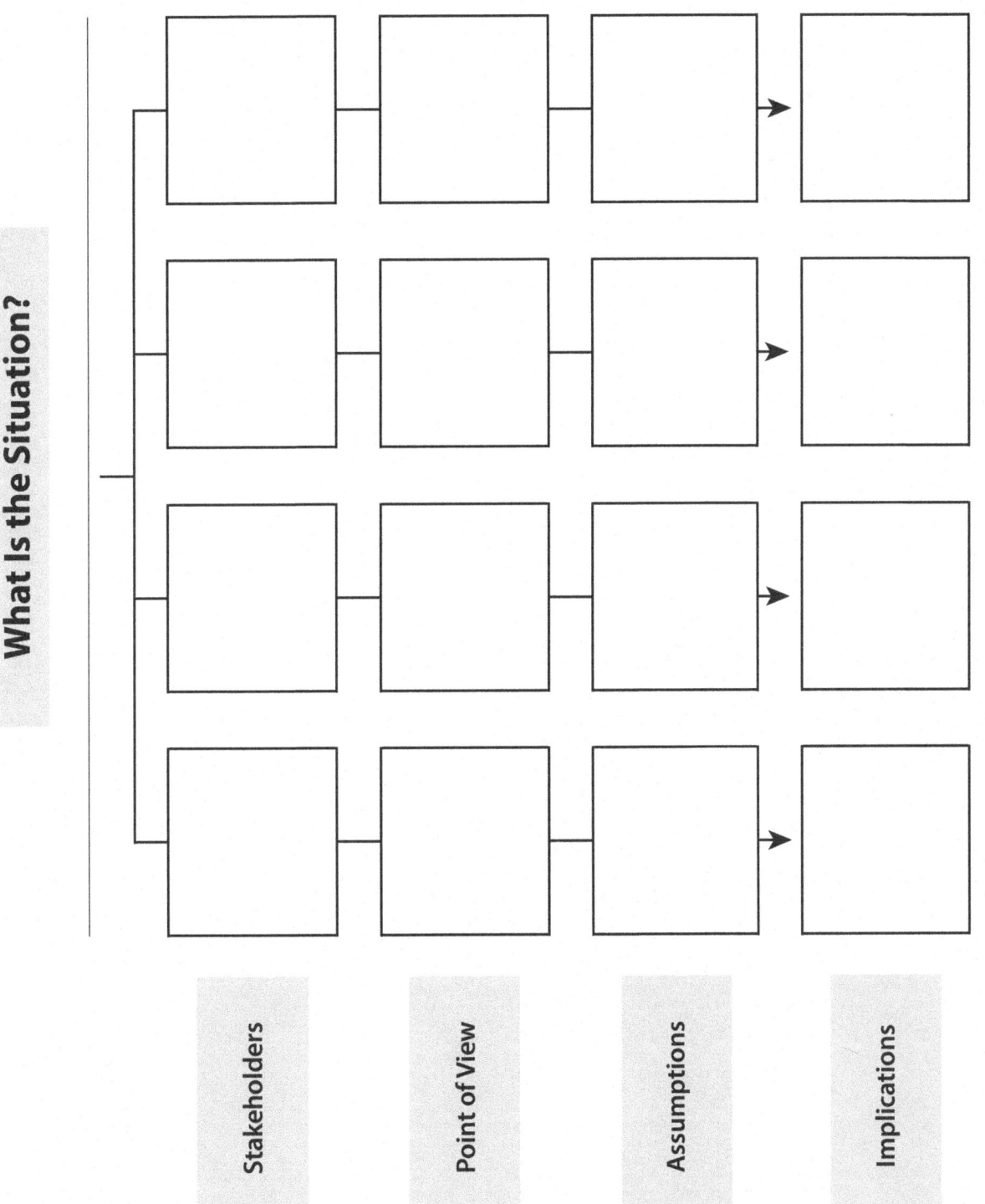

Lesson

Encounters With Situational Archetypes

Key Question

How do encounters with situational archetypes shape our views?

Objectives

Content: To analyze and interpret fiction, nonfiction, and art, students will be able to:
- compare and contrast how literary, visual, informational, and/or primary source texts reveal patterns and themes;
- compare and contrast the use of specific techniques various authors use to approach and develop similar ideas; and
- identify and analyze archetypal patterns in stories, speeches, and real-world contexts and discuss how they are shaped by the author or real-world individuals or events.

Process: To develop interpretation, analysis, and communication skills in the language arts, students will be able to:
- justify inferences with evidence from the text;
- apply evidence to support explanations and opinions relative to a question, text, or issue; and
- respond to an analysis of literature, nonfiction, media, or art by developing arguments and elaborating on explanations through writing a variety of texts (e.g., essays, paragraphs), including relevant and sufficient evidence to support claims.

Concept: To develop conceptual thinking about encounters in language arts and additional content areas, students will be able to:
- explain with evidence how encounters may lead to positive or negative outcomes in literature, media, and real-world examples;
- explain how encounters allow for prediction in literature and real-world examples;

Encounters With Archetypes

- relate encounter generalizations to real-life situations; and
- examine the relationship between encounters and other concepts in multiple contexts.

Accelerated CCSS for ELA

- RI.5.3
- RI.6.9
- RI.7.1
- RI.7.2
- RI.7.5
- W.6.1
- W.7.10
- SL.6.1

Materials

- Video: "Can You Solve the Bridge Riddle? - Alex Gendler" (available at https://www.youtube.com/watch?v=7yDmGnA8Hw0)
- Video: "'Runaway' by Susan Yung, Esther Parobek and Emily Buchanan | Disney Favorite" (available at https://www.youtube.com/watch?v=lOReXHOSnvw)
- Chart paper and markers (per groups of 2–4 students)
- (Optional) Video: "1st Inaugural Address: President Reagans Inaugural Address 1/20/81" (available at https://www.youtube.com/watch?v=LToM9bAnsyM)
- Student copies of excerpt from "On the Pulse of Morning" by Maya Angelou (beginning with "Plant yourself besides the river. Each of you, descendant . . .")
- Handout 1.2: Concept Organizer
- Handout 2.1: Archetype Quick Reference Guide
- Handout 5.1: Excerpt From President Reagan's First Inaugural Address
- Handout 5.2: Blank Rhetorical Analysis Wheel
- Rubric 1: Product Rubric (Appendix C)

Introductory Activities

1. Ask students to work individually or with a partner to complete a challenging brainteaser or riddle, such as "Can You Solve the Bridge Riddle?" (see Materials list). After allowing students to work through a productive struggle, ask them to reflect: *What were your internal and external encounters in this experience?* (Sample response: External encounters might include the challenge, figuring out a different way to approach the problem, cooperation with peers; internal might include frustration, self-doubt, or confidence, if solved.)
2. Remind students that situational archetypes are universal patterns of circumstances that happen in life. Ask students to look over Handout 2.1. Ask:

What situation did you experience while solving the brainteaser/riddle? (Sample response: A difficult task.) *How did the situation shape your view (i.e., how did the situation affect your views on solving riddles?)? Did it cause you to want to solve more, or did it cause frustration?* Explain that in this lesson, students will examine other types of situational archetypes and how these archetypes shape views.

In-Class Activities to Deepen Thinking

1. Referring to Handout 2.1, ask students: *Are all of the situations on this list considered encounters? Why or why not? What might be "encountered" unexpectedly in these situations?* (Sample response: In a quest, an obstacle may be encountered; in initiation, an unexpected disappointment may be encountered; in the battle of good versus evil, an unexpected gain on one side or the other is encountered, etc.)
2. Show the short film *Runaway* (see Materials list). Ask students:
    - What are the major plot elements? (Guide students by showing a plot diagram or the "somebody wanted, but, so, then" structure: Chillie wanted to be loved, but his handle broke, so he thought he would be replaced and ran away to the garbage dump, and then his owner found him and fixed him.)
    - What situational archetypes are present in this plot sequence? Refer to Handout 2.1: Archetype Quick Reference Guide. (Sample response: Situational archetypes include an unhealable wound [the broken handle] and death and rebirth [Chillie is "reborn" with new a handle and new outlook on his relationship]. Note that these situations can be within a hero's journey.)
    - How does the unhealable wound situation shape the views of Chillie? How does the unhealable wound shape the views of the young man? (Sample response: The broken handle causes Chillie to question his worth and value to his owner; the broken handle motivates the owner to help Chillie.)
    - How does the death and rebirth situation shape the views of Chillie? (Sample response: As he receives a new handle, representing a "type" of rebirth situation, he realizes that he is truly valued and loved by his owner.)
    - How is the story in *Runaway* a reversed viewpoint of "The Dog of Pompeii"? (Sample response: "The Dog of Pompeii" focuses more on the companion, and although we see some perspective of the owner companion, *Runaway* focuses more on the character in need of rescue.) How does the same situation (unhealable wound) reveal different insights into

Encounters With Archetypes

the human experience when the point of view is from different character archetypes? (Sample response: "The Dog of Pompeii" reveals the companion's desire to be loyal toward the person with the unhealable wound; in *Runaway*, we see the perspective of the character in need of rescue and more of the appreciation received from the love of the companion/caregiver.)

- Is *Runaway* essentially the same story as *Corduroy*? How do you know? Compare their character and situational archetypes. How do these stories support or deny Jung's view that all cultures unconsciously recognize, experience, and attempt to explain similar behaviors and situations they encounter? What do both stories say about the human experience? (Sample response: Both stories have similar archetypes: unhealable wound, person in need of rescue, darkness, companion; the idea that we all desire to be loved and accepted is evident in both stories.)

3. Have students further examine situational archetypes by selecting another story (from this unit) or a familiar video game (share that video games may display many archetypal situations and the hero's journey; e.g., Minecraft, Zelda, Pokémon, Mario). Divide students into groups based on their selected games or stories and provide each group with chart paper. Ask students to record on the chart paper the title of the story/game and a brief synopsis of the plot using the "somebody, wanted, but, so, then" structure or a plot diagram or game map.

4. Then, ask students to label the plot map with situational archetypes (from Handout 2.1) that they notice in the story/game. Students may need to discuss amongst their small groups:
   - What is the goal of the game for the player?/What is the goal for the main character?
   - What are the obstacles (negative encounters) in the game/story? How is the player/character affected?
   - What are the positive encounters in the game/story? How is the player/character affected?
   - How does the player's "encounter" with the game affect the player as an individual (i.e., consider positive/negative emotions, relationships, internal and external changes, etc.)? How does the reader's "encounter" with the story affect the reader as an individual?

5. Ask groups to share their findings. Then, ask: *How do the encounters within the plot allow for prediction of situational archetypes? In other words, what are some general patterns you notice with character interactions, obstacles,*

and outcomes as they relate to situations? How do these situations shape the views of the character/player?

Read Text

Explain to students that situational archetypes mirror real-world circumstances. Distribute Handout 5.1: Excerpt From President Reagan's First Inaugural Address. Students will read the political speech to examine how situational archetypes are presented and how they may inspire or shape views of listeners. Explain that President Ronald Reagan assumed office in 1981, at a time when the United States was dealing with a variety of national and international crises (hostages in Iran, economic instability and inflation, etc.). Consider showing a photograph of President Reagan or a portion of his inaugural address (see Materials list).

Text-Dependent Questions

Select from the following text-dependent questions for leading a Socratic seminar or class discussion:

1. How does Reagan define *hero*? Why does he use this speech to remind his audience of who heroes are? (Sample response: Reagan defines heroes as the everyday people serving their country and their communities. Due to the economic climate, he is calling on people to step into the role of hero.)
2. What effect does Reagan give listeners when he transitions from using "they" and "their" to "you" and "your"? Why is this narrative technique effective? (Sample response: The shift from they/their to you/your makes the listeners believe that they are the heroes he is referring to in his speech. This is effective because it draws them to share his claim.)
3. Where in the speech does Reagan shift his focus from everyday heroes to heroes who had given their lives? When does he shift back? Why does his focus on who heroes are shift? (Sample response: The shift occurs toward the end of the speech. The emphasis on heroes who have given the ultimate sacrifice implies that the sacrifice he is asking of everyday Americans, although important, does not bear similar consequences.)
4. At what point does Reagan refer to Belleau Wood, Salerno, Guadalcanal, etc.? What is he referring to? Why does he list so many examples? (Sample response: He is referring to foreign battlefields where American soldiers lost their lives. This repetition takes place near the end of the speech.)
5. What evidence of hope does Reagan provide concerning the future? (Sample response: At the close of the speech Reagan says, "our willingness to believe in ourselves and to believe in our capacity to perform great deeds" will help solve our problems. When discussing the problems yet to be solved, he says

Encounters With Archetypes

that an "emphatic yes" is the response when wondering whether solutions would be found.)

Now consider how the speech includes several allusions to situational archetypes. Ask students to highlight or circle references that imply a situational archetype. The following questions may be used to guide students:

1. To Reagan, what is America's "quest"? (Sample response: The quest is to restore the land of America—to address the problems outlined in the speech.)
2. What evidence from the speech supports an idea of "quest"? (Sample response: He opens the speech by talking about a heroic dream—a goal to be pursued. He alludes to restoring the land in paragraph 5, and the challenges that lie ahead—"as for enemies of freedom.")
3. How does the quest bring self-knowledge to America? (Sample response: To perform great deeds, we must confront them together.)
4. How does Reagan allude to "death and rebirth"? (Sample response: He wants to bring back a strong economy; "It is time to reawaken this industrial giant, to get government back within its means, and to lighten our punitive tax burden.")
5. How does Reagan imply good versus evil and human versus technology archetypes? (Sample response: He implies good versus evil through "enemies of freedom" and "I will fight"; he implies technology through "arsenal of weapons.")
6. How might you explain these situational archetypes as a part of the larger context of America's own "hero's journey"? (Sample response: The hero's journey is evidenced through the call to freedom, starting with Washington; the quest with economic, political, and social challenges; and the return to America's core ideals.)
7. Why might the inclusion of archetypes be important to a speech? (Sample response: Archetypes are universal ideas that appeal and relate to human psychology across cultures and time.)
8. How did Reagan use the listeners' encounters with situational archetypes to shape their views? (Sample response: Reagan wants to inspire Americans to see the greatness of America and perform great deeds—go through the quest, battle good versus evil, confront technology, and experience rebirth—together.)
9. How is this speech relevant to real-world issues today? (Sample response: Politicians continue to use rhetoric related to everyday heroes rising to the occasion. As new crises emerge, from hurricanes to food shortages, everyday heroes often step in to provide assistance when encountering those in need.)

Rhetorical Analysis

Ask students to complete Handout 5.2: Blank Rhetorical Analysis Wheel in pairs or in small groups. Explain that in order to evaluate an argument, they have to determine the author's purpose and main argument (claim). They will examine specific appeals (pathos, ethos, and logos) used to support the claim and how these appeals are developed by techniques, organization, and assumptions by the writer. Students may take notes on the wheel and draw arrows to illustrate connections between the various elements. Alternatively, you may guide students to use a simpler version, the Text Analysis Wheel (see Appendix A for a sample lesson), or discuss the wheel as a whole group if these concepts are new. Some sample questions and responses to lead to analysis include:

Simple Questions:
1. **Purpose:** What is Reagan's purpose for delivering this speech? (Sample response: Reagan intends to inspire listeners to believe in the potential of America because of its heroes.)
2. **Claim:** What is Reagan's main claim? What is the main idea he is proving? (Sample response: Reagan claims that America can set an example for freedom by individuals coming together to collectively solve problems.)
3. **Point of View:** What is Reagan's point of view toward America and heroes? What are his assumptions? (Sample response: Reagan assumes that all Americans are willing to make sacrifices for the greater good. He sees Americans not only as descendants of heroes, but also as heroes in the making.)
4. **Structure/Organization:** What is the overall structure of the speech? (Sample response: The speech is organized around problem/solution. Reagan introduces the problems facing America, including issues related to inflation and international adversaries, and then rolls out the solution, American heroes.)
5. **Techniques:** What are some literary techniques used in the speech? (Sample response: Reagan uses imagery to build up the idea of heroes [monuments to heroism, magnificent vista]. Organizationally, he impresses upon listeners ways in which they can be heroes, then alludes to heroes who paid the ultimate sacrifice, then casually infers that they are not expected to make as daunting of a sacrifice. Repetition is used throughout to emphasize specific points and build momentum.)
6. **Pathos:** What emotion(s) does Reagan attempt to invoke in the audience? (Sample response: Reagan uses language with both positive and negative connotations. In referencing God and prayer, he appeals to his listeners' faith and the role that each plays in their solution. By listing the foreign battlefields

where heroes have sacrificed their own lives [good vs. evil], listeners develop connections with those families and are encouraged to do their part.)
7. **Logos:** What are the main points? How does Reagan support his claim(s) with evidence and facts? What are the main reasons that support the claim? (Sample response: Reagan relies on logical claims grounded in history. By referencing founding fathers and documents, he suggests that heroic individuals who "came to greatness reluctantly" are not just a thing of the past.)
8. **Ethos:** Is Reagan credible? How does he establish trust? Is his evidence credible? (Sample response: Having served in the military during World War II in domestic public relations and war bond publicity, and given his work in government as governor of California, Reagan was in many ways seen as an American hero. Although he did not draw on his personal narrative, his historical references and use of 'we' throughout the speech developed trust with his audience.)
9. **Implications:** What are the short- and long-term implications/consequences of this speech? (Sample response: This speech set the stage for his time serving as President of the United States. During his tenure a number of economic and international issues were mitigated.)

Complex Questions:
1. **Pathos + Techniques:** What techniques are used to develop pathos appeals? (Sample response: Within the speech pathos is developed through repetition, the use of a fallen soldier's diary entry [personal experience], and religious imagery.)
2. **Logos + Structure:** How is the argument structured logically? (Sample response: This section of the speech follows a description of a current crisis facing America. Reagan moves from outlining the problem, the current state of the United States, to the solution, which he sees as everyday heroes stepping up to the occasion.)
3. **Ethos + Techniques + Structure:** What techniques are used to establish ethos appeals, and why are they placed where they are? (Sample response: Reagan gives the speech on a platform adjacent to the Capitol Building in Washington, DC, and then compares the monuments to everyday men—Washington, Jefferson, and Lincoln—who rose to become heroes and Arlington National Cemetery, where equally heroic individuals found their final resting place. As the speech progresses, the examples become more specific, from listing foreign battlefields where lives were lost, to mentioning the diary entry of a soldier who saw the meaning in his sacrifice.)
4. **Evaluation:** How effective is Reagan in supporting his claim? Is there a balance of pathos, ethos, and logos appeals? Is the claim fully supported? (Student responses may vary based on their interpretation of the speech.)

Lesson 5

Poem Comparison

1. Distribute copies of an excerpt from "On the Pulse of Morning" by Maya Angelou (starting with the line "Plant yourself beside the river, Each of you, descendant . . ."). Explain that this poem was written for and read at Bill Clinton's 1993 Inauguration. Read the poem aloud (or show a video clip of the poem being read by Maya Angelou; review the poem for age-appropriate content). Address difficult vocabulary. Then, discuss the following questions:
   - What is meant by America being a tree and encountering a new dawn? (Sample response: America is a tree that has stood strong but endured bitter histories over time. If we have courage, a new dawn of "grace" toward each other is coming.)
   - What situational archetypes do you notice? How are these situational archetypes meant to shape listeners' views? (Sample response: A rise from a fall is present. America fell from its ideals but will "rise" to its ideals and move past the darker sides of history into a more positive future. A rebirth is seen in "bright morning dawning for you" and "give birth again to the dream," and death is seen in "history . . . need not be lived again." These archetypes convey ideas of hope for a better future in which we see and value each other, despite history and differences.)

2. Ask students to compare and contrast elements from Maya Angelou's poem to Reagan's speech (see Figure 5). Specifically, compare and contrast situational archetypes, encounter generalizations, and messages about hope, heroes, and courage.

Choice-Based Differentiated Products

Students may choose one of the following to complete (*Note*: Use Rubric 1: Product Rubric in Appendix C to assess student responses):
- Read another inaugural address by a different world leader and complete a Rhetorical Analysis (using the Blank Rhetorical Analysis Wheel, see Appendix B). In a written paragraph, note the rhetorical patterns, similarities, and differences between the two speeches. Also include a comparison of any allusion to situational archetypes within your chosen speech and how the listeners' views might be shaped because of their "encounter" with this speech.
- Learn more about President Reagan's life. In what ways do his life events mirror situational archetypes, and do they fit within the context of a hero's journey? What were the most influential encounters in his life that led to threats and opportunities? How did he respond to those encounters?

Encounters With Archetypes

	Reagan's Speech	Similar Message	Maya Angelou's Poem
Situational Archetypes	Task Rebirth Quest Good vs. evil	Renewal of understanding the values of unity	Rebirth Rise (from Fall)
Links to Encounter Generalizations	Encounters may lead to threats and opportunities. The problems are opportunities for all to come together and be everyday heroes.	Encountering the newness of what's to come requires courage.	Encounters allow for reflection and change. Reflecting on the past inspires a "rise" toward a better future.
Message of Hope and Heroes/Courage	Hope is in the capacity to work together to solve problems. Heroes give ultimate sacrifices, both those who were in battle and everyday heroes.	We all must courageously step forward into what's next by coming together.	If we face the pain of the past with courage, it does not have to be lived again. We do not have to be "wed to fear." Look up and out to new possibilities. The new dawn depends on "grace" to our neighbor.

Figure 5. Poem comparison sample responses.

- Design a game, museum, video game, or adventure ride that allows the player/individual to encounter a situational archetype. In your plan, include the purpose and encounters that bring threats and opportunities along the way, and how the encounter with the situation allows for reflection and change.
- Revisit Handout 4.1. What situational archetypes do you see in each biography? Do any of the notable individuals have an unhealable wound, a rags-to-riches experience, or a fall? Write a paragraph that outlines how encounters and situational archetypes can help us bring about change and shape our views.

Opportunity for Talent Development

Ask students to think about real-world problems within their school or community (hidden hunger, isolated elderly, etc.): *How might the problem be viewed as a situational archetype? Write the problem out as a story plot, specifically as "somebody, wanted, but, so, then," labeling the plot diagram with situational archetypes and developing a solution idea through your "so, then," response.*

Social-Emotional Connection

Ask students to write a brief response: *A situational archetype may involve obstacles and challenges that shape how a character views the world. Think about your own life and a goal you are pursuing. What situational archetype seems to be most relevant (e.g., a short-term quest, such as a goal for the month)? What motivates you to continue through the situation? How does the encounter with the situation lead to positive and negative outcomes? How might you plan to prepare for obstacles? Write an if-then plan (e.g., If I get distracted from doing my homework, then I will not check my phone or look at technology until a part of the work is done).*

ELA Task

Assign the following task as a performance-based assessment for this lesson: *How do situational archetypes affect how a character shapes his or her views? Explain in a well-developed paragraph, using evidence from a story or text you have recently read.*

Concept Connections

1. Lead a class discussion: *Do all situational archetypes lead to reflection and change for a character? Provide examples to support your point of view.*
2. Use Handout 1.2 Concept Organizer (from previous lesson or see Appendix B) to record how the generalizations applied to this lesson. In the last box, students should consider the idea of encounters with our past and present. Consider how encounters as part of situational archetypes change how the characters viewed their past, present, and future.

Assessment

- Examine choice-based differentiated products and rubric criteria, ELA Task responses, and/or Concept Connections. Use Rubric 1: Product Rubric to review the products.

Encounters With Archetypes

90

- Have students complete an exit ticket: *Choose one situational archetype. On a piece of paper, draw a pair of sunglasses. On one lens, write ideas, words, and phrases associated with the situational archetype; on the other lens, write phrases to describe how the situation might shape the character's/person's perspective on life.*

Name: _____ Date: _____

Handout 5.1
Excerpt From President Reagan's First Inaugural Address

Background: *The following excerpt is the second half of President Ronald Reagan's first inaugural address. The speech was given around noon on January 20th, 1981, on a platform erected near the Capitol Building, shortly after he was sworn in as the 40th President of the United States. Earlier in the speech, President Reagan acknowledged some of the economic hardships facing Americans and, in broad statements, suggested how his administration might address the problems.*

We have every right to dream heroic dreams. Those who say that we're in a time when there are not heroes, they just don't know where to look. You can see heroes every day going in and out of factory gates. Others, a handful in number, produce enough food to feed all of us and then the world beyond. You meet heroes across a counter, and they're on both sides of that counter. There are entrepreneurs with faith in themselves and faith in an idea who create new jobs, new wealth and opportunity. They're individuals and families whose taxes support the government and whose voluntary gifts support church, charity, culture, art, and education. Their patriotism is quiet, but deep. Their values sustain our national life.

Now, I have used the words "they" and "their" in speaking of these heroes. I could say "you" and "your," because I'm addressing the heroes of whom I speak—you, the citizens of this blessed land. Your dreams, your hopes, your goals are going to be the dreams, the hopes, and the goals of this administration, so help me God.

We shall reflect the compassion that is so much a part of your makeup. How can we love our country and not love our countrymen; and loving them, reach out a hand when they fall, heal them when they're sick, and provide opportunity to make them self-sufficient so they will be equal in fact and not just in theory?

Can we solve the problems confronting us? Well, the answer is an unequivocal and emphatic "yes." To paraphrase Winston Churchill, I did not take the oath I've just taken with the intention of presiding over the dissolution of the world's strongest economy.

In the days ahead I will propose removing the roadblocks that have slowed our economy and reduced productivity. Steps will be taken aimed at restoring the balance between the various levels of government. Progress may be slow, measured in inches and feet, not miles, but we will progress. It is time to reawaken this industrial giant, to get government back within its means, and to lighten our punitive tax burden. And these will be our first priorities, and on these principles there will be no compromise.

On the eve of our struggle for independence a man who might have been one of the greatest among the Founding Fathers, Dr. Joseph Warren, president of the Massachusetts Congress, said to his fellow Americans, "Our country is in danger, but not to be despaired of . . . . On you depend the fortunes of America. You are to decide the important questions upon which rests the happiness and the liberty of millions yet unborn. Act worthy of yourselves."

Handout 5.1, *continued*

Well, I believe we, the Americans of today, are ready to act worthy of ourselves, ready to do what must be done to ensure happiness and liberty for ourselves, our children, and our children's children. And as we renew ourselves here in our own land, we will be seen as having greater strength throughout the world. We will again be the exemplar of freedom and a beacon of hope for those who do not now have freedom.

To those neighbors and allies who share our freedom, we will strengthen our historic ties and assure them of our support and firm commitment. We will match loyalty with loyalty. We will strive for mutually beneficial relations. We will not use our friendship to impose on their sovereignty, for our own sovereignty is not for sale.

As for the enemies of freedom, those who are potential adversaries, they will be reminded that peace is the highest aspiration of the American people. We will negotiate for it, sacrifice for it; we will not surrender for it, now or ever.

Our forbearance should never be misunderstood. Our reluctance for conflict should not be misjudged as a failure of will. When action is required to preserve our national security, we will act. We will maintain sufficient strength to prevail if need be, knowing that if we do so we have the best chance of never having to use that strength.

Above all, we must realize that no arsenal or no weapon in the arsenals of the world is so formidable as the will and moral courage of free men and women. It is a weapon our adversaries in today's world do not have. It is a weapon that we as Americans do have. Let that be understood by those who practice terrorism and prey upon their neighbors.

I'm told that tens of thousands of prayer meetings are being held on this day, and for that I'm deeply grateful. We are a nation under God, and I believe God intended for us to be free. It would be fitting and good, I think, if on each Inaugural Day in future years it should be declared a day of prayer.

This is the first time in our history that this ceremony has been held, as you've been told, on this West Front of the Capitol. Standing here, one faces a magnificent vista, opening up on this city's special beauty and history. At the end of this open mall are those shrines to the giants on whose shoulders we stand.

Directly in front of me, the monument to a monumental man, George Washington, father of our country. A man of humility who came to greatness reluctantly. He led America out of revolutionary victory into infant nationhood. Off to one side, the stately memorial to Thomas Jefferson. The Declaration of Independence flames with his eloquence. And then, beyond the Reflecting Pool, the dignified columns of the Lincoln Memorial. Whoever would understand in his heart the meaning of America will find it in the life of Abraham Lincoln.

Beyond those monuments to heroism is the Potomac River, and on the far shore the sloping hills of Arlington National Cemetery, with its row upon row of simple white markers bearing crosses or Stars of David. They add up to only a tiny fraction of the price that has been paid for our freedom.

Each one of those markers is a monument to the kind of hero I spoke of earlier. Their lives ended in places called Belleau Wood, The Argonne, Omaha Beach, Salerno, and halfway around the world on Guadalcanal, Tarawa, Pork Chop Hill, the Chosin Reservoir, and in a hundred rice paddies and jungles of a place called Vietnam.

Name: _____ Date: _____

Handout 5.1, *continued*

Under one such marker lies a young man, Martin Treptow, who left his job in a small town barbershop in 1917 to go to France with the famed Rainbow Division. There, on the western front, he was killed trying to carry a message between battalions under heavy artillery fire.

We're told that on his body was found a diary. On the flyleaf under the heading, "My Pledge," he had written these words: "America must win this war. Therefore I will work, I will save, I will sacrifice, I will endure, I will fight cheerfully and do my utmost, as if the issue of the whole struggle depended on me alone."

The crisis we are facing today does not require of us the kind of sacrifice that Martin Treptow and so many thousands of others were called upon to make. It does require, however, our best effort and our willingness to believe in ourselves and to believe in our capacity to perform great deeds, to believe that together with God's help we can and will resolve the problems which now confront us.

And after all, why shouldn't we believe that? We are Americans.

God bless you, and thank you.

Name: _____   Date: _____

Handout 5.2
Blank Rhetorical Analysis Wheel

Directions: Draw arrows across elements to show connections.

Text: _____

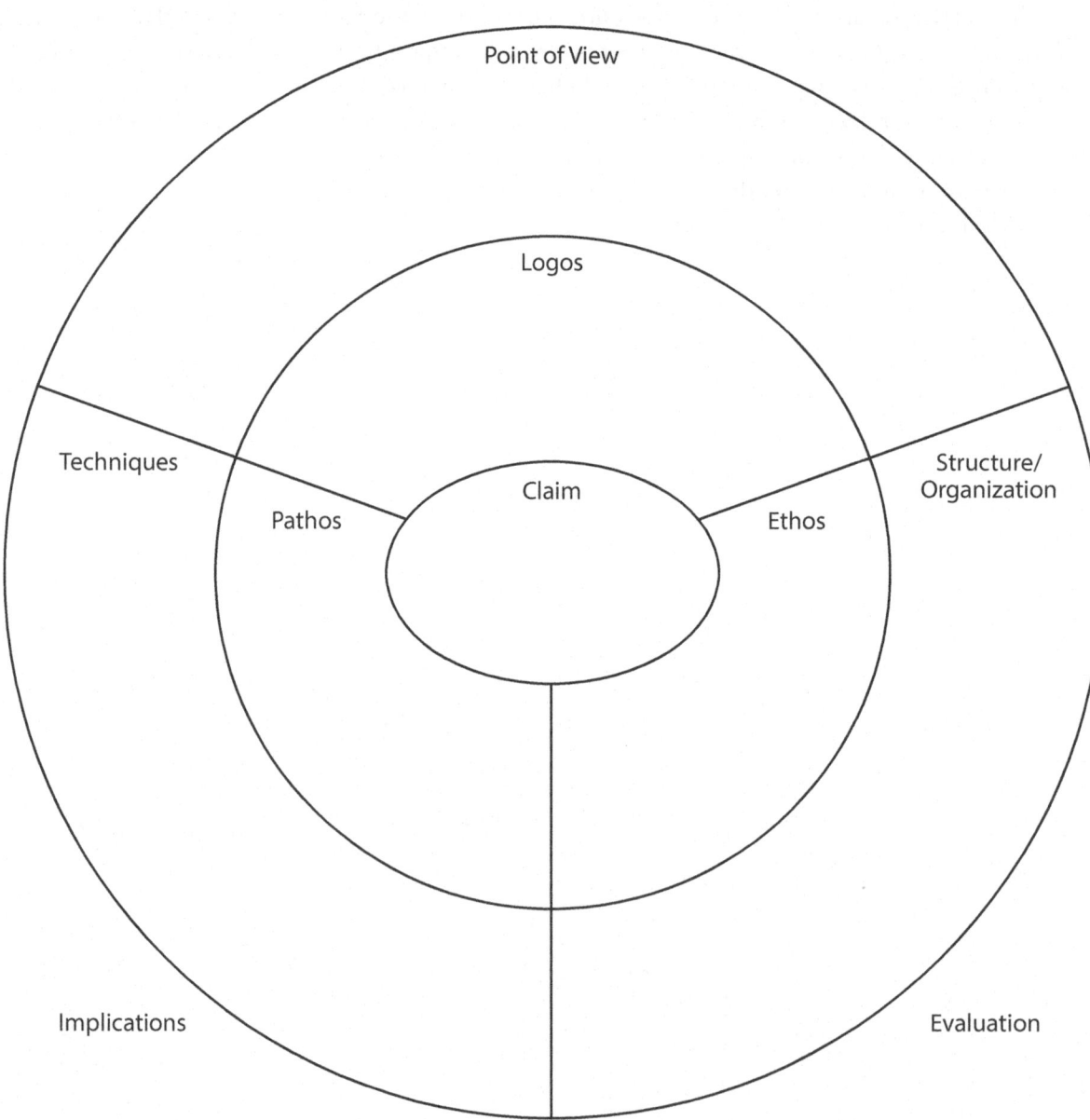

Created by Emily Mofield, Ed.D., & Tamra Stambaugh, Ph.D., 2015.

Lesson 6

Encounters as Experiences

Key Question

Do our experiences shape us, or do we shape our experiences?

Objectives

Content: To analyze and interpret fiction, nonfiction, and art, students will be able to:
- compare and contrast how literary, visual, informational, and/or primary source texts reveal patterns and themes;
- analyze characters' conflicts, motives, values, thoughts, and actions;
- compare and contrast the use of specific techniques various authors use to approach and develop similar ideas;
- identify and analyze archetypal patterns in stories, speeches, and real-world contexts and discuss how they are shaped by the author or real-world individuals or events; and
- analyze how multiple literary elements interact over the course of the text to develop the theme.

Process: To develop interpretation, analysis, and communication skills in the language arts, students will be able to:
- justify inferences with evidence from the text;
- elaborate in discussion or in writing on how authors use language and literary elements to create meaning;
- apply evidence to support explanations and arguments relative to a question, text, or issue; and
- respond to an analysis of literature, nonfiction, media, or art by developing arguments and elaborating on explanations through writing a variety of texts (e.g., essays, paragraphs), including relevant and sufficient evidence to support claims.

Encounters With Archetypes

Concept: To develop conceptual thinking about encounters in language arts and additional content areas, students will be able to:
- explain with evidence how encounters may lead to positive or negative outcomes in literature, media, and real-world examples;
- explain how encounters allow for prediction within literature and real-world examples;
- relate encounter generalizations to real-life situations; and
- examine the relationship between encounters and other concepts in multiple contexts.

Accelerated CCSS for ELA

- RL.6.6
- RL.7.1
- RL.7.3
- RL.8.2
- RL.8.3
- W.6.1
- W.7.10
- SL.6.1

Materials

- Video: Pixar's *La Luna* (available online)
- Handout 1.2: Concept Organizer
- Handout 2.1 Archetype Quick Reference Guide
- Handout 6.1: "The King and the Poisoned Well"
- Handout 6.2: Do We Shape Our Experiences?
- Handout 6.3: "The Emperor's New Clothes" by Hans Christian Andersen
- Handout 6.4: Blank Literary Analysis Wheel
- Rubric 1: Product Rubric (Appendix C)

Introductory Activities

1. Post signs that read "Our experiences shape us" and "We shape our experiences" on opposite sides of the classroom. Have students stand by the sign that they agree with the most.
2. Once students are gathered in groups by the statements, ask them to brainstorm examples that support their statement from real life, movies, or books. Ask each side to share.
3. Explain: *In this lesson, we will continue to explore these statements by examining how character archetypes interact with situational archetypes in stories. A character's encounter with a situation reveals how the character thinks about "our experiences shape us" versus "we shape our experiences."*
4. Distribute Handout 6.1: "The King and the Poisoned Well." After students have read the story, lead a Socratic Seminar:

- What one word describes the king? (Sample responses: Fearful, driven, brave, weak, etc.)
- What problem did the king encounter, and how did he respond? In what ways does this encounter lead to positive and negative outcomes? (Sample response: He encounters the poisoned well and people who are against him; he responds by drinking the water.)
- Is the king a coward, or is he brave? (Sample response: He just wants to be respected again and gives up his sanity; he is brave because good leaders make sacrifices for their people—you cannot be a leader without followers and he was doing the will of the people.)
- Is he a good leader? Did he make the right choice? (Reponses will vary.)
- Did it seem as though the king was in control of the situation, or did the situation control him? (Sample response: The situation likely controlled him because he decided to be insane with the people.)
- Is the king an archetype because of the situation or because of his response to a situation? (Sample response: He is an archetype because of his response; he shows a need to maintain order to be admired.)
- What is the moral of the fable? How does it relate to fear? (Sample response: To be admired, sometimes you must conform, but at the expense of losing your identity. Fear can drive conformity.)
- How do encounters in the story show the king's strengths and weaknesses? (Sample response: The king's weaknesses are revealed in him drinking the water based on fear, but his motive to maintain order is also evident in this decision.)

5. Guide students to identify the character archetypes and situational archetypes in the fable to see if the encounter between them reveals if the king "shapes his experience" or vice versa. Students may continue to use Handout 2.1: Archetype Quick Reference Guide, especially to consider the motivations of characters. Use Handout 6.2: Do We Shape Our Experiences? to guide discussion (Figure 6 includes several sample responses). Ask students:
   - What character archetype is the king? What is his motivation? (Sample response: Leader; he is motivated by a sense of order/control.)
   - What situational archetypes are within the fable? (Students may consider a reverse "cleansing" of the sanity into insanity, shown through the "death" of the king's sanity but "birth" of his insanity.)
   - How does the situation reveal the character's motivation? In what ways does this "encounter" show if the king shapes his experience or if the experience shapes the king?

Encounters With Archetypes

Story	Character	Motivation (Revealed Through Character Encounter With Situation)	Situation	Do We Shape Our Experiences?
"The King and the Poisoned Well"	King (leader)	Needs a sense of order, needs acceptance	Fall; death-rebirth (death of sanity because he needs a sense of order)	Experiences shape us
"The Emperor's New Clothes"	Emperor (leader)	Motivated by pride and vanity	Quest (to have nice things); experience vs. education	Experiences shape us
	Boy (innocent)	Motivated to expose the truth	Education vs. experience	We shape experiences
"Eleven"	Rachel (innocent)	Motivated to want the "good"	Initiation	Experiences shape us
"The Dog of Pompeii"	Bimbo (companion)	Motivated to care for Tito	Quest	We shape experiences
	Tito (person in need of saving)	Needs help with problem	Unhealable wound	Experiences shape us
"We Never Know How High We Are"	Reader (everyday person)	Motivated to rise	Quest	We shape experiences (unless fear interferes)
Reagan speech	Heroes	Motivated to help society	Quest/task	We shape our experiences
"Runaway"	Chillie (person in need of rescuing)	Needs to be cared for	Unhealable wound	Experiences shape us
La Luna	Boy (innocent)	Motivated to show the good	Education vs. experience	We shape our experiences
Corduroy	Corduroy (person in need of rescue; explorer)	Motivated to find his lost button and be accepted	Quest; unhealable wound	Experiences shape us

Figure 6. Sample responses to Handout 6.2.

Read Text

Distribute Handout 6.3: "The Emperor's New Clothes" by Hans Christian Andersen. Ask students to read the text independently.

Text-Dependent Questions

Select from the following prompts to lead small- or whole-group discussion.
1. What can you infer about the emperor's main motivation? What motivates the swindlers, the minister, and the townspeople? How are the character archetypes defined and shaped by their motivations and the motivations of others? (Sample response: The emperor is motivated by pride and vanity; the minister is motivated by fear of loss of prestige; the townspeople are motivated by the fear of not looking intelligent.)
2. Why is the minister so important to the story? What does his role reveal about how humans act? (Sample response: He confirms the "lie" allowing it to be more believable to the emperor.)
3. What does the emperor "encounter," and how does he react to these encounters? What do these reactions reveal about the emperor as a character? List all possibilities of encounters, including encountering "concepts." (Sample response: He encounters lies and truth. His response to the lie is to continue to lie, revealing his motive to stay in power.)
4. What situational archetype does the emperor encounter? (Sample response: He encounters the "experience versus education" situation with the young boy.)
5. Is the emperor an archetype because of the position or because of his response to a situation? (Sample response: Because of his response, he shows a need for control/order to be admired.)
6. What is the author's message about encounters with truth? (Sample response: People are often afraid of exposing the truth.)

Literary Analysis

Distribute Handout 6.4: Blank Literary Analysis Wheel for students to complete in groups. Students should examine different ways in which various story elements interact (arrows on the wheel indicate interactions), including how encounters within a story can shape the message. Guide students through the following questions using the wheel. Additional information and examples can be found in Appendix A.
1. **Point of View + Theme:** In what point of view is the story told? (Sample response: The story is told in third-person omniscient point of view; we

know what the characters' thoughts are.) If we only knew the thoughts of the emperor, what would we not understand as readers? (Sample response: We would not understand that the thread was really invisible.) How does the point of view help enhance the theme of the story? (Sample response: Because we know the truth as readers, we see the absurdity of hiding the truth, which relates to the theme of the story—we should question accepted "truth"; lies often protect us.)

2. **Language + Theme:** Notice the language of the emperor's thoughts and the language of his actions. How does this help us understand him as a character and his internal conflict? What is the emperor's internal conflict? How does this help shape the theme? (Sample response: The emperor is consumed with material things and wanting to know who is competent versus incompetent in his kingdom, evoking a sense of fear. This type of rule spreads a type of fear in which people are afraid to speak truth, supporting the theme—we should question the accepted "truth.")

3. **Characters + Plot:** Think about how the story ends. What archetype would you characterize the boy as (e.g., innocent)? How would the story be different if another character (not the boy) exposed the truth? Would the other townspeople have agreed? (Sample response: If another character pointed out the truth, it is unlikely that others would laugh and admit to seeing the truth because the kingdom was ruled under the assumption that everyone needs to appear competent.)

4. **Theme + Plot:** How does the situational archetype (experience versus education) enhance our understanding of the theme? (Sample response: The theme that truth should be exposed/we should not use lies to protect us is supported in the idea that this is an obvious moral idea—even the young, innocent, and less educated know this wisdom.)

5. **Symbol + Characters:** What does the invisible thread represent about the emperor's life and his rule? (Sample response: The invisible thread serves as a symbol for what he thinks is important.) How does this symbol reveal the emperor's motives and values? (Sample response: This reveals his love for wealth and admiration.)

6. **Mood + Plot + Theme:** How would you describe the mood at the end of the story? What effect does the mood have in conveying the theme of the story? (Sample response: Andersen creates a light, humorous mood, emphasizing the absurdity of the emperor pretending to have a robe. This emphasizes the idea that no one likes to tell the truth because lies often protect us, allowing the idea to be more easily received by the reader.)

In-Class Activities to Deepen Learning

1. Ask students to compare and contrast the king from "The King and the Poisoned Well" to the emperor in "The Emperor's New Clothes." Then, ask students to contrast these characters with the "innocent" boy from "The Emperor's New Clothes" (see Figure 7 for sample responses). Students should compare and contrast:
    - motives (Why do characters act as they do?),
    - values (What is important to characters?),
    - encounters (What do they encounter?), and
    - behaviors/actions (How do they respond to the encounter, and what does that reveal about them?).

2. Revisit the opening question: *Do our experiences shape us, or do we shape our experiences?* Ask students to answer this question as it relates to the emperor's and young boy's perspective in "The Emperor's New Clothes." Students may continue to use Handout 6.2: Do We Shape Our Experiences?

3. Then, watch the Pixar short film *La Luna*. Ask students:
    - How does *La Luna* relate to "The Emperor's New Clothes"? How is it like "Eleven" from Lesson 1? How do the character archetype-situation encounters allow for prediction? (Guide students to see how the innocent relates to the "Education versus experience" situation and also "initiation" in coming-of-age stories.)
    - How do similar character archetypes encounter situations differently? (Sample response: The innocent in "Eleven" was not able to assert herself to bring up the "truth" in her encounter, but the innocent in "The Emperor's New Clothes" was. The innocent in "Eleven" experiences initiation with a negative outcome, but the innocent in *La Luna* experiences a positive one.)

4. Ask students to complete the remaining rows for Handout 6.2: Do We Shape Our Experiences? with at least three additional texts and films from this unit that they particularly like.

5. Divide students into pairs. Ask students to reflect on the stories from this lesson and imagine that the king from "The King and the Poisoned Well" and the emperor in "The Emperor's New Clothes" had a conversation. Have students create a skit/dialogue between the two leaders that shows how they handled various encounters, what they thought about those encounters, and what they learned. Students should make sure to reveal the leaders' thoughts and motives during the skit to reveal how they view the question "Do we shape our experiences?"

Encounters With Archetypes

	Emperor From "The Emperor's New Clothes"	Both	King From "The Poisoned Well"	The Young Boy From "The Emperor's New Clothes"
Motivation	Fear of not appearing wrong; vanity	Fear	To hold power; fear of being overthrown	To show the truth in what he sees
Values	Values nice clothes, praise, others' opinions	Others' opinions	Maintaining the throne, power, and rule/respect of kingdom	Does not value others' opinions; values what is good, the truth
Encounters	Positive encounters with ministers and subjects	Encounters reveal that they want to maintain power	Negative encounters with town subjects	Encounter with truth (the unclothed emperor) and crowd
Behaviors/ Actions	Walks proudly (naked)	Give up identity to be like others	Follows crowd; drinks poison; conforms	Calls out the truth

Figure 7. Sample responses for comparison of texts.

Choice-Based Differentiated Products

Students may choose one of the following to complete (*Note*: Use Rubric 1: Product Rubric in Appendix C to assess student responses):

- In "The Emperor's New Clothes," the young "innocent" archetype encounters the truth and reveals it. Overall, this story conveys the importance of speaking up about truth or what is right. Make a list of five injustices that you notice (from a school perspective, local perspective, or global perspective; e.g., it is not right that by 2050 there will be more trash in the ocean than marine life; it is not right that some girls in the world are not allowed to attend school; it is not right that people have to go into debt to pay for college education). After creating your list, choose one injustice and think about how encounters with problems/truth can lead to change. Develop five ways to bring awareness of this truth to the public in order to lead to change.
- Imagine you were an observer watching the emperor walking down the street in his "invisible" robe. Create a narrative from a spectator's point of

view that provides insight on how this encounter with "truth" and interaction with the innocent boy affects you. Include internal thoughts and dialogue with other spectators, highlighting the contrast between what is said about the event versus what is thought.
- Consider real-world individuals who have used their voices to expose a truth or an unconventional idea about a social justice issue (e.g., Susan B. Anthony, Frederick Douglass). Research this person's life experiences. How do the situational archetypes in this person's life allow for his or her character archetype to emerge? Explain: Do the encounters in the person's life shape the person, or does the person shape the encounters?

Opportunity for Talent Development

Ask students to determine what makes an effective leader. Invite a community leader to discuss effective leadership with students (or ask students to interview a community leader). Ask the leader to focus discussion on the challenges he or she faces, how he or she makes sound decisions (the process he or she uses), how he or she promotes positive change, and how he or she develops solutions to problems. Students should prepare a list of questions pertaining to leaders' encounters (e.g., with others, opportunities, risks, conflicts), personal leadership strengths, and areas to grow. After the visit, ask students to compare the effective leadership components discussed with the guest with the way the leader archetypes in the stories handled their situations and exemplified varying components of leadership.

Social-Emotional Connections

- Lead a class discussion: *In "The Emperor's New Clothes," fear motivated most of the people to go along with a lie. In what situations might students your age feel afraid to stand up for what is right or be different because they don't want to look unintelligent in front of others? Why is it important to be aware of how fear influences our behavior? How might fear interfere with achievement? What kind of "self-talk" can help address fear of standing up for what is right . . . fear of worrying what others think?*
- The stories "The King and the Poisoned Well" and "The Emperor's New Clothes" show the motivations of flawed leaders (e.g., motivated by fear of losing power, motivated by pride, or motivated to stay in control of others): *In the context of school, how can a person's need for "control" lead to negative consequences (e.g., while working on a group project)? What is the difference between being a good leader versus being bossy? Create a list of five dos and don'ts of good leaders.*

Encounters With Archetypes

ELA Task

Assign the following task as a performance-based assessment for this lesson: *Explain how character archetypes' encounters and their encounters with situational archetypes allow for prediction in stories. Answer in a paragraph or two, using examples from at least three texts.*

Concept Connections

1. Lead a class discussion: If encounters are unexpected, can we shape our encounters?
2. Continue to relate lesson ideas to the concept generalizations on the concept map-working wall and/or Handout 2.1: Concept Organizer. Relate encounters to the concept of "truth." Ask: *What did the stories "The King and the Poisoned Well" and "The Emperor's New Clothes" show about encounters with "truth"?* (Sample response: In "The King and the Poisoned Well," truth is based on perception of who is "mad"; in "The Emperor's New Clothes," truth is avoided because people are protected by lies.)

Assessment

- Examine choice-based differentiated products and rubric criteria, ELA Task responses, and/or Concept Connections. Use Rubric 1: Product Rubric to review the products.
- Have students complete an exit ticket: *Create an equation with words to show how encounters between a character and situation lead to a quality or behavior (e.g., hero + good versus evil = acts of courage).*

Name: _____ Date: _____

Handout 6.1
"The King and the Poisoned Well"

There was once a wise king who ruled over a vast kingdom. He was feared for his might and loved for his wisdom. Now in the heart of the city, there was a well with pure and crystalline waters from which the king and all the inhabitants drank. When all were asleep, three witches entered the city and poured seven drops of a strange liquid into the well. They said that henceforth all who drink this water shall become mad.

The next day, all the people drank of the water, but not the king. And the people began to say, "The king is mad and has lost his reason. Look how strangely he behaves. We cannot be ruled by a madman, so he must be dethroned."

The king grew very fearful, for his subjects were preparing to rise against him. He had a difficult choice: risk being destroyed by his beloved subjects or drink from the poisoned well and become mad like them. So that evening, he ordered a golden goblet to be filled from the well, and he drank deeply. The next day, there was great rejoicing among the people, for their beloved king had finally regained his reason.

—Author Unknown

Name: _____ Date: _____

Handout 6.2
Do We Shape Our Experiences?

Directions: Using the chart, identify each character's archetype, his or her motivation(s), and the situational archetype at play. Using what you know, determine how the encounter between the three factors answers the question: Do we shape our experiences?

Story	Archetype Encounters
"The King and the Poisoned Well"	**King** _____ + _____ + _____ = _____ Character Archetype Motivation Situational Archetype Do We Shape Our Experiences?
"The Emperor's New Clothes" by Hans Christian Andersen	**Emperor** _____ + _____ + _____ = _____ Character Archetype Motivation Situational Archetype Do We Shape Our Experiences? **Boy** _____ + _____ + _____ = _____ Character Archetype Motivation Situational Archetype Do We Shape Our Experiences?
La Luna Pixar	**Boy** _____ + _____ + _____ = _____ Character Archetype Motivation Situational Archetype Do We Shape Our Experiences?
"Eleven" by Sandra Cisneros	**Rachel** _____ + _____ + _____ = _____ Character Archetype Motivation Situational Archetype Do We Shape Our Experiences?

Name: _____ Date: _____

Handout 6.2, *continued*

Story	Archetype Encounters
Other Story	**Character:** _____ _____ + _____ + _____ = _____ Character Archetype Motivation Situational Archetype Do We Shape Our Experiences?
Other Story	**Character:** _____ _____ + _____ + _____ = _____ Character Archetype Motivation Situational Archetype Do We Shape Our Experiences?
Other Story	**Character:** _____ _____ + _____ + _____ = _____ Character Archetype Motivation Situational Archetype Do We Shape Our Experiences?
Other Story	**Character:** _____ _____ + _____ + _____ = _____ Character Archetype Motivation Situational Archetype Do We Shape Our Experiences?
Other Story	**Character:** _____ _____ + _____ + _____ = _____ Character Archetype Motivation Situational Archetype Do We Shape Our Experiences?

Name: _____ Date: _____

Handout 6.3
"The Emperor's New Clothes" *by Hans Christian Andersen*

Many years ago there lived an emperor who loved beautiful new clothes so much that he spent all his money on being finely dressed. His only interest was in going to the theater or in riding about in his carriage where he could show off his new clothes. He had a different costume for every hour of the day. Indeed, where it was said of other kings that they were at court, it could only be said of him that he was in his dressing room!

One day two swindlers came to the emperor's city. They said that they were weavers, claiming that they knew how to make the finest cloth imaginable. Not only were the colors and the patterns extraordinarily beautiful, but in addition, this material had the amazing property that it was to be invisible to anyone who was incompetent or stupid.

"It would be wonderful to have clothes made from that cloth," thought the emperor. "Then I would know which of my men are unfit for their positions, and I'd also be able to tell clever people from stupid ones." So he immediately gave the two swindlers a great sum of money to weave their cloth for him.

They set up their looms and pretended to go to work, although there was nothing at all on the looms. They asked for the finest silk and the purest gold, all of which they hid away, continuing to work on the empty looms, often late into the night.

"I would really like to know how they are coming with the cloth!" thought the emperor, but he was a bit uneasy when he recalled that anyone who was unfit for his position or stupid would not be able to see the material. Of course, he himself had nothing to fear, but still he decided to send someone else to see how the work was progressing.

"I'll send my honest old minister to the weavers," thought the emperor. He's the best one to see how the material is coming. He is very sensible, and no one is more worthy of his position than he.

So the good old minister went into the hall where the two swindlers sat working at their empty looms. "Goodness!" thought the old minister, opening his eyes wide. "I cannot see a thing!" But he did not say so.

The two swindlers invited him to step closer, asking him if it wasn't a beautiful design and if the colors weren't magnificent. They pointed to the empty loom, and the poor old minister opened his eyes wider and wider. He still could see nothing, for nothing was there.

"Gracious" he thought. "Is it possible that I am stupid? I have never thought so. Am I unfit for my position? No one must know this. No, it will never do for me to say that I was unable to see the material."

"You aren't saying anything!" said one of the weavers.

"Oh, it is magnificent! The very best!" said the old minister, peering through his glasses. "This pattern and these colors! Yes, I'll tell the emperor that I am very satisfied with it!"

"That makes us happy!" said the two weavers, and they called the colors and the unusual pattern by name. The old minister listened closely so that he would be able say the same things when he reported back to the emperor, and that is exactly what he did.

The swindlers now asked for more money, more silk, and more gold, all of which they hid away. Then they continued to weave away as before on the empty looms.

Name: _____ Date: _____

Handout 6.3, *continued*

The emperor sent other officials as well to observe the weavers' progress. They too were startled when they saw nothing, and they too reported back to him how wonderful the material was, advising him to have it made into clothes that he could wear in a grand procession. The entire city was alive in praise of the cloth. "Magnifique! Nysseligt! Excellent!" they said, in all languages. The emperor awarded the swindlers with medals of honor, bestowing on each of them the title Lord Weaver.

The swindlers stayed up the entire night before the procession was to take place, burning more than sixteen candles. Everyone could see that they were in a great rush to finish the emperor's new clothes. They pretended to take the material from the looms. They cut in the air with large scissors. They sewed with needles but without any thread. Finally they announced, "Behold! The clothes are finished!"

The emperor came to them with his most distinguished cavaliers. The two swindlers raised their arms as though they were holding something and said, "Just look at these trousers! Here is the jacket! This is the cloak!" and so forth. "They are as light as spider webs! You might think that you didn't have a thing on, but that is the good thing about them."

"Yes," said the cavaliers, but they couldn't see a thing, for nothing was there.

"Would his imperial majesty, if it please his grace, kindly remove his clothes." said the swindlers. "Then we will fit you with the new ones, here in front of the large mirror."

The emperor took off all his clothes, and the swindlers pretended to dress him, piece by piece, with the new ones that were to be fitted. They took hold of his waist and pretended to tie something about him. It was the train. Then the emperor turned and looked into the mirror.

"Goodness, they suit you well! What a wonderful fit!" they all said. "What a pattern! What colors! Such luxurious clothes!"

"The canopy to be carried above your majesty awaits outside," said the grandmaster of ceremonies.

"Yes, I am ready!" said the emperor. "Don't they fit well?" He turned once again toward the mirror, because it had to appear as though he were admiring himself in all his glory.

The chamberlains who were to carry the train held their hands just above the floor as if they were picking up the train. As they walked they pretended to hold the train high, for they could not let anyone notice that they could see nothing.

The emperor walked beneath the beautiful canopy in the procession, and all the people in the street and in their windows said, "Goodness, the emperor's new clothes are incomparable! What a beautiful train on his jacket. What a perfect fit!" No one wanted it to be noticed that he could see nothing, for then it would be said that he was unfit for his position or that he was stupid. None of the emperor's clothes had ever before received such praise.

"But he doesn't have anything on!" said a small child.

"Good Lord, let us hear the voice of an innocent child!" said the father, and whispered to another what the child had said.

"A small child said that he doesn't have anything on!"

Finally everyone was saying, "He doesn't have anything on!"

The emperor shuddered, for he knew that they were right, but he thought, "The procession must go on!" He carried himself even more proudly, and the chamberlains walked along behind carrying the train that wasn't there.

Name: _____ Date: _____

Handout 6.4
Blank Literary Analysis Wheel

Directions: Draw arrows across elements to show connections.

Text: _____

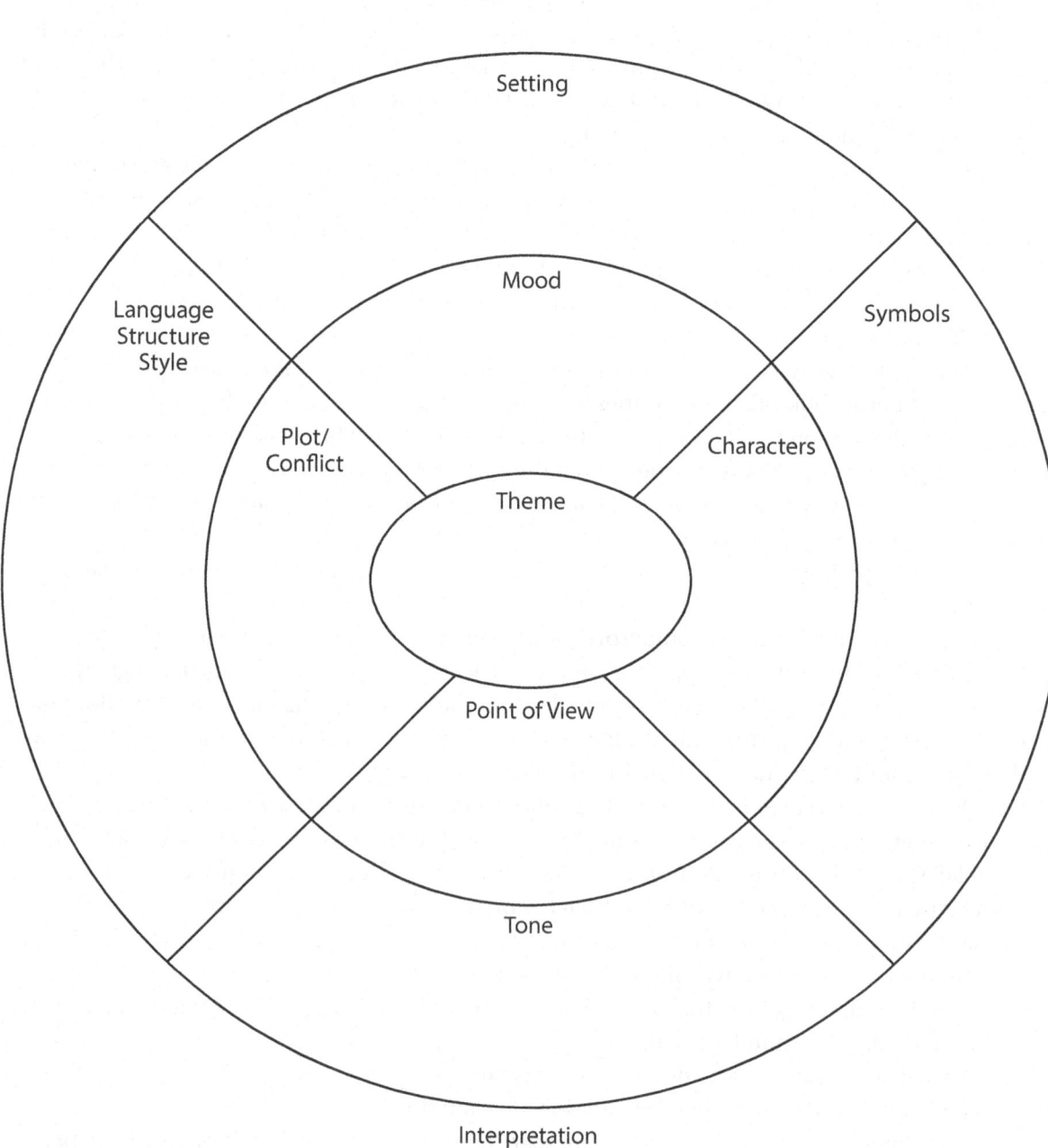

Created by Tamra Stambaugh, Ph.D., & Emily Mofield, Ed.D., 2015.

Lesson

Novel Study: Encounters With Archetypes

Key Question

How do encounters with literature and archetypes allow for reflection and change?

Objectives

Content: To analyze and interpret fiction, nonfiction, and art, students will be able to:
- compare and contrast how literary, visual, informational, and/or primary source texts reveal patterns and themes;
- analyze characters' conflicts, motives, values, thoughts, and actions;
- compare and contrast the use of specific techniques various authors use to approach and develop similar ideas;
- identify and analyze archetypal patterns in stories, speeches, and real-world contexts and discuss how they are shaped by the author or real-world individuals or events; and
- analyze how multiple literary elements interact over the course of the text to develop the theme.

Process: To develop interpretation, analysis, and communication skills in the language arts, students will be able to:
- justify inferences with evidence from the text;
- elaborate in discussion or in writing on how authors use language and literary elements to create meaning;
- apply evidence to support explanations and opinions relative to a question, text, or issue; and
- respond to an analysis of literature, nonfiction, media, or art by developing arguments and elaborating on explanations through writing a variety of texts (e.g., essays, paragraphs), including relevant and sufficient evidence to support claims.

Encounters With Archetypes

Concept: To develop conceptual thinking about encounters in language arts and additional content areas, students will be able to:
- explain with evidence how encounters may lead to positive or negative outcomes in literature, media, and real-world examples;
- explain how encounters allow for reflection and change using literature, media, and real-world examples;
- relate encounter generalizations to real-life situations; and
- examine the relationship between encounters and other concepts in multiple contexts.

Accelerated CCSS for ELA

- RL.6.6
- RL.7.1
- RL.7.3
- RL.8.2
- W.6.1
- W.7.10
- SL.6.1

Materials

- Student copies of *Wonder* by R. J. Palacio or *Counting by 7s* by Holly Goldberg Sloan
- Video: "Wonder (2017 Movie) Official Trailer – #ChooseKind – Julia Roberts, Owen Wilson" (available at https://www.youtube.com/watch?v=ngiK1gQKgK8)
- Video: "Counting by 7s Book Trailer" (available at https://www.youtube.com/watch?v=Yrz41FH6OMM)
- Handout 1.2: Concept Organizer
- Handout 7.1A: *Wonder* Study Guide
- Handout 7.1B: *Counting by 7s* Study Guide
- Handout 7.2: Flash Fiction Quotes
- Rubric 1: Product Rubric (Appendix C)

Note: This lesson includes activities and questions for reading and analyzing an entire novel. It is suggested that students read either *Wonder* by R. J. Palacio or *Counting By 7s* by Holly Goldberg Sloan. They may choose which novel they prefer. Establish a timeline and specific days each week or every few days to discuss specific chapter questions, to provide feedback on students' ongoing activities, and to check for understanding. Product choices are also included for students to engage in upon completion and should be considered when planning the lesson and unit timeline.

Introductory Activities

1. Engage students in a brief discussion:
   - How do our encounters shape our understanding of characters and ourselves?
   - How do archetype patterns support you as a reader? How do they allow for deeper understandings?
   - How do encounters in literature allow for prediction of plot, character actions, and interpretation?

2. Explain that students will continue to explore how encounters with archetypes deepen our understanding of literature. Introduce the novels, and show the book trailers (see Materials list) as inspiration for initial discussions and students' book selections. Ask students to make preliminary observations about the encounters they witness in the book trailers and predict archetypes that may be evident in the novels.

3. Establish a timeline for students to read through the book(s), and explain your expectations for the novel reading, questions, and ongoing activities.

Ongoing Activity

Distribute Handout 7.1A: *Wonder* Study Guide or Handout 7.1B: *Counting by 7s* Study Guide according to students' novel selections. Remind students that that encounters do not just take place with other characters, but can include settings, physical conflicts, and internal emotions, such as hope or fear. As students read, they are responsible for using evidence to determine ways in which particular characters exemplify certain archetypes. This evidence will come from encounters that the character has with internal conflicts, characters, settings, etc.

Chapter Discussion Questions

As students read, explore the texts in more depth using the questions provided. Students may appreciate having a list of questions available to them as they read so they can think about the questions and look for the information. However, questions are not designed to be homework assignments, nor are all questions necessary to ask. Some questions may be considered as reader's response journal entries, but most are intended for class discussions, Socratic seminars, conversations to guide reading groups and teach mini-lessons, checks for understanding, and literary analysis. Selection of questions should be based on student readiness, class goals and outcomes, and students' interest.

Encounters With Archetypes

1. What character archetypes are present in the story? Provide evidence from encounters and details from the text that support your answer.
2. Outline the situational archetypes that are presented. How is the situational archetype tweaked or altered to fit the development of characters, setting, or theme?
3. What symbols appear in the story? How does the use of symbols support your understanding of the characters or plot?
4. The protagonists from both novels exhibit an example of an unhealable wound. How do the wounds present as strengths and then as weaknesses? How do the other characters encounter the unhealable wounds, and what effect do wounds have on character relationships and plot?
5. What positive encounters does the main character in each novel (Willow or Auggie) have, and how do those encounters help shape the archetype of that character and others?
6. What negative encounters does the main character have, and how do those encounters help shape the archetype of that character and others?
7. Is there a situation in which the main character is required to cooperate or work as a team? How did this encounter change what the character believed about him- or herself and others?
8. Consider the conflicts that are explored in each book: man versus himself, man versus others, man versus nature, and man versus society. What types of encounters were present in the story, and how did they help reveal conflict? Was there a pattern that helped you make predictions based on the character or situational archetype?
9. In each story, encounters with other individuals, or even internal encounters with doubt or fear, led to threats or challenges. How did the main character respond to this encounter? In what way was he or she resilient? Was a sage or caretaker archetype character present to help guide the protagonist? What impact did the sage/caretaker have on the protagonist?
10. The following quote is from *Counting by 7s*: "For someone grieving, moving forward is the challenge. Because after extreme loss, you want to go back." Both books present encounters with grief and loss. How do characters respond to these encounters, and how do their responses shape your understanding of their character archetypes?
11. How did certain encounters between/among characters influence the mood of the story?
12. How do encounters and their outcomes influence the author's message or the overall theme of the story?

After Reading

After students have read their novels, explore the texts in more depth using the following questions and activities:
1. Did the main character follow the hero's journey? Plot the main character's encounters to see if the character's journey aligned with Joseph Campbell's original model. (Remember that the stages are call, initiation, adventure, aid, threshold, helper, mentor, revelation, transformation, atonement, return, known, and unknown.)
    - Revisit this question that was discussed earlier in the unit: *Do our experiences shape us, or do we shape our experiences?*
    - Revisit Handout 6.2. If you added the main character from the novel you read to the table, how would he or she respond to the question?
    - How has your response to the question changed after reading through the novel and discussing the experiences and encounters of the characters?

2. How did the main character respond when encountering truth? What connections can you make with encounters with truth (e.g., realization of truth) and generalizations related to opportunities and threats or reflection and change?
3. How is the character's response to a situational archetype (unhealable wound, initiation) different or the same as other stories/resources in this unit? How did the main characters respond to growing up? Refer to Rachel in "Eleven" or the young boy in *La Luna* for comparison.
4. One of the encounters generalizations centers on the idea that encounters allow for reflection and change. In a short essay or journal response, reflect on the themes and messages of the novel you read. How have you changed as a student after encountering the characters and messages from the novel?
5. Handout 7.2: Flash Fiction Quotes features quotes from the two novels. There are many quotes in the stories that can be used for inspiration. Independently or with a partner, select one of the quotes from the book you read or from Handout 7.2. How does the quote exemplify the meaning of the book? Write and share a flash fiction (100-word) story with a similar message to that of your novel that uses the quote as a source of inspiration. (Note: Examples of flash fiction may need to be shared with students.)

Choice-Based Differentiated Products

Students may choose one of the following to complete (*Note*: Use Rubric 1: Product Rubric in Appendix C to assess student responses):

Encounters With Archetypes

- Complete a Blank Literary Analysis Wheel (see Appendix B) on one chapter or section of the novel you read. Explore the interactions among literary components. Consider how certain elements (mood, literary techniques, symbols, etc.) influenced the development of the story and your own understanding of others. Select one or two of the strongest interactions between literary elements and write a paragraph that outlines your analysis and rationale.
- Find a classmate who read a different novel than you. Revisit some of your answers to the questions that you explored as you read the novel and completed Handout 7.1. What patterns do you notice between your answers your classmate's? How did the encounters allow for prediction of archetypal patterns? What was it about the character, situational, or symbolic archetypes that allowed for predictability within the resolution of the plot, character development, etc.?
- Find a classmate who read a different novel than you. Discuss the following ideas and compare responses:
  - In *Counting by 7s*, Willow says, "It is possible that all labels are curses. Unless they are on cleaning products." How does this quote apply to both stories? Cite specific evidence from each novel about how labels can be positive and negative.
  - One novel focuses more on an internal problem or syndrome that manifests externally, while the other focuses on an external problem that manifests internally. Compare these internal and external problems. How does each allow for reflection and change?
  - Are the novels essentially the same story or archetypal pattern, or are they different? Explain your thinking by comparing the situational archetypes and plot structure in a Venn diagram. Then, mutually decide whether or not the stories are patterned in the same or a different way, and be prepared to share your findings with another group.
- Make a diorama of a scene in which a significant encounter took place (e.g., Willow outside of her home as she encounters grief, Auggie encountering bullying at school). Use details from the text to develop the scene. Turn in a written description of the diorama that explains how this scene and the encounter that took place developed your understanding of certain character archetypes. Use symbolic archetypes to convey the power of the selected scene on the plot and message. Relate the setting to other components on the Literary Analysis Wheel to explain the interactions.
- Imagine that characters in novels could jump through the pages and land in another book. Develop a dialogue, either through a script or cartoon, between the main character in your novel and the main character in

another book that you have read. Imagine what their conversation might be like if they were to meet. What would their encounter look like? Would their encounter be positive or negative? To what extent might their encounter change the plot and message of your novel (*Wonder* or *Counting by 7s*)? Think about the situational archetype: Would the situation change, or would the characters change in the new story? Make sure your characters discuss these events.

Opportunities for Talent Development

In the novels, both main characters are different than their same-age peers in a variety of ways. How is being seen as different an asset and a liability? Ask students to interview at least four people about their experiences growing up: *Did they feel different? How did their internal and external encounters support who they are today?* Answer the question "How is being different an asset and a liability?" based on your interviews. Be prepared to discuss what surprised you most about individual responses. What patterns did you notice? How can you use the information you have learned to better support people who do feel different? Make a chart of your findings to share and discuss.

Social-Emotional Connection

Lead students through a discussion using the following prompt: *Do our encounters with characters and the issues they face develop a greater sense of empathy in ourselves?* Empathy can be defined as the ability to understand the feelings of others. Students may choose to share a time when they felt an emotional connection with a character or conflict within a novel. (*Note*: Students may need additional resources to help build their understanding of empathy, such as the animated explanation available at https://www.youtube.com/watch?v=1Evwgu369Jw.)

ELA Task

Assign the following task as a performance-based assessment for this lesson: *Use evidence from the novel you read and the previous information learned in class to write an essay that responds to the following question: Does the main character in your novel follow the hero's journey? Why or why not?*

Concept Connections

1. Revisit the encounter generalizations, and ask students to make connections from the concepts discussed in the previous lessons to the novels read in

class. Develop a large concept visual map for students to link ideas between the previous lessons. Write out explanations for how concepts are related between lessons.
2. Have students continue to add to the concept map-working wall or use Handout 1.2: Concept Organizer (or see Appendix B) to record how the generalizations applied to the text. (Sample response: Encounters may led to reflection and change: Willow's encounter with the loss of her parents leads to a change in terms of her stability and sense of normalcy, but also an opportunity to step out of her comfort zone and make new friends; Auggie's encounter with Summer is a positive one, which leads him to believe that school may not be such a bad place after all.) In the last box, students should relate the idea of encounters to an additional concept, such as power (e.g., the encounters as a source of power, how sources of power, such as pride or fear, are motivating factors within encounters, etc.).

Assessment

- Examine choice-based differentiated products and rubric criteria, ELA Task responses, and/or Concept Connections. Use Rubric 1: Product Rubric to review the products.
- Have students complete an exit ticket: *Consider the generalization "Encounters allow for reflection and change." When you think about the encounters between the main character in your novel and one or two of the supporting characters, which character changed more and in what ways because of the encounter?*

Name: _____   Date: _____

Handout 7.1A
Wonder Study Guide

Directions: Consider how encounters shape your understanding of the archetypes that are embodied by specific characters in the novel. You may discover evidence that suggests a character is a combination of archetypes and that he or she encounters multiple situational archetypes.

Part 1: Recording Encounters

Use the organizer and the following questions to record the various encounters each character has and how that character responds.

1. How do the encounters allow for reflection and change in the character and others the character encounters? Are these encounters internal, external, or both?
2. How does a new encounter lead to opportunities and threats for the character? How does he or she respond and learn as a result?
3. How do the encounters allow readers to predict possible reactions or outcomes?
4. How did the encounters result in positive or negative outcomes?

Wonder by R.J. Palacio	Question 1	Question 2	Question 3	Question 4
Auggie Pullman				
Via Pullman				

123
Encounters With Archetypes © Taylor & Francis

Name: _____ Date: _____

Handout 7.1A, *continued*

Wonder **by R.J. Palacio**	**Question 1**	**Question 2**	**Question 3**	**Question 4**
Summer				
Jack				
Other				

Name: _____ Date: _____

Handout 7.1A, *continued*

Part 2: How Does Our Understanding of Archetypes Help Us Understand the Message?

Complete the chart as you see different examples of character, situational, or symbolic archetypes in the story. Provide a page number or short example.

Character Archetypes	Situational Archetypes	Symbolic Archetypes

Encounter Insight/Generalization

Name: _____ Date: _____

Handout 7.1B
Counting by 7s Study Guide

Directions: Consider how encounters shape your understanding of the archetypes that are embodied by specific characters in the novel. You may discover evidence that suggests a character is a combination of archetypes and that he or she encounters multiple situational archetypes.

Part 1: Recording Encounters

Use the organizer and the following questions to record the various encounters each character has and how that character responds.

1. How do the encounters allow for reflection and change in the character and others the character encounters? Are these encounters internal, external, or both?
2. How does a new encounter lead to opportunities and threats for the character? How does he or she respond and learn as a result?
3. How do the encounters allow readers to predict possible reactions or outcomes?
4. How did the encounters result in positive or negative outcomes?

Wonder by R.J. Palacio	Question 1	Question 2	Question 3	Question 4
Willow Chance				
Dell Duke				

Name: _____ Date: _____

Handout 7.1B, *continued*

***Wonder* by R.J. Palacio**	**Question 1**	**Question 2**	**Question 3**	**Question 4**
Mai				
Patti or Jairo				
Other				

Name: _____ Date: _____

Handout 7.1B, *continued*

Part 2: How Does Our Understanding of Archetypes Help Us Understand the Message?

Complete the chart as you see different examples of character, situational, or symbolic archetypes in the story. Provide a page number or short example.

Character Archetypes	Situational Archetypes	Symbolic Archetypes

Encounter Insight/Generalization

Name: _____ Date: _____

Handout 7.2
Flash Fiction Quotes

Directions: Flash fiction narratives are brief, often limited to 100 words or fewer, but they still have a beginning, middle, and end. Select one of the following quotes as a point of inspiration for your own flash fiction piece. Write out your short narrative on a separate piece of paper. Then, draw an illustration to accompany your flash fiction writing. Use the quote as the introductory sentence for your flash fiction writing.

Wonder *by R. J. Palacio*

- "Kinder than is *necessary*. Because it's not enough to be kind. One should be kinder than needed."
- "Courage. Kindness. Friendship. Character. These are the qualities that define us as human beings, and propel us, on occasion, to greatness."
- "Now that I look back, I don't know why I was so stressed about it all this time. Funny how sometimes you worry a lot about something and it turns out to be nothing."
- "Sometimes you don't have to be mean to hurt someone."

Counting by 7s *by Holly Goldberg Sloan*

- "When you care about other people, it takes the spotlight off your own drama."
- "A second can feel like forever if what follows is heartbreak."
- "And just being there is ninety-nine percent of what matters when your world falls apart"
- "Maybe that happens when you've been through a lot. All of your edges are worn off, like sea glass. Either that, or you shatter."
- "All reality is a blender where hopes and dreams are mixed with fear and despair."
- "I'm not brave; it's just that all other choices have been thrown out the window."

Lesson 8

Encounters With Symbolic Archetypes

Key Question

How do symbols in texts allow for a deeper understanding of the author's message?

Objectives

Content: To analyze and interpret fiction, nonfiction, and art, students will be able to:
- compare and contrast how literary, visual, informational, and/or primary source texts reveal patterns and themes;
- analyze characters' conflicts, motives, values, thoughts, and actions;
- compare and contrast the use of specific techniques various authors use to approach and develop similar ideas;
- identify and analyze archetypal patterns in stories, speeches, and real-world contexts and discuss how they are shaped by the author or real-world individuals or events; and
- analyze how multiple literary elements interact over the course of the text to develop the theme.

Process: To develop interpretation, analysis, and communication skills in the language arts, students will be able to:
- justify inferences with evidence from the text;
- elaborate in discussion or in writing on how authors use language and literary elements to create meaning;
- apply evidence to support explanations and opinions relative to a question, text, or issue; and
- respond to an analysis of literature, nonfiction, media, or art by developing arguments and elaborating on explanations through writing a variety of texts (e.g., essays, paragraphs), including relevant and sufficient evidence to support claims.

Encounters With Archetypes

Concept: To develop conceptual thinking about encounters in language arts and additional content areas, students will be able to:
- explain with evidence how encounters may lead to positive or negative outcomes in literature, media, and real-world examples;
- explain how encounters allow for prediction within literature and real-world examples;
- relate encounter generalizations to real-life situations; and
- examine the relationship between encounters and other concepts in multiple contexts.

Accelerated CCSS for ELA

- RL.6.6
- RL.7.1
- RL.7.3
- RL.8.2
- RI.7.4
- W.6.1
- SL.6.1

Materials

- A variety of colored markers, crayons, or colored pencils, and paper
- Select music videos:
  - "FROZEN | Let It Go Sing-along | Official Disney UK" (available at https://www.youtube.com/watch?v=L0MK7qz13bU)
  - "Get Back Up Again Clip | Trolls" (available at https://www.youtube.com/watch?v=IFuFm0m2wj0)
  - "Olivia Holt- Carry On from DisneyNature Bears" (available at https://www.youtube.com/watch?v=ZysBzkqYA68)
- Teacher's copy of *The Very Hungry Caterpillar* by Eric Carle
- Handout 2.1: Archetypes Quick Reference Guide
- Handout 8.1: Symbol Cards (sets cut out in advance per groups of 3–4 students)
- Handout 8.2: Encounters With Archetypes
- Handout 8.3: "Rikki-Tikki-Tavi" From *The Jungle Book* by Rudyard Kipling
- Handout 8.4: Blank Literary Analysis Wheel
- Rubric 1: Product Rubric (Appendix C)

Introductory Activities

1. Explain that, in this lesson, students will look more closely at symbolic archetypes and how they are used in stories. Distribute sets of cards (face down) from Handout 8.1, paper, and markers to groups of 3–4 students. Have stu-

dents play a form of Pictionary. One group member picks up a card (without showing the rest of the group) and then draws 1–2 images that convey the meaning of the word on the card (without speaking or writing any words). The rest of the group must guess the word. When the group guesses correctly, the next group member draws a card, and play resumes until all cards have been drawn.
2. Afterward, explain that students used symbols to convey meaning as other students guessed what those symbols meant. Authors also use symbols to add deeper meaning to a text. Symbols are generally widely accepted and understood, although there are exceptions. Share examples of commonly used symbols with students (e.g., red = passion or anger, green = growth, white = purity, dove = peace, lion = power and authority, cloak = trickery or deception, dawn = new beginning, etc.).
3. Ask students to refer to Handout 2.1 as needed and to identify symbols in the images and lyrics of a few music videos, including how the symbols enhance other archetypes:
    - "Let It Go" from *Frozen* (mountain, ice, darkness, initiation, rebirth)
    - "Get Back Up Again" from *Trolls* (quest, desert, garden)
    - "Olivia Holt- Carry On" from *DisneyNature Bears* (ice, companion, caregiver, quest, mountain, tree, garden, circle, seasons)
4. Ask students to work in partners or small groups to brainstorm additional symbols from the songs and from other songs, stories, movies, or video games they know. Afterward, discuss the symbols and meanings students noted and generate a class list. Encourage students to share multiple meanings of a given symbol, as symbols can convey different meanings to different people. A symbol's meaning should be understood within its context and the shared meaning associated with it. For example, the colors of the American flag represent purity (white), valor and the blood that has been shed defending the country (red), and perseverance and justice (blue). The blue on Finland's flag, however, symbolizes the country's lakes, and the white represents the country's snow. Explain that although symbols can have varied meanings based on the context, there are patterns in symbol use and meaning.

In-Class Activities to Deepen Learning

1. Read aloud *The Very Hungry Caterpillar*, asking students to pay attention to encounters and the portrayal of archetypes.
2. Distribute Handout 8.2: Encounters With Archetypes and divide students into small groups. Ask students to complete the section of the handout related to *The Very Hungry Caterpillar* (see Figure 8 for sample responses).

Encounters With Archetypes

The Very Hungry Caterpillar		
Character Archetypes	**Situational Archetypes**	**Symbolic Archetypes**
Explorer (caterpillar)	Quest (to fulfill need for hunger); death/rebirth (new identity as butterfly)	Green leaves (set stage for caterpillar's growth)
Encounter Insight		
The explorer (caterpillar) encounters many types of food, which ultimately lead to a big change for him. Change happens as a result of small encounters.		

Figure 8. Sample responses for *The Very Hungry Caterpillar*.

Note that the "Encounters Insight" section of the handout requires students to consider what is learned through the encounters in the story. Guide students to response to that section of the handout by asking: *What is encountered and what is learned from the encounter? What predictions can be made from these encounters?*

3. As a class, review responses to Handout 8.2, paying close attention to the symbols in the story. Ask students: *Which symbols did you notice in* The Very Hungry Caterpillar? Record student responses on the board or chart paper. As symbols are identified, ask: *What do you believe that symbol means in this story?* Possible responses may include:
   - **Blue:** Purity of new life.
   - **Green Leaf:** Growth and hope, looking forward. (Note the prominence of the green leaf at the beginning of the story and again in the middle of the story. Ask: *Why do you think the author/artist displayed the leaf in such a way? What message may the author be trying to convey?*)
   - **White background across multiple pages:** The innocence of the caterpillar.
   - **Golden sun:** Energy. (Note how the rays almost touch the tiny caterpillar.)
   - **Tree displayed midway through the text:** Growth, cycle of life.

4. Allow for various student interpretations. Note that the colors of the fruits and foods, such as the "red" of the apples and strawberries in the story, do not really represent archetypal patterns (i.e., red = passion or violence). Archetypes have to be interpreted in context. Ask: *Considering the placement and use of the symbols in the story, what is the author's message? What is the story about? What does this story say about the human experience? How has the identification of symbols in the text changed and/or deepened your understanding of the text?*

Read Text

1. Distribute Handout 8.3 for students to read "Rikki-Tikki-Tavi" by Rudyard Kipling. This short story is part of a larger work, *The Jungle Book*, which was published in 1894. Biography.com has a thorough biographical sketch of Kipling, which students may read to learn more about how his life impacted his writing. Consider playing a dramatic reading, having students partner read, or conducting a modified reader's theater in which students read assigned parts aloud. As they read, ask students to pay attention to the encounters that occur throughout the story (character and the environment, other characters, themselves, and idea, emotion, etc.).
2. Afterward, have students complete the remainder of Handout 8.2 (see Figure 9 for sample responses).

Text-Dependent Questions

Select from the following text-dependent questions for a Socratic seminar or class discussion:

1. How would you characterize Rikki-Tikki-Tavi? What text evidence supports your characterization? (Rikki may be seen as courageous or foolish depending on the encounter in the story or the perspective of the student.)
2. How does this story relate to the generalization "Encounters lead to positive and negative outcomes"? (Sample response: Rikki's close encounter with death allowed him to fulfill his purpose of becoming a protector and saving lives.)
3. What does the narrator's description of Rikki tell us about his abilities? (Sample response: The narrator describes Rikki as "rather like a little cat in his fur and his tail, but quite like a weasel in his head and his habits. . . ." He is agile.)
4. How would you describe the mood in the beginning of the story? Cite evidence to support your thoughts. (Sample response: There is a mood of excitement when the narrator gives the overview of Rikki winning the "great war.")
5. How does the mood change as the story progresses? Cite evidence to support your thoughts. (Sample response: The mood shifts from excitement in the beginning when the family takes in Rikki, to anxiety and fear when he encounters Nag for the first time.)
6. What is the relevance of Rikki's size? (Sample response: The narrator shows the reader that Rikki is small, "He found a little wisp of grass floating there, and clung to it" and "a big man picked him up between his finger and thumb," emphasizing that Rikki is not yet full-grown. Nag and Nagaina are full-grown. This suggests that it would be very difficult, if not impossible, for Rikki to

Encounters With Archetypes

"Rikki-Tikki-Tavi"		
Character Archetypes	**Situational Archetypes**	**Symbolic Archetypes**
Caregiver (Mom); companion (Teddy); explorer (Rikki); innocent (Rikki); hero (Rikki); sage (Chuchundra); villains (Nag and Nagaina); rebel (Darzee's wife)	Good vs. evil (Rikki vs. Nag and Nagaina); death/rebirth (Rikki's drowning and recovery); initiation (Rikki successfully avoids Nagaina's initial attack); quest (Rikki's quest to restore order and peace to the garden).	Water (the drowning can be seen as a sort of rebirth); evil (Nag, Karait and Nagaina); passion/determination (Rikki's red eyes); order/safety (garden); wilderness (garden)
Encounter Insight		
Knowing that water may represent birth or renewal, the reader can anticipate that Rikki may have grown or changed in some way from the young, curious mongoose that he was before the drowning.		

Figure 9. Sample responses for "Rikki-Tikki-Tavi."

fight and win against them, "[Rikki] knew that all a grown mongoose's business in life was to fight and eat snakes.")

7. What significant information do we gain about Rikki when he encounters Karait? (Sample response: This encounter shows that Rikki is overconfident and lacks knowledge.)
8. Why are both Chuchundra and Rikki concerned with the open space? (Sample response: Snakes can move quickly in open spaces.)
9. What similarities can you draw between Nag and Nagaina and the Father and Mother? (Sample response: The father and Nag both have families to protect and ways to protect them: Nag has his bite; the father has his gun and Rikki.)
10. What does Rikki mean by "he must catch her, or all the trouble would begin again"? (Sample response: Nagaina has taken her egg from the veranda and headed toward the tall grass.)
11. What is the significance of the snakes in the garden? (Sample response: We often view a garden as a safe space, but this serves as a reminder that beauty can hide real danger.)
12. What does the snake in the garden allude to? (Sample response: Gardens symbolize paradise, but in some instances there is evil or temptation. The interactions with the snake lead to/represent evil.)

13. What symbolic archetypes are present in the story? (Sample response: Snake = evil; Rikki's red eyes = passion or anger; garden = paradise/deception; father's gun = power.)
14. Is there a difference between Nagaina's willingness to kill Teddy and Rikki's willingness to kill Nagaina's young? (Responses will vary.)

Literary Analysis

Use Handout 8.4: Blank Literary Analysis Wheel to explore the interactions among elements in the wheel, paying special attention to the influence that symbols within the story have on our understanding of other elements (character, conflict, plot, mood, etc.). Pose the following questions for discussion by combining multiple elements on the wheel to help students make additional connections:

1. **Symbol + Setting:** How does the author's use of symbols add deeper meaning to the setting? (Sample response: The garden may be viewed as a place of safety. But, because it is only "partially cultivated," the garden is not entirely safe.)
2. **Symbol + Setting + Plot:** How does the understanding of the symbolism of the garden setting serve to develop the major conflict felt by Rikki-Tikki-Tavi? (Sample response: Rikki recognizes that the "partially cultivated" garden means that he will have to be watchful of danger. As the setting moves from the garden to the house, the plot is propelled forward as the black snakes enter the center—or heart—of the garden.)
3. **Character + Symbol + Theme:** How does the author's choice of characters and their symbolic meaning develop the theme? (Sample response: The choice of the mongoose battling the black snake suggests the battle of good versus evil.)
4. **Character + Theme:** How does the author's choice of characters help us understand the theme? (Sample response: The author chooses a young mongoose to battle against the older more experienced snakes [experience versus education], showing that the young have the power to bring about change through action.)
5. **Setting + Characters + Theme:** Which impacted the theme the most—the interactions between the setting and the characters or the interactions between characters and the theme? (Sample response: The changing settings for the encounters between Rikki and the snakes serves to increase the tension, revealing the evolving resilience and strength of Rikki and the increasing desperation of Nag and Nagaina. Each encounter moves closer and closer to the heart of the garden, with the final encounter resulting in Rikki chasing Nagaina out of the heart—the home—back into the darkness of her rat hole.)

Encounters With Archetypes

6. **Symbols + Characters + Techniques:** How did the symbolism of certain characters combined with the author's word choice support your understanding of characters' development and how that development allows for predictions? (Sample response: The snakes symbolized evil and represented the story's villains. The author reinforced the evil by emphasizing the snakes' black color and repeatedly referring to their broad hoods, both of which are also associated with evil and danger. In addition, with each encounter between Rikki and one of the snakes, the author emphasized the increasing tension through the color of Rikki's eyes, which change from "red and hot" to "eyes like hot coals" during one of the final encounters between Rikki and Nagaina. Knowing the different character and symbolic archetypes allowed the reader to predict how the character would respond and what might happen next. The symbols allowed the reader to understand some of the themes, such as good versus evil.)
7. **Choice of Literary Elements:** What additional connections or interactions of literary elements did you identify? What made those important to the story? (Responses will vary.)

Refer back to the Handout 2.1: Archetypes Quick Reference Guide as needed. Discuss the following questions:
1. What archetypal patterns do you notice (e.g., specific interactions of archetype characters with other types of characters, situations, symbols, etc.)? (Sample response: The encounters with Karait and with Nag show that Rikki is more than an explorer; Rikki is a warrior hero. He acts as a hero when battling Karait and when taking on Nag in the bathroom. By acting in a courageous manner, he ended the conflict between Nag, Nagaina, and the family.)
2. How do obstacles during the quest help reveal character archetypes? For example, how does the sage respond differently than a hero? (Sample response: Chuchundra acts as a sage, giving guidance and sharing knowledge. Had he acted as a hero, Chuchundra may have attempted to challenge Nag himself.)
3. How might the plot have been impacted if the characters responded in a different archetypal manner? (Sample response: Had Rikki acted as the explorer archetype, he may have chosen to just observe Nag or to travel into the sluice, and/or he may have followed the snakes and not been present to protect Teddy from Karait or to protect Father from Nag.)
4. What qualities of the character's archetype help that character resolve the conflicts encountered during the quest? (Sample response: Had Mother acted as leader, she may have had the funeral for Rikki, rather than taking time to heal him.)

5. What other archetypes (character, symbols, situations) did you notice in the story?
6. How do the encounters in the story allow for prediction? (Sample responses may include: Knowing that water may represent a rebirth or renewal, the reader can anticipate that Rikki may have grown or changed in some way from the young, curious mongoose that he was before the drowning. Knowing that snakes oftentimes represent evil and danger prepares the reader to anticipate that there will be a battle against safety and order; the author creates a twist for readers, setting Rikki on his quest to restore order and peace to the garden. Knowing that Rikki's eye color changes and intensifies with impending danger enables the reader to anticipate approaching encounters with dangerous situations that may bring about change.)

Choice-Based Differentiated Products

Students may choose one of the following to complete (*Note*: Use Rubric 1: Product Rubric in Appendix C to assess student responses):

- Rewrite "Rikki-Tikki-Tavi" as though Rikki-Tikki-Tavi represents a different archetype, while maintaining the overall theme. Be purposeful in your selection and use of symbols within three different encounters in your story. Consider using different types of animals and settings to enhance the impact of your selected symbols to show how encounters allow for prediction.
- Create three visual metaphors that symbolize three key plot points from "Rikki-Tikki-Tavi." The metaphors must convey the tension or significance of each key plot using a combination of color and imagery. You may create images or use images from magazines. Select a keyword that summarizes the encounter and explain how it relates to "encounters may lead to threats and opportunities" by writing a short paragraph. Use text evidence to support your thinking.
- Examine symbolic archetypes in a selected song or a video of a song from a movie. Identify the character, symbol, and situational archetypes that relate to the song and explain how our understanding of the singer's "encounter" is enhanced through the use of symbols. Present your findings to the class.

Opportunity for Talent Development

Have students research why and how various symbols and symbol systems originated (e.g., hieroglyphics, mathematics, sign language, Morse code): *What was the purpose or goal of these originations? Create a presentation to answer the question "Why are symbols an important part of one's culture?"*

Social-Emotional Connection

Symbols are an important part of conveying how we feel, hence the popularity of emoji. Ask students: *How do symbols enhance our expression of emotion (consider various expressions and forms)? Why are graphics, such as emoji, so important in today's form of communication? Create a new emoji to symbolize an idea or emotion you have that is unique to you and/or your friend group.*

ELA Task

Assign the following task as a performance-based assessment for this lesson: *Write a compare-and-contrast essay in which you explore similarities and differences between the symbols used in "Rikki-Tikki-Tavi" and one of the other short stories from this unit. Discuss how the use of symbols enhances our understanding of the meaning in a story.*

Concept Connections

1. Have students use at least three of following words to create a true statement about a real-world message of "Rikki-Tikki-Tavi": *encounter, change, risk, fear, rebirth, rise, hero, safe, rely.*
2. Continue to add to the concept map-working wall or use Handout 1.2: Concept Organizer (from Lesson 1 or see Appendix B) to record how encounter generalizations are applied to the story. In the last box, students should relate the idea of encounter to the concept of conflict.

Assessment

- Examine choice-based differentiated products and rubric criteria, ELA Task responses, and/or Concept Connections. Use Rubric 1: Product Rubric to review the products.
- Have students complete an exit ticket: *Select another story you know and explain how symbols are used to enhance the encounters one of the characters has with his or her world. Provide specific evidence from the story you select, as well as symbols.*

Handout 8.1
Symbol Cards

Wisdom	Strength	Hope
Courage	Peace	Evil
Love	Life	Idea
Time	Paradise	Innocence

Name: _____ Date: _____

Handout 8.2
Encounters With Archetypes

Directions: Identify the archetypes in each story and how the archetypes "encounter" or influence each other. Refer to Handout 2.1 as needed.

The Very Hungry Caterpillar		
Character Archetypes	**Situational Archetypes**	**Symbolic Archetypes**
Encounter Insight/Generalization		

"Rikki-Tikki-Tavi"		
Character Archetypes	**Situational Archetypes**	**Symbolic Archetypes**
Encounter Insight/Generalization		

Name: _____ Date: _____

Handout 8.3
Rikki-Tikki-Tavi From *The Jungle Book* by Rudyard Kipling

At the hole where he went in
Red-Eye called to Wrinkle-Skin.
Hear what little Red-Eye saith:
"Nag, come up and dance with death!"

Eye to eye and head to head, (Keep the measure, Nag.)
This shall end when one is dead; (At thy pleasure, Nag.)
Turn for turn and twist for twist-- (Run and hide thee, Nag.)
Hah! The hooded Death has missed! (Woe betide thee, Nag!)

This is the story of the great war that Rikki-tikki-tavi fought single-handed, through the bath-rooms of the big bungalow in Segowlee cantonment. Darzee, the Tailorbird, helped him, and Chuchundra, the musk-rat, who never comes out into the middle of the floor, but always creeps round by the wall, gave him advice, but Rikki-tikki did the real fighting.

He was a mongoose, rather like a little cat in his fur and his tail, but quite like a weasel in his head and his habits. His eyes and the end of his restless nose were pink. He could scratch himself anywhere he pleased with any leg, front or back, that he chose to use. He could fluff up his tail till it looked like a bottle brush, and his war cry as he scuttled through the long grass was: "Rikk-tikk-tikki-tikki-tchk!"

One day, a high summer flood washed him out of the burrow where he lived with his father and mother, and carried him, kicking and clucking, down a roadside ditch. He found a little wisp of grass floating there, and clung to it till he lost his senses. When he revived, he was lying in the hot sun on the middle of a garden path, very draggled indeed, and a small boy was saying, "Here's a dead mongoose. Let's have a funeral."

"No," said his mother, "let's take him in and dry him. Perhaps he isn't really dead."

They took him into the house, and a big man picked him up between his finger and thumb and said he was not dead but half choked. So they wrapped him in cotton wool, and warmed him over a little fire, and he opened his eyes and sneezed.

"Now," said the big man (he was an Englishman who had just moved into the bungalow), "don't frighten him, and we'll see what he'll do."

It is the hardest thing in the world to frighten a mongoose, because he is eaten up from nose to tail with curiosity. The motto of all the mongoose family is "Run and find out," and Rikki-tikki was a true mongoose. He looked at the cotton wool, decided that it was not good to eat, ran all round the table, sat up and put his fur in order, scratched himself, and jumped on the small boy's shoulder.

"Don't be frightened, Teddy," said his father. "That's his way of making friends."

"Ouch! He's tickling under my chin," said Teddy.

Handout 8.3, *continued*

Rikki-tikki looked down between the boy's collar and neck, snuffed at his ear, and climbed down to the floor, where he sat rubbing his nose.

"Good gracious," said Teddy's mother, "and that's a wild creature! I suppose he's so tame because we've been kind to him."

"All mongooses are like that," said her husband. "If Teddy doesn't pick him up by the tail, or try to put him in a cage, he'll run in and out of the house all day long. Let's give him something to eat."

They gave him a little piece of raw meat. Rikki-tikki liked it immensely, and when it was finished he went out into the veranda and sat in the sunshine and fluffed up his fur to make it dry to the roots. Then he felt better.

"There are more things to find out about in this house," he said to himself, "than all my family could find out in all their lives. I shall certainly stay and find out."

He spent all that day roaming over the house. He nearly drowned himself in the bath-tubs, put his nose into the ink on a writing table, and burned it on the end of the big man's cigar, for he climbed up in the big man's lap to see how writing was done. At nightfall he ran into Teddy's nursery to watch how kerosene lamps were lighted, and when Teddy went to bed Rikki-tikki climbed up too. But he was a restless companion, because he had to get up and attend to every noise all through the night, and find out what made it. Teddy's mother and father came in, the last thing, to look at their boy, and Rikki-tikki was awake on the pillow. "I don't like that," said Teddy's mother. "He may bite the child." "He'll do no such thing," said the father. "Teddy's safer with that little beast than if he had a bloodhound to watch him. If a snake came into the nursery now–"

But Teddy's mother wouldn't think of anything so awful.

Early in the morning Rikki-tikki came to early breakfast in the veranda riding on Teddy's shoulder, and they gave him banana and some boiled egg. He sat on all their laps one after the other, because every well-brought-up mongoose always hopes to be a house mongoose some day and have rooms to run about in; and Rikki-tikki's mother (she used to live in the general's house at Segowlee) had carefully told Rikki what to do if ever he came across white men.

Then Rikki-tikki went out into the garden to see what was to be seen. It was a large garden, only half cultivated, with bushes, as big as summer-houses, of Marshal Niel roses, lime and orange trees, clumps of bamboos, and thickets of high grass. Rikki-tikki licked his lips. "This is a splendid hunting-ground," he said, and his tail grew bottle-brushy at the thought of it, and he scuttled up and down the garden, snuffing here and there till he heard very sorrowful voices in a thorn-bush.

It was Darzee, the Tailorbird, and his wife. They had made a beautiful nest by pulling two big leaves together and stitching them up the edges with fibers, and had filled the hollow with cotton and downy fluff. The nest swayed to and fro, as they sat on the rim and cried.

"What is the matter?" asked Rikki-tikki.

"We are very miserable," said Darzee. "One of our babies fell out of the nest yesterday and Nag ate him."

"H'm!" said Rikki-tikki, "that is very sad–but I am a stranger here. Who is Nag?"

Name: _____ Date: _____

Handout 8.3, *continued*

Darzee and his wife only cowered down in the nest without answering, for from the thick grass at the foot of the bush there came a low hiss—a horrid cold sound that made Rikki-tikki jump back two clear feet. Then inch by inch out of the grass rose up the head and spread hood of Nag, the big black cobra, and he was five feet long from tongue to tail. When he had lifted one-third of himself clear of the ground, he stayed balancing to and fro exactly as a dandelion tuft balances in the wind, and he looked at Rikki-tikki with the wicked snake's eyes that never change their expression, whatever the snake may be thinking of.

"Who is Nag?" said he. "I am Nag. The great God Brahm put his mark upon all our people, when the first cobra spread his hood to keep the sun off Brahm as he slept. Look, and be afraid!"

He spread out his hood more than ever, and Rikki-tikki saw the spectacle-mark on the back of it that looks exactly like the eye part of a hook-and-eye fastening. He was afraid for the minute, but it is impossible for a mongoose to stay frightened for any length of time, and though Rikki-tikki had never met a live cobra before, his mother had fed him on dead ones, and he knew that all a grown mongoose's business in life was to fight and eat snakes. Nag knew that too and, at the bottom of his cold heart, he was afraid.

"Well," said Rikki-tikki, and his tail began to fluff up again, "marks or no marks, do you think it is right for you to eat fledglings out of a nest?"

Nag was thinking to himself, and watching the least little movement in the grass behind Rikki-tikki. He knew that mongooses in the garden meant death sooner or later for him and his family, but he wanted to get Rikki-tikki off his guard. So he dropped his head a little, and put it on one side.

"Let us talk," he said. "You eat eggs. Why should not I eat birds?"

"Behind you! Look behind you!" sang Darzee.

Rikki-tikki knew better than to waste time in staring. He jumped up in the air as high as he could go, and just under him whizzed by the head of Nagaina, Nag's wicked wife. She had crept up behind him as he was talking, to make an end of him. He heard her savage hiss as the stroke missed. He came down almost across her back, and if he had been an old mongoose he would have known that then was the time to break her back with one bite; but he was afraid of the terrible lashing return stroke of the cobra. He bit, indeed, but did not bite long enough, and he jumped clear of the whisking tail, leaving Nagaina torn and angry.

"Wicked, wicked Darzee!" said Nag, lashing up as high as he could reach toward the nest in the thorn-bush. But Darzee had built it out of reach of snakes, and it only swayed to and fro.

Rikki-tikki felt his eyes growing red and hot (when a mongoose's eyes grow red, he is angry), and he sat back on his tail and hind legs like a little kangaroo, and looked all round him, and chattered with rage. But Nag and Nagaina had disappeared into the grass. When a snake misses its stroke, it never says anything or gives any sign of what it means to do next. Rikki-tikki did not care to follow them, for he did not feel sure that he could manage two snakes at once. So he trotted off to the gravel path near the house, and sat down to think. It was a serious matter for him.

If you read the old books of natural history, you will find they say that when the mongoose fights the snake and happens to get bitten, he runs off and eats some herb that cures

Name: _____   Date: _____

Handout 8.3, *continued*

him. That is not true. The victory is only a matter of quickness of eye and quickness of foot—snake's blow against mongoose's jump—and as no eye can follow the motion of a snake's head when it strikes, this makes things much more wonderful than any magic herb. Rikki-tikki knew he was a young mongoose, and it made him all the more pleased to think that he had managed to escape a blow from behind. It gave him confidence in himself, and when Teddy came running down the path, Rikki-tikki was ready to be petted.

But just as Teddy was stooping, something wriggled a little in the dust, and a tiny voice said: "Be careful. I am Death!" It was Karait, the dusty brown snakeling that lies for choice on the dusty earth; and his bite is as dangerous as the cobra's. But he is so small that nobody thinks of him, and so he does the more harm to people.

Rikki-tikki's eyes grew red again, and he danced up to Karait with the peculiar rocking, swaying motion that he had inherited from his family. It looks very funny, but it is so perfectly balanced a gait that you can fly off from it at any angle you please, and in dealing with snakes this is an advantage. If Rikki-tikki had only known, he was doing a much more dangerous thing than fighting Nag, for Karait is so small, and can turn so quickly, that unless Rikki bit him close to the back of the head, he would get the return stroke in his eye or his lip. But Rikki did not know. His eyes were all red, and he rocked back and forth, looking for a good place to hold. Karait struck out. Rikki jumped sideways and tried to run in, but the wicked little dusty gray head lashed within a fraction of his shoulder, and he had to jump over the body, and the head followed his heels close.

Teddy shouted to the house: "Oh, look here! Our mongoose is killing a snake." And Rikki-tikki heard a scream from Teddy's mother. His father ran out with a stick, but by the time he came up, Karait had lunged out once too far, and Rikki-tikki had sprung, jumped on the snake's back, dropped his head far between his forelegs, bitten as high up the back as he could get hold, and rolled away. That bite paralyzed Karait, and Rikki-tikki was just going to eat him up from the tail, after the custom of his family at dinner, when he remembered that a full meal makes a slow mongoose, and if he wanted all his strength and quickness ready, he must keep himself thin.

He went away for a dust bath under the castor-oil bushes, while Teddy's father beat the dead Karait. "What is the use of that?" thought Rikki-tikki. "I have settled it all;" and then Teddy's mother picked him up from the dust and hugged him, crying that he had saved Teddy from death, and Teddy's father said that he was a providence, and Teddy looked on with big scared eyes. Rikki-tikki was rather amused at all the fuss, which, of course, he did not understand. Teddy's mother might just as well have petted Teddy for playing in the dust. Rikki was thoroughly enjoying himself.

That night at dinner, walking to and fro among the wine-glasses on the table, he might have stuffed himself three times over with nice things. But he remembered Nag and Nagaina, and though it was very pleasant to be patted and petted by Teddy's mother, and to sit on Teddy's shoulder, his eyes would get red from time to time, and he would go off into his long war cry of "Rikk-tikk-tikki-tikki-tchk!"

Teddy carried him off to bed, and insisted on Rikki-tikki sleeping under his chin. Rikki-tikki was too well bred to bite or scratch, but as soon as Teddy was asleep he went off for his nightly walk round the house, and in the dark he ran up against Chuchundra,

Handout 8.3, *continued*

the musk-rat, creeping around by the wall. Chuchundra is a broken-hearted little beast. He whimpers and cheeps all the night, trying to make up his mind to run into the middle of the room. But he never gets there.

"Don't kill me," said Chuchundra, almost weeping. "Rikki-tikki, don't kill me!"

"Do you think a snake-killer kills muskrats?" said Rikki-tikki scornfully.

"Those who kill snakes get killed by snakes," said Chuchundra, more sorrowfully than ever. "And how am I to be sure that Nag won't mistake me for you some dark night?"

"There's not the least danger," said Rikki-tikki. "But Nag is in the garden, and I know you don't go there."

"My cousin Chua, the rat, told me–" said Chuchundra, and then he stopped.

"Told you what?"

"H'sh! Nag is everywhere, Rikki-tikki. You should have talked to Chua in the garden."

"I didn't–so you must tell me. Quick, Chuchundra, or I'll bite you!"

Chuchundra sat down and cried till the tears rolled off his whiskers. "I am a very poor man," he sobbed. "I never had spirit enough to run out into the middle of the room. H'sh! I mustn't tell you anything. Can't you hear, Rikki-tikki?"

Rikki-tikki listened. The house was as still as still, but he thought he could just catch the faintest scratch-scratch in the world–a noise as faint as that of a wasp walking on a window-pane–the dry scratch of a snake's scales on brick-work.

"That's Nag or Nagaina," he said to himself, "and he is crawling into the bath-room sluice. You're right, Chuchundra; I should have talked to Chua."

He stole off to Teddy's bath-room, but there was nothing there, and then to Teddy's mother's bathroom. At the bottom of the smooth plaster wall there was a brick pulled out to make a sluice for the bath water, and as Rikki-tikki stole in by the masonry curb where the bath is put, he heard Nag and Nagaina whispering together outside in the moonlight.

"When the house is emptied of people," said Nagaina to her husband, "he will have to go away, and then the garden will be our own again. Go in quietly, and remember that the big man who killed Karait is the first one to bite. Then come out and tell me, and we will hunt for Rikki-tikki together."

"But are you sure that there is anything to be gained by killing the people?" said Nag.

"Everything. When there were no people in the bungalow, did we have any mongoose in the garden? So long as the bungalow is empty, we are king and queen of the garden; and remember that as soon as our eggs in the melon bed hatch (as they may tomorrow), our children will need room and quiet."

"I had not thought of that," said Nag. "I will go, but there is no need that we should hunt for Rikki-tikki afterward. I will kill the big man and his wife, and the child if I can, and come away quietly. Then the bungalow will be empty, and Rikki-tikki will go."

Rikki-tikki tingled all over with rage and hatred at this, and then Nag's head came through the sluice, and his five feet of cold body followed it. Angry as he was, Rikki-tikki was very frightened as he saw the size of the big cobra. Nag coiled himself up, raised his head, and looked into the bathroom in the dark, and Rikki could see his eyes glitter.

"Now, if I kill him here, Nagaina will know; and if I fight him on the open floor, the odds are in his favor. What am I to do?" said Rikki-tikki-tavi.

Name: _____ Date: _____

Handout 8.3, *continued*

Nag waved to and fro, and then Rikki-tikki heard him drinking from the biggest water-jar that was used to fill the bath. "That is good," said the snake. "Now, when Karait was killed, the big man had a stick. He may have that stick still, but when he comes in to bathe in the morning he will not have a stick. I shall wait here till he comes. Nagaina—do you hear me?—I shall wait here in the cool till daytime."

There was no answer from outside, so Rikki-tikki knew Nagaina had gone away. Nag coiled himself down, coil by coil, round the bulge at the bottom of the water jar, and Rikki-tikki stayed still as death. After an hour he began to move, muscle by muscle, toward the jar. Nag was asleep, and Rikki-tikki looked at his big back, wondering which would be the best place for a good hold. "If I don't break his back at the first jump," said Rikki, "he can still fight. And if he fights—O Rikki!" He looked at the thickness of the neck below the hood, but that was too much for him; and a bite near the tail would only make Nag savage.

"It must be the head'" he said at last; "the head above the hood. And, when I am once there, I must not let go."

Then he jumped. The head was lying a little clear of the water jar, under the curve of it; and, as his teeth met, Rikki braced his back against the bulge of the red earthenware to hold down the head. This gave him just one second's purchase, and he made the most of it. Then he was battered to and fro as a rat is shaken by a dog—to and fro on the floor, up and down, and around in great circles, but his eyes were red and he held on as the body cart-whipped over the floor, upsetting the tin dipper and the soap dish and the flesh brush, and banged against the tin side of the bath. As he held he closed his jaws tighter and tighter, for he made sure he would be banged to death, and, for the honor of his family, he preferred to be found with his teeth locked. He was dizzy, aching, and felt shaken to pieces when something went off like a thunderclap just behind him. A hot wind knocked him senseless and red fire singed his fur. The big man had been wakened by the noise, and had fired both barrels of a shotgun into Nag just behind the hood.

Rikki-tikki held on with his eyes shut, for now he was quite sure he was dead. But the head did not move, and the big man picked him up and said, "It's the mongoose again, Alice. The little chap has saved our lives now."

Then Teddy's mother came in with a very white face, and saw what was left of Nag, and Rikki-tikki dragged himself to Teddy's bedroom and spent half the rest of the night shaking himself tenderly to find out whether he really was broken into forty pieces, as he fancied.

When morning came he was very stiff, but well pleased with his doings. "Now I have Nagaina to settle with, and she will be worse than five Nags, and there's no knowing when the eggs she spoke of will hatch. Goodness! I must go and see Darzee," he said.

Without waiting for breakfast, Rikki-tikki ran to the thornbush where Darzee was singing a song of triumph at the top of his voice. The news of Nag's death was all over the garden, for the sweeper had thrown the body on the rubbish-heap.

"Oh, you stupid tuft of feathers!" said Rikki-tikki angrily. "Is this the time to sing?"

"Nag is dead—is dead—is dead!" sang Darzee. "The valiant Rikki-tikki caught him by the head and held fast. The big man brought the bang-stick, and Nag fell in two pieces! He will never eat my babies again."

Name: _____ Date: _____

Handout 8.3, *continued*

"All that's true enough. But where's Nagaina?" said Rikki-tikki, looking carefully round him.

"Nagaina came to the bathroom sluice and called for Nag," Darzee went on, "and Nag came out on the end of a stick–the sweeper picked him up on the end of a stick and threw him upon the rubbish heap. Let us sing about the great, the red-eyed Rikki-tikki!" And Darzee filled his throat and sang.

"If I could get up to your nest, I'd roll your babies out!" said Rikki-tikki. "You don't know when to do the right thing at the right time. You're safe enough in your nest there, but it's war for me down here. Stop singing a minute, Darzee."

"For the great, the beautiful Rikki-tikki's sake I will stop," said Darzee. "What is it, O Killer of the terrible Nag?"

"Where is Nagaina, for the third time?"

"On the rubbish heap by the stables, mourning for Nag. Great is Rikki-tikki with the white teeth."

"Bother my white teeth! Have you ever heard where she keeps her eggs?"

"In the melon bed, on the end nearest the wall, where the sun strikes nearly all day. She hid them there weeks ago."

"And you never thought it worth while to tell me? The end nearest the wall, you said?"

"Rikki-tikki, you are not going to eat her eggs?"

"Not eat exactly; no. Darzee, if you have a grain of sense you will fly off to the stables and pretend that your wing is broken, and let Nagaina chase you away to this bush. I must get to the melon-bed, and if I went there now she'd see me."

Darzee was a feather-brained little fellow who could never hold more than one idea at a time in his head. And just because he knew that Nagaina's children were born in eggs like his own, he didn't think at first that it was fair to kill them. But his wife was a sensible bird, and she knew that cobra's eggs meant young cobras later on. So she flew off from the nest, and left Darzee to keep the babies warm, and continue his song about the death of Nag. Darzee was very like a man in some ways.

She fluttered in front of Nagaina by the rubbish heap and cried out, "Oh, my wing is broken! The boy in the house threw a stone at me and broke it." Then she fluttered more desperately than ever.

Nagaina lifted up her head and hissed, "You warned Rikki-tikki when I would have killed him. Indeed and truly, you've chosen a bad place to be lame in." And she moved toward Darzee's wife, slipping along over the dust.

"The boy broke it with a stone!" shrieked Darzee's wife.

"Well! It may be some consolation to you when you're dead to know that I shall settle accounts with the boy. My husband lies on the rubbish heap this morning, but before night the boy in the house will lie very still. What is the use of running away? I am sure to catch you. Little fool, look at me!"

Darzee's wife knew better than to do that, for a bird who looks at a snake's eyes gets so frightened that she cannot move. Darzee's wife fluttered on, piping sorrowfully, and never leaving the ground, and Nagaina quickened her pace.

Handout 8.3, *continued*

Rikki-tikki heard them going up the path from the stables, and he raced for the end of the melon patch near the wall. There, in the warm litter above the melons, very cunningly hidden, he found twenty-five eggs, about the size of a bantam's eggs, but with whitish skin instead of shell.

"I was not a day too soon," he said, for he could see the baby cobras curled up inside the skin, and he knew that the minute they were hatched they could each kill a man or a mongoose. He bit off the tops of the eggs as fast as he could, taking care to crush the young cobras, and turned over the litter from time to time to see whether he had missed any. At last there were only three eggs left, and Rikki-tikki began to chuckle to himself, when he heard Darzee's wife screaming:

"Rikki-tikki, I led Nagaina toward the house, and she has gone into the veranda, and–oh, come quickly–she means killing!"

Rikki-tikki smashed two eggs, and tumbled backward down the melon-bed with the third egg in his mouth, and scuttled to the veranda as hard as he could put foot to the ground. Teddy and his mother and father were there at early breakfast, but Rikki-tikki saw that they were not eating anything. They sat stone-still, and their faces were white. Nagaina was coiled up on the matting by Teddy's chair, within easy striking distance of Teddy's bare leg, and she was swaying to and fro, singing a song of triumph.

"Son of the big man that killed Nag," she hissed, "stay still. I am not ready yet. Wait a little. Keep very still, all you three! If you move I strike, and if you do not move I strike. Oh, foolish people, who killed my Nag!"

Teddy's eyes were fixed on his father, and all his father could do was to whisper, "Sit still, Teddy. You mustn't move. Teddy, keep still."

Then Rikki-tikki came up and cried, "Turn round, Nagaina. Turn and fight!"

"All in good time," said she, without moving her eyes. "I will settle my account with you presently. Look at your friends, Rikki-tikki. They are still and white. They are afraid. They dare not move, and if you come a step nearer I strike."

"Look at your eggs," said Rikki-tikki, "in the melon bed near the wall. Go and look, Nagaina!"

The big snake turned half around, and saw the egg on the veranda. "Ah-h! Give it to me," she said.

Rikki-tikki put his paws one on each side of the egg, and his eyes were blood-red. "What price for a snake's egg? For a young cobra? For a young king cobra? For the last–the very last of the brood? The ants are eating all the others down by the melon bed."

Nagaina spun clear round, forgetting everything for the sake of the one egg. Rikki-tikki saw Teddy's father shoot out a big hand, catch Teddy by the shoulder, and drag him across the little table with the tea-cups, safe and out of reach of Nagaina.

"Tricked! Tricked! Tricked! Rikk-tck-tck!" chuckled Rikki-tikki. "The boy is safe, and it was I–I–I that caught Nag by the hood last night in the bathroom." Then he began to jump up and down, all four feet together, his head close to the floor. "He threw me to and fro, but he could not shake me off. He was dead before the big man blew him in two. I did it! Rikki-tikki-tck-tck! Come then, Nagaina. Come and fight with me. You shall not be a widow long."

Name: _____ Date: _____

Handout 8.3, *continued*

Nagaina saw that she had lost her chance of killing Teddy, and the egg lay between Rikki-tikki's paws. "Give me the egg, Rikki-tikki. Give me the last of my eggs, and I will go away and never come back," she said, lowering her hood.

"Yes, you will go away, and you will never come back. For you will go to the rubbish heap with Nag. Fight, widow! The big man has gone for his gun! Fight!"

Rikki-tikki was bounding all round Nagaina, keeping just out of reach of her stroke, his little eyes like hot coals. Nagaina gathered herself together and flung out at him. Rikki-tikki jumped up and backward. Again and again and again she struck, and each time her head came with a whack on the matting of the veranda and she gathered herself together like a watch spring. Then Rikki-tikki danced in a circle to get behind her, and Nagaina spun round to keep her head to his head, so that the rustle of her tail on the matting sounded like dry leaves blown along by the wind.

He had forgotten the egg. It still lay on the veranda, and Nagaina came nearer and nearer to it, till at last, while Rikki-tikki was drawing breath, she caught it in her mouth, turned to the veranda steps, and flew like an arrow down the path, with Rikki-tikki behind her. When the cobra runs for her life, she goes like a whip-lash flicked across a horse's neck.

Rikki-tikki knew that he must catch her, or all the trouble would begin again. She headed straight for the long grass by the thorn-bush, and as he was running Rikki-tikki heard Darzee still singing his foolish little song of triumph. But Darzee's wife was wiser. She flew off her nest as Nagaina came along, and flapped her wings about Nagaina's head. If Darzee had helped they might have turned her, but Nagaina only lowered her hood and went on. Still, the instant's delay brought Rikki-tikki up to her, and as she plunged into the rat-hole where she and Nag used to live, his little white teeth were clenched on her tail, and he went down with her—and very few mongooses, however wise and old they may be, care to follow a cobra into its hole. It was dark in the hole; and Rikki-tikki never knew when it might open out and give Nagaina room to turn and strike at him. He held on savagely, and stuck out his feet to act as brakes on the dark slope of the hot, moist earth.

Then the grass by the mouth of the hole stopped waving, and Darzee said, "It is all over with Rikki-tikki! We must sing his death song. Valiant Rikki-tikki is dead! For Nagaina will surely kill him underground."

So he sang a very mournful song that he made up on the spur of the minute, and just as he got to the most touching part, the grass quivered again, and Rikki-tikki, covered with dirt, dragged himself out of the hole leg by leg, licking his whiskers. Darzee stopped with a little shout. Rikki-tikki shook some of the dust out of his fur and sneezed. "It is all over," he said. "The widow will never come out again." And the red ants that live between the grass stems heard him, and began to troop down one after another to see if he had spoken the truth.

Rikki-tikki curled himself up in the grass and slept where he was—slept and slept till it was late in the afternoon, for he had done a hard day's work.

"Now," he said, when he awoke, "I will go back to the house. Tell the Coppersmith, Darzee, and he will tell the garden that Nagaina is dead."

The Coppersmith is a bird who makes a noise exactly like the beating of a little hammer on a copper pot; and the reason he is always making it is because he is the town crier to

Name: _____   Date: _____

Handout 8.3, *continued*

every Indian garden, and tells all the news to everybody who cares to listen. As Rikki-tikki went up the path, he heard his "attention" notes like a tiny dinner gong, and then the steady "Ding-dong-tock! Nag is dead—dong! Nagaina is dead! Ding-dong-tock!" That set all the birds in the garden singing, and the frogs croaking, for Nag and Nagaina used to eat frogs as well as little birds.

When Rikki got to the house, Teddy and Teddy's mother (she looked very white still, for she had been fainting) and Teddy's father came out and almost cried over him; and that night he ate all that was given him till he could eat no more, and went to bed on Teddy's shoulder, where Teddy's mother saw him when she came to look late at night.

"He saved our lives and Teddy's life," she said to her husband. "Just think, he saved all our lives."

Rikki-tikki woke up with a jump, for the mongooses are light sleepers.

"Oh, it's you," said he. "What are you bothering for? All the cobras are dead. And if they weren't, I'm here."

Rikki-tikki had a right to be proud of himself. But he did not grow too proud, and he kept that garden as a mongoose should keep it, with tooth and jump and spring and bite, till never a cobra dared show its head inside the walls.

Name: _____ Date: _____

Handout 8.4
Blank Literary Analysis Wheel

Directions: Draw arrows across elements to show connections.

Text: _____

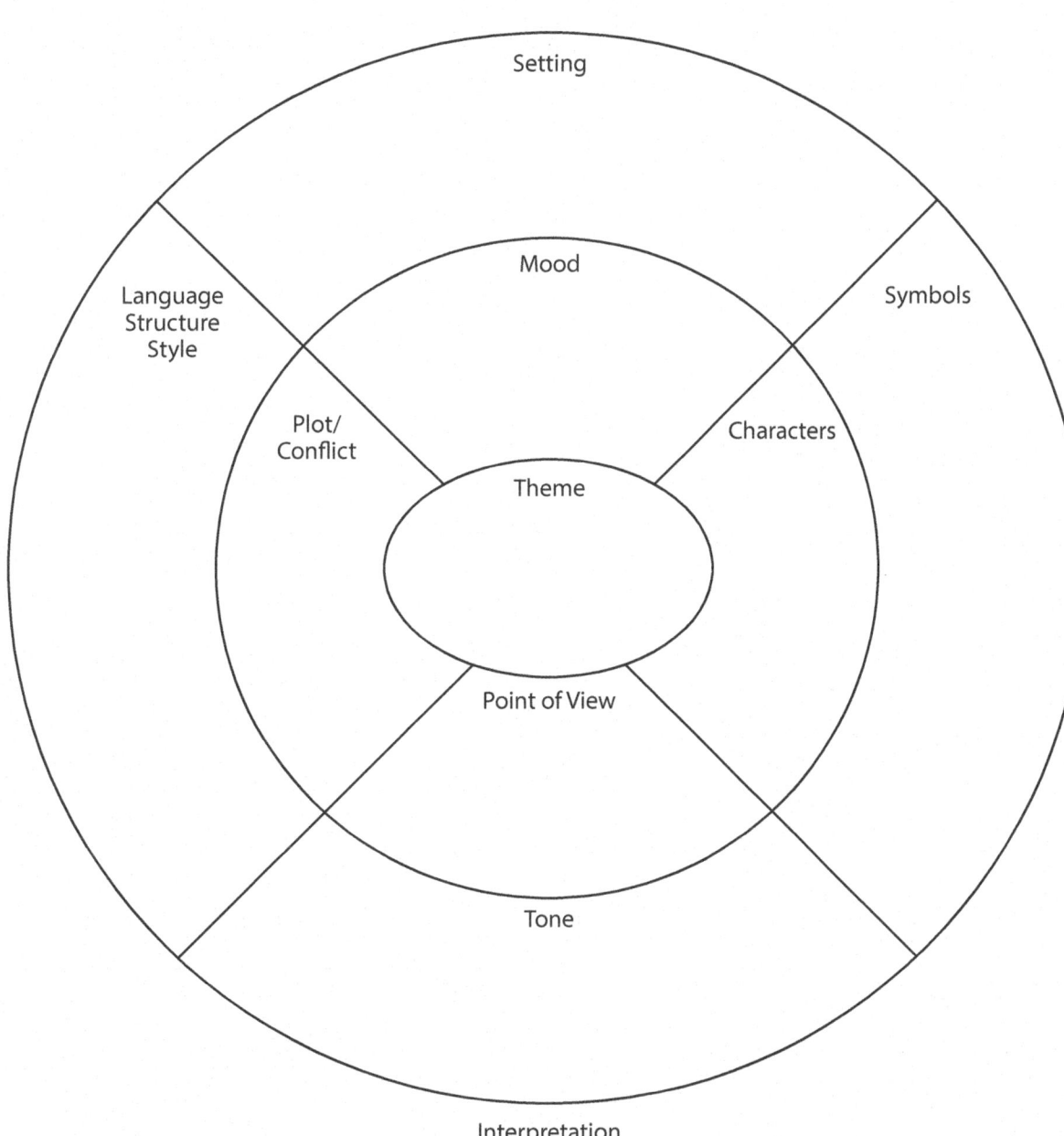

Created by Tamra Stambaugh, Ph.D., & Emily Mofield, Ed.D., 2015.

153
Encounters With Archetypes © Taylor & Francis

Lesson 9

Encounters With Symbols, Images, and Visual Media

Key Question

How are messages conveyed through encounters with images and symbols?

Objectives

Content: To analyze and interpret fiction, nonfiction, and art, students will be able to:
- compare and contrast how literary, visual, informational, and/or primary source texts reveal patterns and themes;
- compare and contrast the use of specific techniques various authors use to approach and develop similar ideas; and
- identify and analyze archetypal patterns in stories, speeches, and real-world contexts and discuss how they are shaped by the author or real-world individuals or events.

Process: To develop interpretation, analysis, and communication skills in the language arts, students will be able to:
- justify inferences with evidence from the text;
- apply evidence to support explanations and opinions relative to a question, text, or issue; and
- respond to an analysis of literature, nonfiction, media, or art by developing arguments and elaborating on explanations through writing a variety of texts (e.g., essays, paragraphs), including relevant and sufficient evidence to support claims.

Concept: To develop conceptual thinking about encounters in language arts and additional content areas, students will be able to:
- explain with evidence how encounters may lead to positive or negative outcomes in literature, media, and real-world examples;
- explain how encounters allow for prediction within literature and real-world examples;

Encounters With Archetypes

- relate encounter generalizations to real-life situations; and
- examine the relationship between encounters and other concepts in multiple contexts.

Accelerated CCSS for ELA

- RL.8.3
- W.7.10
- SL.6.1

Materials

- Video: "Eagle Whirlpool ad TV - 1970s" (available at https://www.youtube.com/watch?v=wcHufFQ8UnA)
- A variety of commercials that rely on archetypes to market their product (for students to complete Handout 8.1)
    - "Toyota Verso - My Dad, My Hero Commercial" (available at https://www.youtube.com/watch?v=o4loLINsV6I)
    - "Brotherly Love #EnjoytheFeeling" (available at https://www.youtube.com/watch?v=S5h2lmROw5A)
    - "Video Capital One CreditWise® Tai Chi TV Commercial Ad Advertisement 2017" (available at https://www.youtube.com/watch?v=wQL1QJsIt6k)
    - "Ford Mustang Shelby GT350 and GT350R – 'Be a Kid Again' TV Commercial" (available at https://www.youtube.com/watch?v=cb5jld1a2l0)
- Video: "Official Ram Trucks Super Bowl Commercial | Dr. Martin Luther King, Jr. | Built to Serve" (available https://www.youtube.com/watch?v=SlbY1tGARUA)
- Handout 2.1: Archetypes Quick Reference Guide
- Handout 9.1: Encounters With Archetypes in Advertising
- Handout 9.2: Blank Rhetorical Analysis Wheel
- Rubric 1: Product Rubric (Appendix C)

Introductory Activities

1. Show "Eagle Whirlpool ad TV - 1970s" (see Materials list) without sound. Pause the video at the 55-second mark or before the logo appears. Ask: *What do you think this commercial is for? What is the ad trying to sell by showing you the eagle hunting for fish?* Guide students to make a connection between the eagle and what it symbolizes (courage, strength, freedom).
2. Show the full video, this time with sound. Ask students:
    - What is being advertised?

- Why is the eagle used, and what does it symbolize? (Sample response: The eagle symbolizes courage, strength, work ethic, and the shared value that the company and the customer have; without even showing its product, Whirlpool sells its brand as one that is synonymous with the values of its customers.)
- How do the image of the eagle and the uplifting music reinforce the message shared in the voiceover? (Sample response: As viewers listen to the narrator, they are shown images that symbolize America, freedom, etc.)

3. Select a series of brands that students are familiar with, such as Kit Kat, Crayola, etc. Ask: *When you see this brand or logo, what archetype comes to mind?* (Sample responses: Kit Kat = everyday person, Crayola = creator, M&M = jester, Jeep = explorer.)
4. Explain to students that advertisements often incorporate archetypes. Ask: *Why might archetypes be such a powerful tool in advertising?* (Help students understand that archetypes allow a product to remain or become relevant; archetypes also allow advertisers to convey a message in a shorter amount of time because patterns are common, known, and established. Aligning a brand with a particular archetype also sets a brand apart from the competition.)

In-Class Activities to Deepen Learning

1. Distribute Handout 9.1: Encounters With Archetypes in Advertising for students to complete as they watch a series of commercials. Show 3–4 commercials (see Materials list or select other ads that may be relevant to your students). You may want to guide students through one example as an entire class. Students may need to view commercials 2–3 times to complete the handout.
2. As you show each commercial, ask students a series of questions, such as the following, to help them complete their handouts (sample responses are for the Toyota commercial). They may discuss these questions in small- or whole-group settings:
   - What encounters take place within the commercial? How do encounters reveal an archetype? (Sample response: Dad encounters the problem of fitting the family's gear into the car; he is the hero for solving all of the family's problems and keeping them safe.)
   - What major archetypes are present? What other archetypes are present, and how do they relate to and influence each other? (Sample response: The dad is an everyday person who is seen as a hero when he has the car; with the car the family can go on adventures, have enough room to store everything kids need, and have fun as a family. The car's route may symbolize a quest, as well as purity and innocence [because of its color].

Encounters With Archetypes

The person in need of rescue may be represented by the family's need for gas; the desert may symbolize a hopeless situation.)

- To whom is this commercial appealing? What makes it relevant to this audience? (Sample response: The everyday "dad" wants to take care of and protect his family.)
- What happens when the product is encountered? What happens without the product? (Sample response: Dad is seen as a hero when he has the car; he can take his family on adventures, keep them safe, etc. Without the car, he might not be seen as a hero.)
- How does the archetypal pattern help make the commercial relatable (i.e., what problem is solved, what need does it fill, and what might we predict or assume because of the characters or situations?)? (Sample response: The commercial is relatable to parents who want to provide for their families, go on adventures with them, and have space in a car to carry everything they need.)
- How does an encounter with that product (or lack thereof) allow for a positive or negative outcome, allow for opportunities or threats, allow for reflection and change, and/or allow for prediction? (*Note*: Not all generalizations may be represented in every commercial.) (Sample response: The car allows for opportunities for a dad to keep his family safe and to carry all of their things; owning the car has positive outcomes, as his family has fun and views him as a hero; one may predict that an encounter with the car is good for families.)
- What message is conveyed? (Sample response: You can be the hero of your family if you buy this car.)

Rhetorical Analysis

Show "Official Ram Trucks Super Bowl Commercial | Dr. Martin Luther King, Jr. | Built to Serve" (see Materials list). Have students complete Handout 9.2: Blank Rhetorical Analysis Wheel about the commercial. (*Note*: This ad may be seen as controversial. Any ad with a substantial emphasis on a particular archetype may serve as a substitute.) Explain that in order to evaluate an argument, students have to determine the purpose and main argument (claim). They will examine specific appeals (pathos, ethos, and logos) used to support the claim and how these appeals are developed by techniques, organization, and assumptions of those who developed the commercial. If students are not familiar with pathos, ethos, and logos, consider substituting words such as "emotions or feelings" instead of pathos, "facts and logic" instead of logos, and "credibility" instead of ethos. Students may take notes on the wheel and draw arrows to illustrate connections between the various elements. Some sample questions and responses to lead to analysis include:

Simple questions:
1. **Purpose:** What is the purpose of the commercial? (Sample response: The ad sells trucks.)
2. **Claim:** What is the commercial's main claim? (Sample response: The ad claims that the truck can help you if you want to help your community as an everyday person or hero.)
3. **Point of View:** What is the point of view of the commercial's creators toward everyday people? (Sample response: The creators of the commercial saw everyday people as part of the heart and soul of communities. Their point of view is reflected in the voiceover of Dr. King, which suggests that serving others is the highest form of greatness.)
4. **Structure/Organization:** What is the overall structure of the commercial? (Sample response: The ad quickly cuts from one example of an individual serving his or her community to the next: a cowboy, a teacher, a firefighter, a community moving a historic church, etc. The snapshots of everyday people engaged in service to their communities help support the point of view.)
5. **Techniques:** What are some rhetorical techniques that are used in the ad? (Sample response: Repetition of everyday people using their trucks to help their communities reinforces the idea that the truck is necessary to serve. Blue tones are used throughout, which may represent the moral purity of helping others.)
6. **Pathos:** What emotion(s) do the commercial's creators attempt to evoke? (Sample response: Images of serving others and Dr. King's voiceover help deliver an emotional appeal of hope to the audience.)
7. **Logos:** What are the main points? How do the creators of the commercial support their claim(s) with evidence and facts? (Sample response: The creators use syllogism [if $x = y$ and $y = z$, then $x = z$]: If you want to be great [x], then you need to serve your community [y]. If you want to serve your community [y], then you need the truck [z]. Therefore, if you want to be great [x], you need the truck [z].)
8. **Ethos:** Is the commercial credible? How is trust established? (Sample response: The use of Dr. King's speech as a voiceover establishes trust.)
9. **Implications:** What are the short- and long-term implications/consequences of this commercial? (Sample response: People will think about ways that they can serve their communities and whether or not a Ram truck would help them accomplish that purpose.)

Encounters With Archetypes

Complex questions:
1. **Pathos + Techniques:** What techniques are used to develop pathos appeals? (Sample response: The images of people serving their communities appeal to the audience's emotions. Viewers might also be motivated to get involved in their communities. Using the audio from Dr. King's famous speech also appeals to the audience's emotions.)
2. **Logos + Structure:** How is the argument structured logically? (Sample response: The syllogism is reinforced by the structure of the commercial. The short clips of people serving their communities spliced with Ram trucks helping make that work possible reinforce the logic.)
3. **Ethos + Techniques:** What techniques are used to establish ethos appeals? (Sample response: The use of a speech by Dr. King, a credible advocate of everyday people serving in their community, lends itself to the overall ethos of the commercial.)
4. **Evaluation:** How effective is the commercial in supporting its claim? Is there a balance of pathos, ethos, and logos appeals? Is the claim fully supported? (Responses will vary.)

Choice-Based Differentiated Products

Students may choose one of the following to complete (*Note*: Use Rubric 1: Product Rubric in Appendix C to assess student responses):

- Choose a commercial from this lesson. Explain how the brand used encounters and archetypes, especially symbols, to develop the main message of the ad. Analyze the commercial's use of archetypes in a well-developed paragraph that includes specific examples cited from the ad. Discuss specific encounters, the portrayal of the archetype(s), and which generalization about encounters is best represented and why.
- Create your own commercial that incorporates at least three encounters with archetypes (e.g., with a person, circumstance, idea) and uses those encounters to encourage others that they need the product without explicitly stating so. Show your commercial to your classmates and ask them to identify the symbolic archetypes, encounters, and message. Solicit feedback and make edits as needed.

Opportunity for Talent Development

Have students research business psychology and learn more about how advertisers use archetypes to sell products: *Select one of the commercials presented, and analyze it based on the information you gathered in your research. Then, generate a list of questions you have about that marketing strategy and the commercial. E-mail five questions to the company's marketing department (with teacher and parent permission) and share your insights about the commercial as well. Create a presentation for the class that explains principles for effectively using archetypes in marketing. Present your findings to the class using specific examples to illustrate your ideas and lessons learned.*

Social-Emotional Connection

Have students think about a commercial from this lesson: *Advertisers rely on emotion (pathos appeals) to convey their ideas. Our response to messages in the media (whether we buy things or receive the message) can be guided by emotion or critical thought. Why is it important to reflect on the emotional appeals and logical appeals in media? How might individuals with a different point of view feel about the message? Why is it important to practice perspective-taking? Create a T-chart to show how different points of view may interpret the message, including their emotions.* (Note: You may choose to explore how the "Built to Serve" commercial was received by different audiences. A general search for reactions to the commercial will yield a variety of audience responses.)

ELA Task

Assign the following task as a performance-based assessment for this lesson: *How do commercials use different encounters to address real-world problems? Answer the question in an explanatory essay, using at least three texts from this unit. Cite relevant and sufficient evidence in your response.*

Concept Connections

1. Lead a class discussion: Think about the concepts that you saw in the commercials (e.g., courage, change, power, fear, doubt, kindness). How does your encounter with these concepts allow for reflection and change for you, the viewer?
2. Use Handout 1.2: Concept Organizer or continue to add to the concept map-working wall to record how encounter generalizations are applied to the media viewed in today's lesson. (Sample response: Encounters lead to positive and negative outcomes: Encounters with seeing people serving their community may lead to a positive outcome for action in one's own community.) In the last box, students should relate the idea of encounters to the concept of persuasion (i.e., our unexpected encounters with messages in media means that we need to be aware of how media intends to persuade our views).

Assessment

- Examine choice-based differentiated products and rubric criteria, ELA Task responses, and/or Concept Connections. Use Rubric 1: Product Rubric to review the products.
- Have students complete an exit ticket: *What is one of your favorite quotes or speeches? How does it relate to an idea of archetype (character, situation, or symbol)? Convey the meaning of this quote or speech through a symbol.*

Name: _____ Date: _____

Handout 9.1
Encounters With Archetypes in Advertising

Directions: Complete the chart. Note the major character, situation, and symbol archetypes, and the ideas or messages in each commercial.

Commercial	Advertisement 1	Advertisement 2	Advertisement 3	Advertisement 4
Encounters and the Archetypes Revealed				
Audience Appeal or Relevance				
Encounters With Product Result in Threats and Opportunities				

Name: _____ Date: _____

Handout 9.1, continued

Commercial	Advertisement 1	Advertisement 2	Advertisement 3	Advertisement 4
Encounters With Product Allow for Prediction				
Encounters With Product Can Be Internal, External, or Both				
Encounters With Product Allow for Reflection and Change				
Message				

Name: _____   Date: _____

Handout 9.2
Blank Rhetorical Analysis Wheel

Directions: Draw arrows across elements to show connections.

Text: _____

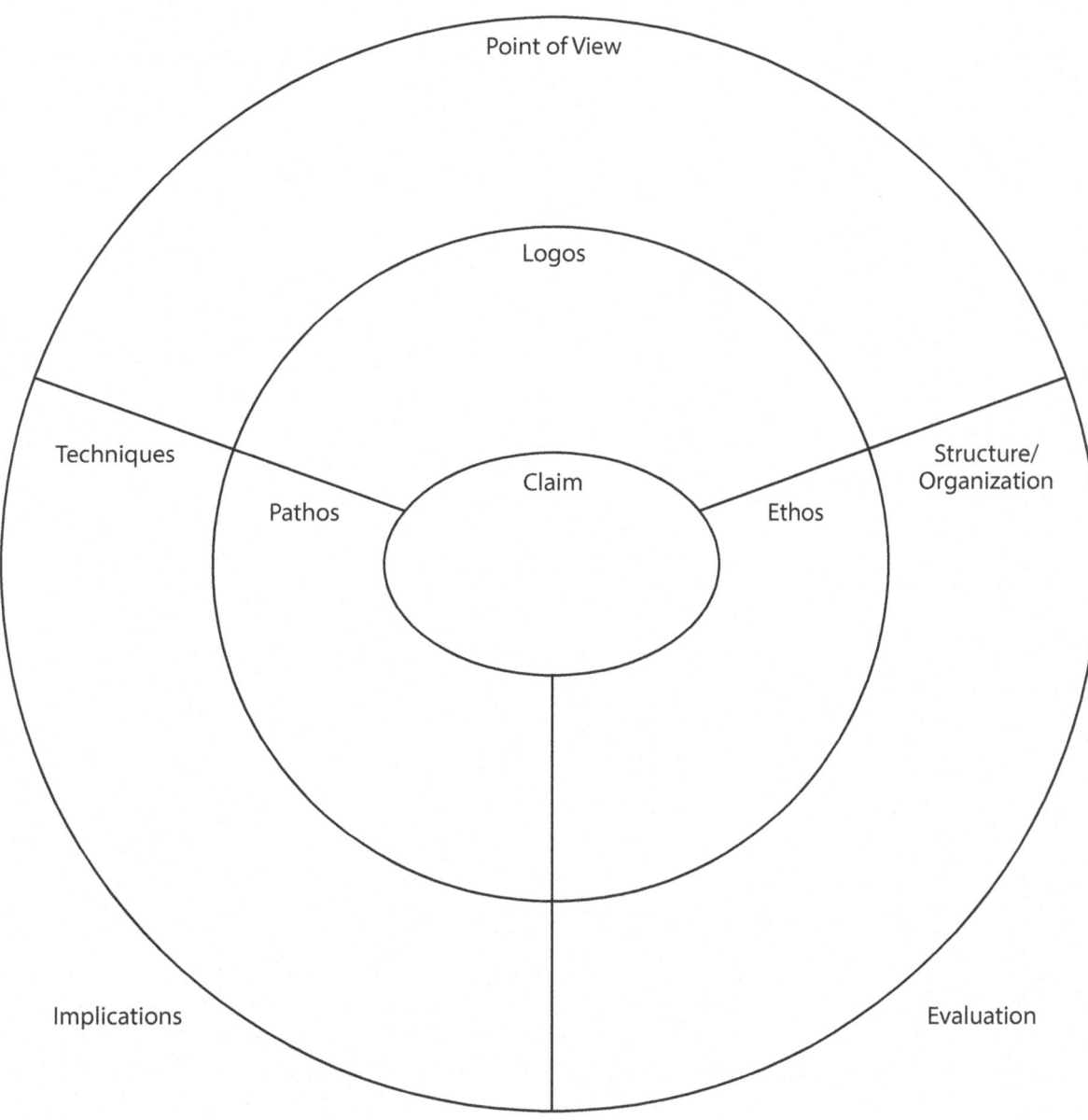

Created by Emily Mofield, Ed.D., & Tamra Stambaugh, Ph.D., 2015.

Lesson 10

Encounters With Art

Key Question

How do artists use their work to convey messages?

Objectives

Content: To analyze and interpret fiction, nonfiction, and art, students will be able to:
- compare and contrast how literary, visual, informational, and/or primary source texts reveal patterns and themes;
- analyze characters' conflicts, motives, values, thoughts, and actions;
- compare and contrast the use of specific techniques various authors use to approach and develop similar ideas; and
- identify and analyze archetypal patterns in stories, speeches, and real-world contexts and discuss how they are shaped by the author or real-world individuals or events.

Process: To develop interpretation, analysis, and communication skills in the language arts, students will be able to:
- justify inferences with evidence from the text;
- elaborate in discussion or in writing on how authors use language and literary elements to create meaning;
- apply evidence to support explanations and opinions relative to a question, text, or issue; and
- respond to an analysis of literature, nonfiction, media, or art by developing arguments and elaborating on explanations through writing a variety of texts (e.g., essays, paragraphs), including relevant and sufficient evidence to support claims.

Encounters With Archetypes

Concept: To develop conceptual thinking about encounters in language arts and additional content areas, students will be able to:
- explain with evidence how encounters may lead to positive or negative outcomes in literature, media, and real-world examples;
- explain how encounters allow for prediction (within literature and real-world examples);
- relate encounter generalizations to real-life situations; and
- examine the relationship between encounters and other concepts in multiple contexts.

Accelerated CCSS for ELA

- W.6.1
- W.7.10
- SL.6.1

Materials

- Various art supplies (crayons, markers, colored pencils, etc.) and paper (per student)
- *Invisible Homeless* by Luke Jerram (to display; available at https://www.lukejerram.com/invisible-homeless)
- *Landscape With the Fall of Icarus* attributed to Pieter Bruegel (to display; available online)
- Examples of art by Pieter Bruegel: *Landscape With the Flight Into Egypt*, 1563; *The Hunters in the Snow*, 1565; *The Peasant Wedding*, 1566–1569; *Winter Landscape With (Skaters and) a Bird Trap*, 1565; *The Harvesters*, 1565 (to display; available online)
- *Crashed Aeroplane* (1918) by John Singer Sargent (to display; available online)
- Handout 1.2: Concept Organizer
- Handout 10.1: Blank Visual Analysis Wheel
- Rubric 1.1: Product Rubric (Appendix C)

Note: Additional teacher resources may be required in order to guide students through the visual analysis in this lesson. An online search for analysis of the main painting, *Landscape With the Fall of Icarus*, or of artist Pieter Bruegel's background and techniques, may be helpful. Resources to consider may include http://www.artinsociety.com/bruegels-icarus-and-the-perils-of-flight.html and https://artsandculture.google.com/exhibit/MgIyXpmuNdcLJg.

Introductory Activities

1. Provide each student with a variety of art supplies and a blank sheet of white paper. Ask students to create a poster using only images and symbols that convey a message about a problem they want to see addressed within their school or community. For example, a student might draw a picture of a bully with a "no" symbol. Invite students to share their posters with the class and have others determine the message of their work.
2. Explain that artists often use their work to convey messages using characters, symbols, or situations. Often, artists hope that their audience's encounter with the specific piece of art will lead to reflection and change.
3. Display a photo of Luke Jerram's sculpture *Invisible Homeless*. Provide some background: Formed out of glass, this sculpture was designed to draw attention to the growing number of homeless individuals in the United Kingdom. The sculpture has been moved to a variety of locations since it was first created. Share with students what the artist had to say about the work:

   > For every person you see sleeping on the streets, there are many others sleeping in hostels, squats and other forms of unsatisfactory and insecure accommodation. I was interested to see whether the sculpture would be ignored and treated like street furniture as homeless people often are in a city. I hope the artwork will raise awareness of the problem and that the public will feel moved to support the charity, to make a difference. (Jerram, n.d., para. 4)

4. Ask students:
   - What do you notice about the sculpture and the techniques that the artist used? (Students may mention the blown glass technique and how fragile glass is to work with as a medium for art.)
   - What does the art symbolize? (Beyond the initial symbolism of homelessness, students may mention indifference and how people had started turning a blind eye to those in need.)
   - What do you think the artist hoped the audience would take away from its encounter with the sculpture? Why do you think he designed it in a way that allowed for it to be moved from one location to the next? (Sample response: Having the sculpture move to outdoor areas where homelessness is an issue draws greater attention, compared to having it sit in a gallery.)
   - How does this artwork relate to ideas from "The Emperor's New Clothes"? (Sample response: The sculpture's message reveals an obvious truth that no one is acknowledging because of fear.)

- What are some examples of art you have encountered that have a clearly intended message? What kinds of messages might an artist seek to convey through his or her art? (Answers will vary. Encourage students to use evidence from the art featured to justify their thinking.)

In-Class Activities to Deepen Learning

1. Explain to students that they will examine another piece of art as they consider ways that encounters with art and archetypes allow for reflection and change.
2. Provide a brief summary of the story of Daedalus and Icarus (*Note*: You may also choose to provide students with a copy of the story or show a brief video that reimagines the tale.): *Daedalus was a servant of King Minos. Having designed the labyrinth on the island of Crete, Daedalus was seen as a threat to the king, so he held Daedalus prisoner on his island. With escape by air as the only option, Daedalus made two pairs of wings, one for him and one for his son, Icarus, out of branches, wax, and bird feathers. Daedalus warned his son not to fly too close to the sun because the heat would melt the wax. As they flew away, Icarus became carried away with flying, flew too close to the sun, his wings melted, and he plunged into the sea.*
3. Display paintings attributed to Pieter Bruegel (see Materials list), and provide background and context for Bruegel and his style of painting: *Bruegel (1525–1569) was a 16th-century painter who contributed to the Dutch and Flemish Renaissance movement. Bruegel was the first of many in his family to take up painting. Early on in his career, Bruegel was known for his engravings; he produced more than 40 during the late 1550s and early 1560s. He later shifted into oil paintings that depicted everyday life and Flemish traditions amid sweeping landscapes set in particular seasons. His art is considered a precursor to art in the Dutch Golden Age of the 17th century* (Pieter-bruegel-the-elder.org, n.d.; Wisse, 2002).
4. Display *Landscape With the Fall of Icarus*. Explain that some scholars believe that this painting is attributed to Bruegel, although others believe that it is an early copy of a lost Bruegel original. This is one of his most notable works and a prime example of a 16th-century Renaissance landscape painting.
5. As a class, play a version of "I Spy" with the painting. Students should take turns pointing out a different feature or object in the painting that they notice. (Students may point to the plow, the ships in the harbor, the sheep, the sword, the setting sun, the legs of Icarus in the water.)
6. Afterward, ask:
   - What event is represented in this painting? (Sample response: Icarus has fallen into the sea.) What evidence supports this? (Sample response: Icarus's legs are poking out of the water, and the sun is setting.)

- Bruegel incorporated aspects of everyday life into his paintings. What figures or objects would be related to life in the Netherlands at that time? (Sample response: A man is plowing the field; a boy is herding sheep.)
- What do you notice about the people in relation to Icarus's body? (Sample response: The people are not paying attention to Icarus. *Note*: Scholars suggest that this is Bruegel's way of saying that people at the time had stopped looking out for each other.)
- What do you notice about the colors used in the painting? (*Note*: The artist only uses red twice, with the plowman and the fisherman. In this context, red does not symbolize anger or passion. Red serves as a bright color that draws the audience's eye—first to the plowman, then to the fisherman, where viewers should find the legs of Icarus. Students may also notice the fade from brown to green to blue—a technique that adds depth to a painting.)
- What symbolism exists in the painting? (Sample response: The setting sun symbolizes the end of a journey or an ending of life [Icarus's]; the sword is symbolic of war, while the plow symbolizes peace and prosperity; the furrowed soil and the presence of new sheep with a flock are symbolic of spring or new beginnings; the faces turned away symbolize indifference.)

Visual Analysis

Using Handout 10.1: Visual Analysis Wheel, guide students through analyzing the painting further. Students may take notes on the wheel and draw arrows to illustrate connections between elements. See Appendix A for detailed instructions.

Simple Questions:
1. **Images:** What are the main images that you notice in the painting? Why did the artist choose the subjects that he did? What do you notice about the individuals drawn in the painting? What do their actions suggest about society at the time? (Sample response: The sun is a central image; it plays a role in the downfall of Icarus and is connected to the crops being planted in the field. The plowman and the shepherd are looking away from the crashing body of Icarus, the fisherman is fixated on the position of his pole in the water, and even the horse that is used to plow the field is wearing blinders. [Their combined lack of awareness is discussed in the main idea section.] The painting also includes a number of images, such as the island prison, which reference the story of Daedalus and Icarus.)
2. **Organization:** What are your eyes drawn to first? How do the subjects and use of color impact the meaning of the work? (Sample response: The artist painted Icarus in the lower right-hand corner of the painting to intentionally

make him somewhat inconspicuous. The bright red of the plowman's shirt draws the audience's attention there first. The red used in the fisherman then draws the audience in to Icarus' body in the water.)

3. **Techniques:** What techniques does the artist use? (Sample response: The artist downplayed the size of the characters in comparison to the landscape surrounding them. His use of color, especially red, draws viewers to look first at the plowman, then at the fisherman, and then to Icarus's body. He also used three distinct color palletes that give way to one another, moving from brown, to green, and then to blue, which provides the illusion of depth.)
4. **Artist's Background:** What do we know about Pieter Bruegel?
5. **Emotions:** How do you feel when you see this painting? What emotions are most present? How did the artist achieve this? If you did not know the story of Icarus and Daedalus, would the emotions be different? (Responses will vary.)
6. **Purpose:** What do you think Bruegel's purpose was in making this art? (Sample response: Bruegel connected a well-known story to what he saw as a social issue—people not paying attention to the needs or suffering of others.)
7. **Main Idea:** What do you think the main idea of this artwork is? (*Note*: A number of interpretations have emerged, supported mostly by the images in the paining. Given the inaction of the characters in the foreground, a common theme emerges around man's willingness to turn away from others in need or inhumanity. This is seen not only in Icarus' drowning, but also in the unattended body in the bushes. Another interpretation points to the need for people to focus not on reaching for the heavens, as Icarus did, but on the earthly tasks at hand.)
8. **Point of View:** What is the artist's point of view? (*Note*: Modern interpretations assert that Bruegel assumed audiences would receive his intended message and cease to turn away from their fellow man in times of need.)
9. **Evaluation:** Do you like this art? Why or why not? Is this art impactful?
10. **Concept Connections:** How does this painting apply to a generalization about encounters? What other concepts are presented (e.g., change, patterns, conformity)? (Students may explain how encounters with society lead to changes in behavior as part of societal norms. Explain that encounters happen in art as well. Knowing that encounters lead to change, artists can use their work to send a message or encourage action within the audience. The audience might encounter a piece of artwork and notice archetypal patterns, characters, and symbols, which others recognize. Such artists can convey a message without words by capitalizing on the viewer's knowledge of archetypes.)

Complex Questions:
1. **Images + Techniques:** What techniques does the artist use to enhance images? (Sample response: The artist uses color to draw the audience to certain images in the painting. The red of the plowman's shirt, which was not a traditional style or color worn at the time, focuses the audience's attention on that portion of the painting before moving on to other parts. The scale of certain images, moving from larger in the foreground to smaller in the background, gives the painting depth.)
2. **Images + Structure/Organization:** How does the artist intentionally place the objects in the painting to reveal meaning? (Sample response: The men in the foreground, representative of peasant life at the time, are one of the first things that the audience is drawn to. The men's size and the dash of red in the shirt give way to smaller, more muted images in the painting. This organization of large to small images, coupled with the fade from brown, to green, and to blue, structures the painting in a way that adds depth.)
3. **Emotions + Structure/Organization:** How did the artist organize the painting to portray or evoke emotion? Are parts of the artwork more powerful than others? What techniques were used to evoke or portray emotion? (Sample response: The painting is organized in a way that draws viewers from the foreground, where the plowman and shepherd are, to the quadrant where the fisherman and the legs of Icarus are located. As the audience moves throughout the painting, their emotions may change. The realization that there are three characters who are indifferent to the suffering of Icarus may bring about a negative emotion.)
4. **Artist Background + Purpose/Context:** How was Bruegel influenced by the historical context of his time? How does he influence the historical context of his time? (Sample response: Bruegel used his own encounters with the world, in which he saw humanity turning away from one another, indifferent to the sufferings of fellow men, to influence his purpose. Using the context of a well-known myth, he merged the myth with elements from his own world.)

Display the painting *Crashed Aeroplane* (1918) by John Singer Sargent. Explain that *Landscape With the Fall of Icarus* and *Crashed Aeroplane* were painted more than 300 years apart. Ask students:
1. How do these images portray similar messages through the use of archetypes? (*Note*: In both paintings, the main subjects are choosing not to engage or offer support to those in need. There was someone in need of saving and antiheroes or everyday persons who ignored them, symbolizing society's condition of indifference.)
2. What similarities do you notice with regard to the encounters with character archetypes in the two works of art? (Sample response: In both pieces, the art-

ists may want to bring about reflection and change by showing an unhealable wound, initiation, or the impact of an antihero as an everyday person who ignores others in society in need of saving.)
3. What situational archetype(s) do the artists want you to experience? (Sample response: They may want us to experience initiation, show an example of a rise and fall of society, or encourage others to embark on a hero's journey and take action as companions, caregivers, or heroes in society.)
4. What connections can you make with other ideas in this unit regarding how truth is encountered through art and stories? (Students may make connections between the art and "The Emperor's New Clothes" in which the boy pointed out—just as the glass sculpture does—the obvious truth that is evaded by society; students may make connections to the idea of unhealable wound as it relates to the need for citizens to be the companion to those in need.)

Choice-Based Differentiated Products

Students may choose one of the following to complete (*Note*: Use Rubric 1: Product Rubric in Appendix C to assess student responses):

- Select one of the subjects depicted in *Landscape With the Fall of Icarus*, and create a short story or poem that imagines his encounter with Icarus if the subject heard the splash and saved Icarus. Use detail to paint a narrative, using words instead of colors. Consider the following as you plan your story: What is the subject's background? How did he find himself on the hillside on that sunny spring afternoon? If he had encountered Icarus how would his story have changed? Is he an everyday person archetype or a hero? Is saving Icarus the beginning of his journey or the end? How does this impact the story?
- Icarus and Daedalus took a risk with fashioning wings to fly away from the island. Artists take risks when sharing art with the public (criticism). In some ways, all character archetypes encounter risk with the situations they face. Create a flowchart or poster that outlines how different character archetypes approach risk-taking. Use examples from stories, songs, and other resources introduced in the unit, as well as your own examples.
- Create a short dialogue between Jerram and Bruegel. What would they say about their encounters with society and how those encounters allow for reflection and change? Use specific examples of their art interpretations and the encounter generalizations in the conversation.

Opportunities for Talent Development

- Have students learn more about the life and work of Pieter Bruegel or Luke Jerram through online research. In a couple of paragraphs, explain how artists or patrons who encountered Bruegel or Jerram's other pieces of art were influenced and why. *What encounter generalizations were most evident?*
- Ask students to create their own artwork that uses one of the resources used throughout the unit or a well-known myth or fable as inspiration: *In the same way that Bruegel included the legs of Icarus, select one object or symbol from the story or poem to be included in your art. What message do you want your audience to take away from your art? How will the positioning of the characters and objects, colors, techniques, and other artistic elements support your message? What symbolic archetypes will you use to make your message recognizable?*
- Use a Blank Visual Analysis Wheel (Handout 10.1) to analyze another work by one of your favorite artists. *How does your artwork reveal archetypal patterns?*

Social-Emotional Connection

Lead a class discussion: *In the case of some artists, a great deal of rejection occurs before he or she finds success. Vincent Van Gogh received little to no acknowledgement during his lifetime. Consider a time when something you have worked hard on has been met with criticism or rejection. How did it make you feel? How should people respond to encounters with rejection regarding work that they are passionate about? What steps can be taken after criticism of an individual's artwork or creation to help him or her continue refining and producing work?*

ELA Task

Assign the following task as a performance-based assessment for this lesson: *In what ways can archetypes be present in art? How does the audience's encounter with art help convey the message of the artist?*

Concept Connection

1. Have students reflect in writing or discussion: *How does the story of Icarus and Daedalus and/or the painting* Landscape With the Fall of Icarus *relate to one of the encounters generalizations discussed earlier in this unit?* Students may record relevant responses on Handout 1.2: Concept Organizer or record the key points of their discussion on a sticky note and add it to the concept

map-working wall. It is not necessary for students to make connections to every generalization.
2. Lead a class discussion: *How are encounter generalizations evident when an audience interacts with a piece of art?*

Assessment

- Examine choice-based differentiated products and rubric criteria, ELA Task responses, and/or Concept Connections. Use Rubric 1: Product Rubric to review the products.
- Have students complete an exit ticket: *How can artists' encounters with the world around them influence the message of their artwork?* Use the Visual Analysis Wheel and encounters generalizations to explain your thinking.

Name: _____ Date: _____

Handout 10.1
Blank Visual Analysis Wheel

Directions: Draw arrows across elements to show connections.

Text: _____

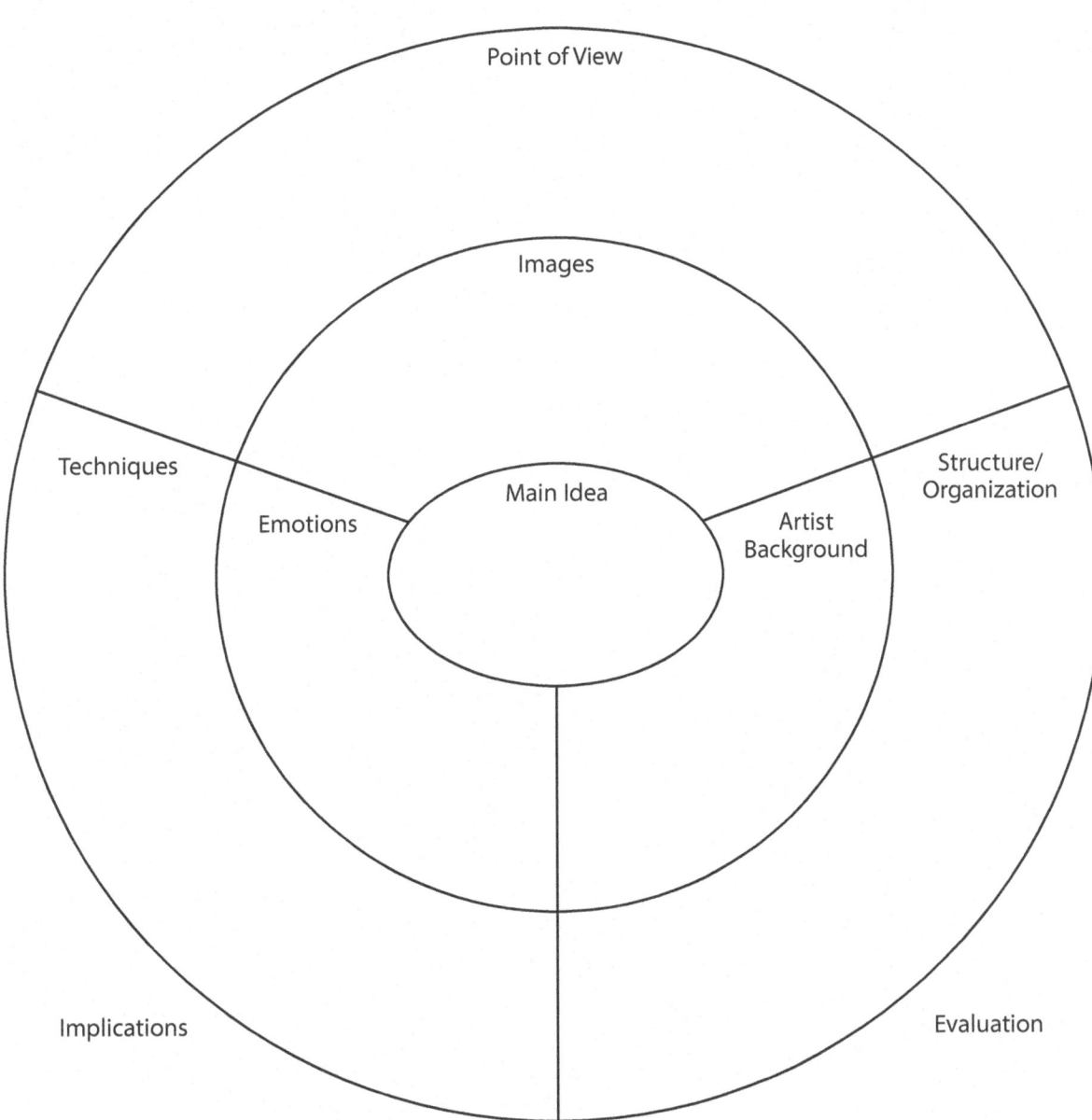

Created by Tamra Stambaugh, Ph.D., & Emily Mofield, Ed.D., 2015.

Lesson 11

Writing Narratives With Archetypes

Key Question

How do authors use encounters with archetypes to convey meaning?

Objectives

Content: To analyze and interpret fiction, nonfiction, and art, students will be able to:
- analyze characters' conflicts, motives, values, thoughts, and actions; and
- identify and analyze archetypal patterns in stories, speeches, and real-world contexts and discuss how they are shaped by the author or real-world individuals or events.

Process: To develop interpretation, analysis, and communication skills in the language arts, students will be able to:
- justify inferences with evidence from the text;
- apply evidence to support explanations and opinions relative to a question, text, or issue; and
- develop character archetypes through encounters with other characters, situations, and symbols.

Concept: To develop conceptual thinking about encounters in language arts and additional content areas, students will be able to:
- explain with evidence how encounters may lead to positive or negative outcomes in literature, media, and real-world examples;
- explain how encounters allow for prediction within literature and real-world examples;
- relate encounter generalizations to real-life situations; and
- examine the relationship between encounters and other concepts in multiple contexts.

Encounters With Archetypes

Accelerated CCSS for ELA

- W.7.3
- W.7.4
- SL.6.1

Materials

- Video: "Pixar in a Box: Introduction to Storytelling" (available at https://www.youtube.com/watch?v=1rMnzNZkIX0)
- Video: Pixar's *Lifted* (available online)
- Blank piece of paper and pencil (one per student)
- Paper lunch sack or jar (for skit bags; one per small group)
- Handout 11.1: Skit Bag (cut out in advance and placed in skit bags; two character archetype cards, one form card, one internal and external encounter card, one situational card, and one symbol card per small group)
- Handout 11.2: Character Development Guide
- Handout 11.3: Narrative Writing Checklist
- Rubric 1: Product Rubric (Appendix C)

Introductory Activities

1. Ask students: *What is your favorite story? What makes it your favorite? How do you come up with ideas for a great story?* Make a list of student responses.
2. Show "Pixar in a Box: Introduction to Storytelling" (see Materials list). Explain that this is a short video from writers who design Pixar films. As the video is shown, ask students to make a list of criteria that might be appropriate for creating a good story, such as writing about one's own experiences and feelings, making a character relevant to the audience so that the story evokes feelings, and having an interesting story line.
3. Ask: *How does a story and its purpose reveal patterns in the human condition?* (Sample response: Stories relate to the human experience in some way and help the audience connect.) *How does this compare to Jung's idea of an archetype?* (Students may say that archetypes are patterns that share the human condition; therefore, story patterns and recognizable characters reveal lessons or situations in society that are common to most people.)

In-Class Activities to Deepen Learning

1. Divide students into groups of 3–4, and provide each group with a skit bag (see Handout 11.1). Give groups 5 minutes to create and plan a skit using all of the character archetypes, encounters, situations and symbols provided in their bags. (Sample response: If the cards are self-doubt [internal], trickster ogre [character], rise [situation], and green [symbol], the skit might be about an ogre who doubts he has the courage to keep scaring people, does a lot of self-talk, and rises to fulfill his job of tricking young children in the

lush green forest. After many failed attempts or encounters, he succeeds.) Remind groups that they need to make sure archetypal patterns are followed but are not too obvious.
2. Have groups perform their skits. Allow others to guess the archetypes.
3. With their groups, have students create a different story scenario by applying a new character archetype to the same situations. How does their story change or remain the same? (Students may note that different character archetypes will respond differently to the same situation. This may or may not change the theme or outcome. A rise and fall will always be a rise and fall, but may take a different shape depending upon who the character is and his or her motivation or purpose. A sidekick whose purpose is to become the hero will reveal a different plot than a sidekick who is loyal beyond fault. Archetypes help us predict, but still allow for individuality and creativity in, stories. Similarly, setting may or may not impact the story. Sometimes location drives the entire story; whereas other times the same story could occur in any setting.)
4. Show the Pixar short film *Lifted* and discuss the following questions:
    - What "skit bag" archetypes and encounters are present in this short film? (Sample response: There is an alien trying to pass his saucer flying exam, failure, companion, etc.)
    - What archetypes or person in need of saving are present? (Sample response: The smaller alien could be a companion; the older alien could be a mentor; operating the switchboard could be seen as initiation.)
    - What encounters do you notice, and how do they influence your understanding of the characters? (Sample response: The small alien encounters failure and is then given another opportunity to try working the controls. The larger alien encounters frustration with the alien in training, which leads the audience to see him in a negative light.)
    - How does an encounter lead to change and reflection? (Sample response: The older alien encounters the crying of the younger alien. This leads the older alien to reconsider and give him another chance.)
    - How does perspective shape how the second attempt at navigating the controls is viewed by the characters? (Sample response: The younger alien sees the second attempt as an opportunity, and the older alien sees it as a threat.)
5. Walk students through the story elements that are present in the short film. Clearly outline the characters (younger/older aliens), setting (flying saucer), plot (exam for flying the saucer and using the tractor beam), conflict (failure on the part of the younger alien), and resolution (second chances). Discuss any symbols used, as well as clearly defined beginning, middle, and end features. If needed, complete a plot outline with students.

Encounters With Archetypes

Writing a Narrative

1. Explain that students are going to write their own short narratives to develop an archetypal main character, situation, and symbols.
2. Distribute Handout 11.2: Character Development Guide for students to complete. As students think about the development of their stories and main characters, ask them to consider: *How do the character's archetypal qualities help resolve the conflict?* Remind students to focus their planning around the development of a character archetype, rather than a stereotype, and that each character archetype will resolve conflicts differently (leaders seek order, explorers take risks, companions will make sacrifices, etc.). Also help them consider how they will make their character relatable. Students may choose to add a few characteristics from other archetypes for authenticity while making a primary archetypal pattern. This makes the character more believable.
3. Explain to students that stories are a way for authors to use their voices to portray a theme—a message that the author gives about an idea or topic (e.g., hope, friendship, loyalty, facing obstacles, persevering, fitting in, abuse of power, lies, truth, perception, etc.). Ask: *What message do you think should be portrayed about these ideas?* (Sample responses: Power should be shared, friendship involves sacrifice, etc.). These messages are themes. Writers think about how plot events, character interactions, and other elements shape their message.
4. Students should consider additional use of structure, techniques, voice, use of perspective, etc., and how these elements interact and cause the character change. Remind students that characters generally experience change in a story, so they must consider how that change is portrayed. What encounters lead to changes? How do those encounters lead to reflection? Are the encounters internal, external, or both? Is the change a small or a big one? Does one character stay the same while others change?
5. As students write, ask them to pay attention to developing the voice of their character through dialogue. How does the character talk? How does the character express him- or herself? Does the character have a catch phrase or a style that shows who he or she is? Emphasize the use of sensory details and the use of shifts (e.g., when the character's desires are thwarted and the plot changes due to a new or different encounter with setting, experience, emotions, or another character). Shifts move the plot along, keep the story interesting, and help readers understand what motivates the character or how he or she responds.
6. Allow time for students to write, revise, peer review, and edit their drafts. During peer review, direct students to use Handout 11.3: Narrative Writing Checklist.

7. Students may share their finished products (with the class or in small groups). Celebrate the process and writing accomplishment.

Choice-Based Differentiated Products

Students may choose one of the following to complete (*Note*: Use Rubric 1: Product Rubric in Appendix C to assess student responses):

- Create a book cover for your story. Include important details that relate to your character archetype and encounters. Incorporate archetype colors or other symbols that relate to your story as part of the cover.
- Develop a piece of art or draw a portrait of your character archetype and show (with words and/or symbols) the thoughts, motives, and values within his or her head. Use color and object symbols as part of your drawing to help explain the situation or characters.
- Create a comic book representation of your writing. Be sure to show how the character's internal thoughts and encounters with other archetype characters, situations, and symbols shape the reader's understanding of the character.
- Select a book or short film to analyze from a writer's perspective. Consider how the story was structured, the archetypes used, and how encounters with one's emotions or ideas, others, or the environment shaped the theme. As you read, create a list of questions in the margins of the story about the author's technique. Then write a book/film review analyzing the techniques and use of encounters and archetypes.

Opportunities for Talent Development

- After revising their drafts, have students submit their final narratives to a writing competition or publication (e.g., *Stone Soup*).
- Ask students to create a presentation: *Do you have a favorite author or know of a local author that you could interview? Is there an "Ask the Author" page on your favorite author's website? Ask an author about his or her creative process. How does he or she develop characters? To what extent does he or she rely on archetypes when developing a story? What is his or her favorite character, situation, or symbol archetype to incorporate into a story? Share a presentation with your class.*

Social-Emotional Connection

Introduce the following activity to students: *Sometimes our strengths are also our weaknesses. Well-developed characters (that may resemble archetypes but have*

Encounters With Archetypes

a well-developed personality) can experience many different types of emotions or show strengths and weaknesses at the same time, given their complexities and the changes they undergo. How are your character's strengths and weaknesses one and the same? How did your character experience a duality of emotions (e.g., joy and sadness at the same time) when exhibiting his or her strengths and weaknesses? When have you experienced opposite emotions at the same time? What role do these emotions and traits play in shaping our own actions and relationships with others? Create a symbol, illustration, or meme that shows how one's strengths, weaknesses, and emotions are a paradox.

ELA Task

Assign the following task as a performance-based assessment for this lesson: *How does an author's understanding of encounters with archetypes support the writing process and the development of characters and situations within a story?*

Concept Connections

Lead a class discussion: *How did your personal experience of writing a narrative relate to an encounter generalization? Think of the encounter as "me + writing assignment." How was this an opportunity and a threat? How does the idea of creativity relate to encounters? What archetype did you, as a writer, experience during this assignment (e.g., perhaps you were an explorer, confronting the unknown territory of developing an archetype, etc.)?*

Assessment

- Examine choice-based differentiated products and rubric criteria, ELA Task responses, and/or Concept Connections. Use Rubric 1: Product Rubric to review the products.
- Have students create a model or flowchart that outlines ways in which writers develop characters and stories using encounters. Students should provide examples from their own writing process.
- Have students complete an exit ticket: *What did you find most rewarding about developing and writing your own story using encounters and archetypes as a starting point? What was difficult about the process? As you think ahead to the next story that you will write, what will you continue doing as part of the writing process? What will you change?*

Handout 11.1
Skit Bag

Character(s)

Leader	Trickster	Sidekick
Rebel	Sage	Caregiver
Jokester	Companion	Everyday Person

Form My Character Archetype Takes

Monkey	Grandparent	Girl
Wicked Stepmother	Boy	Owl
Mouse	Police Officer	Angel

Internal or External Conflict, or Encounter

Self-Doubt	Fear	Doesn't Want to Be on the Basketball Team
Meets His or Her Worst Enemy Who Moved Next Door	Broke His or Her Leg	Travels in Time to Outer Space
Can't Get Rid of the Hiccups	Doesn't Want to Move	Refuses to do Homework

Situation Archetype

Rebirth	Unhealable Wound	Initiation
Meets His or Her Worst Enemy	Rise	Quest
Task	Good Versus Evil	

Name: _____ Date: _____

Handout 11.2
Character Development Guide

Directions: Think through and answer the following questions about the main character of your story. Remember, the goal is to create a relatable and realistic character. Use a separate sheet of paper if necessary.

1. Choose a character archetype to build (or combination of archetypes, such as sage-companion). What is your character's name? How does this name enhance your idea for the character?

2. What are some particular mannerisms or quirks your character has?

3. What is the main challenge your character faces? What emotions does your character feel when confronting the challenge?

4. What are your character's thoughts when he or she goes to bed at night?

5. What does the character want more than anything? What emotions are associated with this desire?

Name: _____ Date: _____

Handout 11.2, *continued*

6. What keeps the character from getting what he or she desires?

7. What do other people think about this character (characteristics that are unknown to this character)? Who or what is most important to the character? Describe your character's best friend. What draws the two together?

8. What would be in this character's backpack or purse? What does this say about his or her personality?

9. What does your character fear?

10. What distracts your character? Why does your character get distracted?

11. What other character archetypes will your character encounter? How will they cause your character to change? Who are your character's enemies or friends?

Name: _____ Date: _____

Handout 11.2, *continued*

12. What situational archetypes will your character encounter? How will these situations cause your character to change? What does the character learn from these situations?

13. What symbol archetypes, images, or colors can you use to enhance your story?

14. Look over the encounters generalizations. What situations will you create so that connections can be made to at least two of these?

15. How will you showcase the character's strengths and weaknesses through his or her encounters?

Name: _____ Date: _____

Handout 11.3
Narrative Writing Checklist

	Evidence in Story	Suggestions
Character archetype is multidimensional with strengths and weaknesses and changes throughout the story.		
Use of shift: Characters change with new situations or encounters.		
Use of symbols: Symbols, images, or color help enhance the message.		
Use of a situation archetype propels the story and character development.		
There is a clear beginning, middle, and end.		

Name: _____ Date: _____

Handout 11.3, *continued*

	Evidence in Story	**Suggestions**
Reader understands the setting. Setting is important to the story.		
Use of sensory details is evident (sight, smell, hearing, touch, taste) and enhances the story.		
Use of figurative language (e.g., simile, metaphor, etc.) is present.		
Use of appropriate transition words to propel the story (*first, then, ultimately, immediately*, etc.) is present.		
Character's voice is crafted with specific language, diction, and dialogue.		
There is an implied theme (a message about an idea applied to real life).		

Lesson 12

Encounters With Archetypes

Key Question

How do encounters with archetypes in real life and fiction allow for a deeper understanding of ourselves and our world?

Objectives

Choose specific unit objectives as they relate to each product option (see pp. 14–15).

Materials

- Handout 1.2: Concept Organizer (completed from previous lessons or see Appendix B)
- Handout 12.1: Culminating Project
- Rubric 1: Product Rubric (Appendix C)

Discussion

Remind students about the concept generalizations explored in this unit. They may revisit Handout 1.2: Concept Organizer or the class concept map:
- Encounters allow for reflection and change.
- Encounters allow for prediction.
- Encounters can result in positive and negative outcomes.
- Encounters may result in threats and opportunities.

Ask: *How do the lessons in this unit connect?*

Student Reflection

Ask students to reflect on their learning throughout the unit.
1. What have you learned about yourself as a learner? What questions do you have?
2. Consider how you noticed the encounters generalizations across multiple resources (short stories, novels, videos, media, etc.) or even in your own life. Provide an example for each generalization. Create a chart, similar to Handout 1.2, but use your own real-life examples, as well as examples from other subject areas.
3. What is the relationship between encounters with archetypes in literature and encounters in real life? How are these the same and different? Create a symbol that illustrates the similarities between the two. Explain in two paragraphs why your symbol is appropriate, using information you have learned from this unit.

Choice-Based Differentiated Products

- Assign the culminating project (Handout 12.1). Students may choose based on their interests. At teacher discretion, students can present parts of the project to the class.
- Use Rubric 2: Culminating Project Rubric (Appendix C) to assess student products.

ELA Practice Task

Assign the following task as a culminating performance-based assessment. *How does your understanding of encounters allow for reflection and change? After reading the texts, analyzing art, and learning about encounters and ways in which they inform our understanding of archetypes, write an essay to answer the question. Refer to at least three lesson ideas to develop your response and cite specific evidence from the works.*

Name: _____ Date: _____

Handout 12.1
Culminating Project

Directions: Choose one product choice to demonstrate your understanding of what you have learned throughout this unit.

1. Select at least five of the character archetypes that you learned about in this unit. Create a playlist with songs that describe an encounter and archetypes. For example, in the song "Go the Distance" from the movie *Hercules*, the main character encounters an internal struggle with who he is and who he wants to be. Write a one-paragraph explanation of how lyricists and musicians rely on our understanding of archetypes to create relatable or appealing songs.
2. Revisit the Paradox of Theseus's Ship. Do you think the paradox of the ship is a metaphor for one's journey in life? Why or why not? Create a video blog that explains the paradox and your thinking in response to this question. Use examples from the stories and biographies you have read in this unit as well as your own life.
3. Write a play or script that has at least three characters talking about their encounters in life and how the encounters affected them. Using their own words, have the characters make connections with encounters. For example, one character might discuss how what he or she first saw as a threat ended up being more of an opportunity. As you establish your characters, consider incorporating some sort of symbolic archetype for their lives or for a specific encounter.
4. Think of a real-world problem that needs to be addressed. Develop a way to bring awareness to this issue through use of character, situational, and symbolic archetypes in a way that connects with the audience. Through the use of archetypes, show how participation will lead to a positive encounter that leads to change for others.
5. Create a digital collage of quotes and pictures that represent the archetypes that are present in your everyday life. With each quote or picture, make a connection to one of the archetype examples that you encountered in the unit. For example, you may add a picture of someone you see as a caregiver and make a connection with one of the adults (Mr. Tushman in *Wonder* or Pattie in *Counting by 7s*). With each example and connection, explain how your understanding of the world around you is informed by your understanding of encounters and archetypes.
6. Read another short story, such as "The Circuit" by Francisco Jiménez or "Thank You Ma'am" by Langston Hughes, and complete a Blank Literary Analysis Wheel. Identify ways in which literary elements interact with one another to develop meaning within the text. Write an essay that outlines the character, situational, and symbolic archetypes that are evident in the story. How did your understanding of encounters with archetypes provide opportunities for deeper understanding?
7. In many of the texts you read throughout this unit, encounters resulted in opportunities that led to more opportunities. Develop a list of how this was seen in the

Name: _____ Date: _____

Handout 12.1, *continued*

stories, texts, media, or biographies studied. Conduct an interview with a role model and ask him or her how encounters in his or her life resulted in opportunities that led to more opportunities. What threats were evident, and how did the individuals overcome those threats?

8. Throughout the unit, many concepts related to encounters were incorporated into lessons: growing up, self-sacrifice, risk, loyalty, truth, obstacles, conflict, power, courage, fear, opportunity, identity, self-awareness. Make a word map with "encounters" in the middle. Choose eight concepts and make a word map with arrows and words to show how they relate to encounters and to each other. Write several general statements about the interactions between the two concepts chosen.

Name: _____ Date: _____

Posttest
"Jack and the Beanstalk" *by Joseph Jacobs*

Directions: Read the passage and respond to the following questions, citing evidence from the text. Complete the questions within 35 minutes, using a separate sheet of paper if necessary.

There was once upon a time a poor widow who had an only son named Jack, and a cow named Milky-White. And all they had to live on was the milk the cow gave every morning, which they carried to the market and sold. But one morning Milky-White gave no milk, and they didn't know what to do. "What shall we do, what shall we do?" said the widow, wringing her hands. "Cheer up, Mother, I'll go and get work somewhere," said Jack. "We've tried that before, and nobody would take you," said his mother. "We must sell Milky-White and with the money start a shop, or something." "All right, Mother," says Jack. "It's market day today, and I'll soon sell Milky-White, and then we'll see what we can do."

So he took the cow's halter in his hand, and off he started. He hadn't gone far when he met a funny-looking old man, who said to him, "Good morning, Jack." "Good morning to you," said Jack, and wondered how he knew his name. "Well, Jack, and where are you off to?" said the man. "I'm going to market to sell our cow here." "Oh, you look the proper sort of chap to sell cows," said the man. "I wonder if you know how many beans make five." "Two in each hand and one in your mouth," says Jack, as sharp as a needle. "Right you are," says the man, "and here they are, the very beans themselves," he went on, pulling out of his pocket a number of strange-looking beans. "As you are so sharp," says he, "I don't mind doing a swap with you—your cow for these beans."

"Go along," says Jack. "Wouldn't you like it?" "Ah! You don't know what these beans are," said the man. "If you plant them overnight, by morning they grow right up to the sky." "Really?" said Jack. "You don't say so." "Yes, that is so. And if it doesn't turn out to be true you can have your cow back." "Right," says Jack, and hands him over Milky-White's halter and pockets the beans.

Back goes Jack home, and as he hadn't gone very far, it wasn't dusk by the time he got to his door. "Back already, Jack?" said his mother. "I see you haven't got Milky-White, so you've sold her. How much did you get for her?" "You'll never guess, Mother," says Jack. "No, you don't say so. Good boy! Five pounds? Ten? Fifteen? No, it can't be twenty." "I told you, you couldn't guess. What do you say to these beans? They're magical. Plant them overnight and—"

"What!" says Jack's mother. "Have you been such a fool, such a dolt, such an idiot, as to give away my Milky-White, the best milker in the parish, and prime beef to boot, for a set of paltry beans? Take that! Take that! Take that! And as for your precious beans here they go out of the window. And now off with you to bed. Not a sup shall you drink, and not a bit shall you swallow this very night." So Jack went upstairs to his little room in the attic, and

Posttest, continued

sad and sorry he was, to be sure, as much for his mother's sake as for the loss of his supper. At last he dropped off to sleep.

When he woke up, the room looked so funny. The sun was shining into part of it, and yet all the rest was quite dark and shady. So Jack jumped up and dressed himself and went to the window. And what do you think he saw? Why, the beans his mother had thrown out of the window into the garden had sprung up into a big beanstalk, which went up and up and up till it reached the sky. So the man spoke truth after all. The beanstalk grew up quite close past Jack's window, so all he had to do was to open it and give a jump onto the beanstalk, which ran up just like a big ladder. So Jack climbed, and he climbed, and he climbed, and he climbed, and he climbed, and he climbed, and he climbed till at last he reached the sky. And when he got there he found a long broad road going as straight as a dart. So he walked along, and he walked along, and he walked along till he came to a great big tall house, and on the doorstep there was a great big tall woman.

"Good morning, Mum," says Jack, quite polite-like. "Could you be so kind as to give me some breakfast?" For he hadn't had anything to eat, you know, the night before, and was as hungry as a hunter.

"It's breakfast you want, is it?" says the great big tall woman. "It's breakfast you'll be if you don't move off from here. My man is an ogre, and there's nothing he likes better than boys broiled on toast. You'd better be moving on or he'll be coming." "Oh! please, Mum, do give me something to eat, Mum. I've had nothing to eat since yesterday morning, really and truly, Mum," says Jack.

Well, the ogre's wife was not half so bad after all. So she took Jack into the kitchen, and gave him a hunk of bread and cheese and a jug of milk. But Jack hadn't half-finished these when thump! thump! thump! the whole house began to tremble with the noise of someone coming. "Goodness gracious me! It's my old man," said the ogre's wife. "What on earth shall I do? Come along quick and jump in here." And she bundled Jack into the oven just as the ogre came in.

He was a big one, to be sure. At his belt he had three calves strung up by the heels, and he unhooked them and threw them down on the table and said, "Here, wife, broil me a couple of these for breakfast. Ah! what's this I smell? Fee-fi-fo-fum, I smell the blood of an Englishman, be he alive, or be he dead, I'll have his bones to grind my bread."

"Nonsense, dear," said his wife. "You're dreaming. Or perhaps you smell the scraps of that little boy you liked so much for yesterday's dinner. Here, you go and have a wash and tidy up, and by the time you come back your breakfast I'll be ready for you." So off the ogre went, and Jack was just going to jump out of the oven and run away when the woman told him not. "Wait till he's asleep," says she; "he always has a doze after breakfast."

Well, the ogre had his breakfast, and after that he goes to a big chest and takes out a couple of bags of gold, and down he sits and counts till at last his head began to nod, and he began to snore till the whole house shook again. Then Jack crept out on tiptoe from his oven, and as he was passing the ogre, he took one of the bags of gold under his arm, and off he pelters till he came to the beanstalk, and then he threw down the bag of gold, which, of course, fell into his mother's garden, and then he climbed down and climbed down till at last

Name: _____ Date: _____

Posttest, *continued*

he got home and told his mother and showed her the gold and said, "Well, mother, wasn't I right about the beans? They are really magical, you see."

So they lived on the bag of gold for some time, but at last they came to the end of it, and Jack made up his mind to try his luck once more at the top of the beanstalk. So one fine morning he rose up early, and got onto the beanstalk, and he climbed, and he climbed, and he climbed, and he climbed, and he climbed, and he climbed till at last he came out onto the road again and up to the great tall house he had been to before. There, sure enough, was the great tall woman a-standing on the doorstep.

"Good morning, mum," says Jack, as bold as brass, "could you be so good as to give me something to eat?" "Go away, my boy," said the big tall woman, "or else my man will eat you up for breakfast. But aren't you the youngster who came here once before? Do you know, that very day my man missed one of his bags of gold." "That's strange, mum," said Jack, "I dare say I could tell you something about that, but I'm so hungry I can't speak till I've had something to eat."

Well, the big tall woman was so curious that she took him in and gave him something to eat. But he had scarcely begun munching it as slowly as he could when thump! thump! they heard the giant's footstep, and his wife hid Jack away in the oven. All happened as it did before. In came the ogre as he did before, said, "Fee-fi-fo-fum," and had his breakfast of three broiled oxen.

Then he said, "Wife, bring me the hen that lays the golden eggs." So she brought it, and the ogre said, "Lay," and it laid an egg all of gold. And then the ogre began to nod his head, and to snore till the house shook. Then Jack crept out of the oven on tiptoe and caught hold of the golden hen, and was off before you could say "Jack Robinson." But this time the hen gave a cackle which woke the ogre, and just as Jack got out of the house he heard him calling, "Wife, wife, what have you done with my golden hen?"

And the wife said, "Why, my dear?" But that was all Jack heard, for he rushed off to the beanstalk and climbed down like a house on fire. And when he got home he showed his mother the wonderful hen, and said "Lay" to it; and it laid a golden egg every time he said "Lay."

Well, Jack was not content, and it wasn't long before he determined to have another try at his luck up there at the top of the beanstalk. So one fine morning he rose up early and got to the beanstalk, and he climbed, and he climbed, and he climbed, and he climbed till he got to the top. But this time he knew better than to go straight to the ogre's house. And when he got near it, he waited behind a bush till he saw the ogre's wife come out with a pail to get some water, and then he crept into the house and got into the copper. He hadn't been there long when he heard thump! thump! thump! as before, and in came the ogre and his wife. "Fee-fi-fo-fum, I smell the blood of an Englishman," cried out the ogre. "I smell him, wife, I smell him."

"Do you, my dearie?" says the ogre's wife. "Then, if it's that little rogue that stole your gold and the hen that laid the golden eggs he's sure to have got into the oven." And they both rushed to the oven. But Jack wasn't there, luckily, and the ogre's wife said, "There you are again with your fee-fi-fo-fum. Why, of course, it's the boy you caught last night that I've just

Name: _____   Date: _____

Posttest, continued

broiled for your breakfast. How forgetful I am, and how careless you are not to know the difference between live and dead after all these years."

So the ogre sat down to the breakfast and ate it, but every now and then he would mutter, "Well, I could have sworn — " and he'd get up and search the larder and the cupboards and everything, only, luckily, he didn't think of the copper. After breakfast was over, the ogre called out, "Wife, wife, bring me my golden harp." So she brought it and put it on the table before him. Then he said, "Sing!" and the golden harp sang most beautifully. And it went on singing till the ogre fell asleep, and commenced to snore like thunder.

Then Jack lifted up the copper lid very quietly and got down like a mouse and crept on hands and knees till he came to the table, when up he crawled, caught hold of the golden harp and dashed with it towards the door.

But the harp called out quite loud, "Master! Master!" and the ogre woke up just in time to see Jack running off with his harp. Jack ran as fast as he could, and the ogre came rushing after, and would soon have caught him, only Jack had a start and dodged him a bit and knew where he was going. When he got to the beanstalk the ogre was not more than 20 yards away when suddenly he saw Jack disappear like, and when he came to the end of the road he saw Jack underneath climbing down for dear life. Well, the ogre didn't like trusting himself to such a ladder, and he stood and waited, so Jack got another start.

But just then the harp cried out, "Master! Master!" and the ogre swung himself down onto the beanstalk, which shook with his weight. Down climbs Jack, and after him climbed the ogre. By this time Jack had climbed down and climbed down and climbed down till he was very nearly home. So he called out, "Mother! Mother! bring me an ax, bring me an ax." And his mother came rushing out with the ax in her hand, but when she came to the beanstalk she stood stock still with fright, for there she saw the ogre with his legs just through the clouds.

But Jack jumped down and got hold of the ax and gave a chop at the beanstalk, which cut it half in two. The ogre felt the beanstalk shake and quiver, so he stopped to see what was the matter. Then Jack gave another chop with the ax, and the beanstalk was cut in two and began to topple over. Then the ogre fell down and broke his crown, and the beanstalk came toppling after.

Then Jack showed his mother his golden harp, and what with showing that and selling the golden eggs, Jack and his mother became very rich, and he married a great princess, and they lived happily ever after.

Name: _____ Date: _____

Posttest, *continued*

QUESTIONS

1. Explain how the different elements of the story (e.g., use of words, point of view, setting, characters, ideas, plot/conflict, images/symbols, etc.) interact to contribute to the overall meaning of the text.

2. What archetypes are present in the story? How did the encounters reveal those archetypes? Cite evidence from the text to support your answer.

3. What does this story suggest about encounters? Write at least two true statements about encounters in the story with evidence to support your ideas.

Name: _____ Date: _____

Posttest Rubric
"Jack and the Beanstalk" *by Joseph Jacobs*

	0	1	2	3	4
Question 1: Content: Literary Analysis	Provides no response.	Response is limited and vague. There is no connection to how literary elements contribute to the meaning, main idea, or theme. A literary element is merely named.	Response is accurate with 1–2 literary techniques described with vague or no connection to a main idea or theme. Response includes limited or no evidence from text.	Response is appropriate and accurate, describing at least two literary elements and a main idea or theme. Response is literal and includes some evidence from the text.	Response is insightful and well-supported, describing at least two literary elements and how they enhance the theme. Response includes abstract connections and adequate evidence from the text.
Question 2: Process: Inference From Evidence	Provides no response.	Response is limited, vague, and/or inaccurate. There is no justification for answers given.	Response is accurate, but lacks adequate explanation. Response includes some justification about how encounters revealed archetypes.	Response is accurate and makes sense. Response includes some justification about how encounters revealed archetypes.	Response is accurate, insightful, interpretive, and well-written. Response includes thoughtful justification about how encounters revealed archetypes.
Question 3: Concept/Theme Applied to Literature	Provides no response.	Response is limited, vague, and/or inaccurate.	Response lacks adequate explanation. Response does not relate or create a generalization about encounters. Little or no evidence from text.	Response is accurate and makes sense. Response relates to or creates an idea about encounters with some relation to the text.	Response is accurate, insightful, and well-written. Response relates to or creates two generalizations about encounters with evidence from the text.

Note: Adapted with permission from Stambaugh & VanTassel-Baska, 2011.

References

Adamski, A. (2011). Archetypes and the collective unconscious of Carl G. Jung in the light of quantum psychology. *NeuroQuantology, 9,* 563–571.

Archetypes. (n.d.). Retrieved from https://www.hccfl.edu/media/724354/archetypesforliteraryanalysis.pdf

Assouline, S., Colangelo, N., VanTassel-Baska, J., & Lupkowski-Shoplik, A. (Eds.). (2015). *A nation empowered: Evidence trumps the excuses holding back America's brightest students.* Iowa City: University of Iowa, The Connie Belin & Jacqueline N. Blank International Center for Gifted Education and Talent Development.

Booth, A., & Mays, K. J. (n.d.). Glossary. *LitWeb.* Retrieved from http://www.wwnorton.com/college/english/litweb10/glossary/A.aspx

Guerin, W. L., Labor, E., Morgan, L., Reesman, J. C., & Willingham, J. R. (1992). *Mythological and archetypal approaches.* Retrieved from http://mjoseph.comminfo.rutgers.edu/c-guerin.html

Jerram, L. (n.d.). *Invisible homeless.* Retrieved from https://www.lukejerram.com/invisible-homeless

Jonas, J. J. (n.d.). *The twelve archetypes.* Retrieved from http://www.uiltexas.org/files/capitalconference/Twelve_Character_Archetypes.pdf

Kulik, J. A., & Kulik, C.-L. C. (1992). Meta-analytic findings on grouping programs. *Gifted Child Quarterly, 36,* 73–77.

Literary Terms. (n.d.). *Archetype.* Retrieved from https://literaryterms.net/archetype

M. C. Escher Foundation. (2017). *Biography.* Retrieved from http://www.mcescher.com/about/biography

Morris, S. B., & DeShon, R. P. (2002). Combining effect size estimates in meta-analysis with repeated measures and independent-groups designs. *Psychological Methods, 7*(1), 105–125.

Pieter-bruegel-the-elder.org. (n.d.). *Pieter the Elder Bruegel.* Retrieved from https://www.pieter-bruegel-the-elder.org

Protas, A., Brown, G., Smith, J., & Jaffe, E. (2001). *Ice.* Retrieved from http://www.umich.edu/~umfandsf/symbolismproject/symbolism.html/I/ice.html

Rogers, K. B. (2007). Lessons learned about educating the gifted and talented: A synthesis of the research on educational practice. *Gifted Child Quarterly, 51,* 382–396.

Stambaugh, T., & VanTassel-Baska, J. (2011). *Jacob's Ladder Reading Comprehension Program: Level 4.* Waco, TX: Prufrock Press.

Steenbergen-Hu, S., Makel, M. C., & Olszewski-Kubilius, P. (2016). What one hundred years of research says about the effects of ability grouping and acceleration on K-12 students' academic achievement. *Review of Education Research, 86,* 849–899.

VanTassel-Baska, J. (1986). Effective curriculum and instruction models for talented students. *Gifted Child Quarterly, 30,* 164–169.

VanTassel-Baska, J., & Stambaugh, T. (2016). *Jacob's Ladder Reading Comprehension Program: Nonfiction, Grade 4.* Waco, TX: Prufrock Press.

Wisse, J. (2002). *Pieter Bruegel the Elder (ca. 1525–1569).* Retrieved from https://www.metmuseum.org/toah/hd/brue/hd_brue.htm

Appendix A

Instructions for Using the Models

LITERARY ANALYSIS WHEEL INSTRUCTIONS

The Literary Analysis Model is used to guide students through analyzing how an author uses literary techniques to develop meaning within a work. The model allows students to see connections between multiple literary elements (e.g., setting impacts conflict, conflict reveals character motives and values, characterization impacts theme, etc.).

Using the Literary Analysis Wheel

The Literary Analysis Wheel can be used to guide students through an analysis of a short story, poem, or novel. First, guide students to identify elements of the wheel separately, and then emphasize a deeper analysis by asking how elements relate to each other (e.g., point of view impacts theme, setting creates mood, etc.).

The Literary Analysis Wheel is meant to be interactive. The inner wheel conceptually spins so that its elements interact with each other and the outer wheel. Each element can relate to each other, regardless of its placement on the wheel.

The Literary Analysis Wheel Guide (Appendix B) shows specific prompts for each element of the wheel. The teacher may simply refer to the model during instruction, or students may take notes on the Blank Literary Analysis Wheel using arrows to show how the various elements relate. It is suggested that students note the answers to the "simple" questions on the graphic organizer, and then discuss interactions with other elements. Consider making a poster of the Literary Analysis Wheel Guide and posting it in your classroom for students to refer to throughout the unit.

Once students are accustomed to using the wheel, encourage students to develop their own questions about the relationship between elements.

Students can make their own interactive paper-plate model of the wheel. Two different colored papers may be used for the inner and outer circles, secured with a brass paper fastener. Students may use the wheels as visuals in small groups.

Encounters With Archetypes

Sample questions for literary analysis. The following questions can be asked to support students in analyzing literature. Note that complexity is added by combining elements.

- **Simple:**
  - **Character:** *What are the values and motives of the characters? What evidence supports this? How does the author reveal character?*
  - **Setting:** *What is the time and place of the story?*
  - **Tone:** *What is the author's attitude toward the subject? With what attitude does the author approach the theme?*
  - **Symbols:** *How do objects or names represent more abstract ideas?*
  - **Point of View:** *What is the narrator's point of view (first person, third person objective, third person limited, third person omniscient)?*
  - **Language/Style/Structure:** *What figurative language and imagery does the author use? What is the author's style?*
  - **Plot/Conflict:** *What are the significant internal and external conflicts of the story? What are the significant parts of the plot?*
  - **Mood:** *What is the feeling the reader gets from the story? How is this established?*
  - **Theme:** *What is the author's main message that can be generalized to broader contexts? (The theme is the author's point of view on a given subject or idea.)*

- **Complex:**
  - Setting+
    - *How does the setting influence the development of the theme?*
    - *How does the setting affect the mood?*
    - *What language does the author use to describe the setting (e.g., use of imagery, similes, etc.)?*
    - *How does the setting enhance conflict? How does the setting provoke plot events?*
    - *How is the setting symbolic of a larger idea (e.g., autumn, twilight)?*
    - *How does the setting affect and change the characters?*
    - *How does the setting help reveal the author's tone/attitude toward the theme/subject?*
    - *What conflicts could only happen in this setting? How does this influence the plot and theme?*

  - Symbols+
    - *How do symbols help develop the theme?*
    - *How does the author use figurative language to establish symbolism?*
    - *How do symbols relate to key plot elements and conflicts?*

- *How do symbols contribute to establishing the mood?*
- *Is the setting symbolic of a larger idea (e.g., twilight, autumn)?*
- *How does the author's use of symbols reveal the author's tone?*
- *How are characters symbolic of archetypes? What symbols are associated with the characters?*

- Character+
  - *How do the characters' actions/beliefs/attitudes/struggles influence the theme?*
  - *How do the qualities of the characters affect the conflict as it relates to significant parts of the plot?*
  - *How do the characters' actions and responses establish mood?*
  - *What characters' thoughts/feelings are hidden and/or revealed by the narrator's point of view? How does this impact the reader's experience of the story?*
  - *How does the author use language to develop character? Consider dialect, descriptions, use of figurative language, and names.*
  - *Are characters revealed by symbols?*
  - *How does the setting affect character actions?*
  - *How does the author's tone toward the subject influence the development of characters?*

- Tone+
  - *How does the author's tone help establish the theme? What attitude does the author take in approaching the theme?*
  - *How is the author's tone revealed in the narrator's point of view (e.g., the narrator's words and feelings will reveal the attitude of how the author approaches the theme)?*
  - *What words/phrases does the author use to establish tone? How does the tone change throughout the story? How is this established through the author's style?*
  - *How is the author's tone revealed in the plot and conflicts? What specific textual evidence supports this?*
  - *How do the characters' conflicts reveal the author's tone toward a subject?*
  - *How does the author's tone aid in developing the mood of the story?*
  - *How do symbols help reveal the author's tone?*
  - *How do character actions, values, and conflicts reveal the author's tone?*
  - *How does the setting help reveal the author's tone/attitude toward the subject?*

Encounters With Archetypes

- Point of View+
    - *How does the narrator's point of view shape the theme?*
    - *How does the narrator's point of view establish mood (e.g., the reader depends on the narrator's perspective in telling the story, so the reader feels the way the narrator does about what is being described)?*
    - *How does the narrator's point of view affect the way the reader views the significant conflicts and plot events?*
    - *What is the style of the narrator? How does the narrator's point of view (specifically, voice and diction) affect the story?*
    - *How is the author's tone revealed in the narrator's point of view (e.g. the narrator's words and feelings will reveal the attitude of how the author approaches the theme)?*
    - *What character thoughts are revealed or hidden because of the narrator's point of view? How does this impact the reader's experience of the story?*

- Language/Style/Structure+
    - *How does the author's use of figurative language or imagery contribute to literary elements?*
    - *How does the dialect of the characters contribute to our understanding of literary elements?*
    - *How does the author's style and sentence structure enhance the mood?*

- Mood+
    - *How does the mood help develop the theme? What if the mood were different? How would this change the theme of the story?*
    - *How does the author's point of view help create mood?*
    - *How does the author's tone create mood for the reader?*
    - *How do the characters' actions, thoughts, and conflicts contribute to the mood?*
    - *How does the setting contribute to the mood?*
    - *How does the author use specific language to develop the mood?*
    - *How do specific symbols help establish the mood?*

- Plot/Conflict+
    - *How does the plot develop the theme? How would the theme be different if the story had a different ending?*
    - *How does the conflict reveal the character's values and motives?*
    - *How does setting impact the conflict and plot?*

- *What insight about the conflict does the reader have (or not have) as a result of the narrator's point of view?*
- *How do symbols represent aspects of the conflict (also consider foreshadowing devices)?*
- *How do character actions, thoughts, and conflicts reveal the author's tone?*
- *How do the plot and conflict reveal and/or change the mood?*
- *How does the author's style contribute to the development of the plot? Why does the author use more language/description on certain aspects of the plot than others?*

- Theme+
  - *How does the plot impact the theme? How would the theme change if key parts of the plot or ending were changed?*
  - *How does the theme impact the development of the plot? If the author wanted to show a different theme, how would he or she have to change the plot of the story? How would the characters' values, motives, and actions change?*
  - *How do the literary elements contribute to the development of the theme?*

- Interpretation:
  - *Taken altogether, what is your interpretation of the work (e.g., what is the explanation or meaning of this work given the author's use of various literary elements)? How did literary elements combine to create meaning? Support your interpretation by referring to the interaction of multiple elements in shaping your understanding of the work.*

Example Literary Analysis Lesson 1

Read the poem "Child Moon" by Carl Sandburg.

Step 1: Text-dependent questions. Lead students through a close reading of the text.

- What makes this poetry? Does it rhyme? What makes this structure different from prose? What makes it different from other styles of poetry? (*Note*: Poetry expresses thoughts and ideas in a distinctive style, often through rhyme or rhythm.)
- How many sentences do you notice? What is important about the length of the sentences as they relate to the poem's ideas? (Sample response: The poem starts out with a short sentence, reflecting simplicity in the child's wonder. The next long sentence shows more of an elaborate description of

Encounters With Archetypes

the "thing," followed by an incomplete sentence showing how she falls back asleep, perhaps back from interrupted sleep to see the moon.)
- How does the lack of rhyme contribute to any literary elements (or the meaning) of the poem? (Sample response: It evokes a sense of broken sleepiness, stream of conscious thought, as if following a child's thought process of the moon while half-awake.)
- Examine the first three lines of the poem. What contrast do you notice, and why is it significant? (Sample response: Young vs. old conveys the point of view of looking at something old through fresh eyes.)
- Why might the author refer to the moon as "the yellow thing"? Why is this important to the overall idea of the poem? (Sample response: This conveys more of the child's point of view, revealing more unknown wonder.)
- What are the major concepts or ideas in the poem? (Sample response: Wonder, innocence, perspective.) Literature, including poetry, reflects the human experience. What might the author want readers to consider about life? (Sample response: Appreciate the wonder of nature as a child appreciates it.)

Step 2: Literary Analysis Wheel, separate elements. Lead students through a simple analysis by completing the separate parts of the wheel (some of the separate elements can be noted while leading the text-dependent questions, and not every part of the wheel has to be completed).
- **Setting:** What is the setting of the poem? What words convey the setting? (Sample response: It is night in little girl's bedroom.)
- **Point of View:** What can you tell about the child's point of view about the moon? Does she like it? What are her thoughts about it? How do you know?
- **Character:** What can you tell about the child in the poem? How old do you think she is? What makes you think this?
- **Language/Structure:** What words are interesting to you? What is important about the contrast between child and "old moon"? How many sentences are there? Are these complete sentences? Why is this important? (Sample response: The incomplete sentences convey ideas of her thoughts as a child about to fall asleep.) What words stand out to you? Why do you think the author chose to use the word "babblings"?
- **Symbols:** What symbols do you notice? (Sample response: golden sand.) What does this represent? (Sample response: the light of the moon.)
- **Plot/Conflict:** (Because this is a poem, this does not have to be completed; you may ask: What's the main event happening in this poem?)
- **Theme:** What might be the overall message of the poem? What idea does the author want us to think about, and what is his message about this idea? (Sample response: Wonder. Appreciate nature as a child.)

Step 3: Combined elements for complexity. Discuss how multiple elements interact to establish an overall interpretation of the poem. Draw arrows across elements to show connections.

- **Point of View + Mood:** How does the author's use of point of view affect the mood of the poem? (Sample response: The point of view is from a child, conveying an innocent, childlike, warm mood).
- **Setting + Character:** How does the setting help us understand more about the character? (Sample response: Because this is set during the evening when the little girl is supposed to be sleeping, this helps us understand more about her intense wonder about the moon and the impact it has on her thoughts while going to sleep.)
- **Structure + Theme:** How does the author's structure (e.g., punctuation, rhyme scheme, etc.) contribute to the overall big idea of the poem? (Sample response: The lack of rhyme and fragmented sentences convey the thoughts of a child about to go to sleep; refer to the main idea that the poem reminds the reader to appreciate the moon as a child does.)
- **Language + Point of View + Theme:** How does the author's use of language reveal the point of view in the poem? How does this contribute to the overall theme? (Sample response: "Yellow thing" reveals the child's simple point of view about the moon, implying an overall message to appreciate the moon through a child's eyes.)

Example Literary Analysis Lesson 2

Read the poem "I like to see it lap the Miles" by Emily Dickinson.

Step 1: Text-dependent questions. Lead students through a close reading of text. (*Note:* Do not give away that the poem is about a train; students should continue to hypothesize and discuss with textual evidence.)

- According to the poem, does the author enjoy watching this object? How do you know? (Sample response: Yes, the first line of the poem states, "I like to see it . . . ")
- According to the poem, does the author like the object itself? How do you know? (Sample response: No, negative connotations about the object—supercilious, complaining, horrid, hooting—are combined with its omnipotence. It carves out the quarry to fit its own needs, to "fit its sides"—which is not welcomed in Dickinson's world.)
- What feelings can we associate with some of the words in this poem (horrid, hooting, omnipotent, supercilious, complaining, docile, punctual)? Are the connotations positive or negative?
- How do these connotations change, and what effect does it have on the poem? (Sample response: They change from negative to positive.)

Encounters With Archetypes

- After a second reading, students should respond to a partner: What is this poem about? (Most may say a horse, but help students understand that it is being compared to a horse; continue to guide them as they "discover" it is a railway train.) What evidence is there to support your idea? (The poem is about a train that is compared to a horse. Ask students to highlight or underline all comparisons of the train symbolized through a horse. Note that a train was referred to as an "iron horse" during the time period.)

Step 2: Literary Analysis Wheel, separate elements. Lead students through a simple analysis by completing the separate parts of the wheel.

- **Setting:** What is the setting? What words are used to describe the setting?
- **Character:** Considering the train as a character, what are the train's values and motives? (Sample response: The train is the "iron horse," which is proud and powerful, changing the landscape to fit its own needs. The train's values are to be efficient and strong, with a motivation to arrive punctually at its destination.)
- **Point of View:** What is Dickinson's point of view toward the object? How do you know? (Sample response: She sees both the negative and positive qualities.) (*Note*: Because this is a poem, we are considering the author's point of view—however, in short stories and novels, consider first person, third limited, omniscient, and objective point of view.)
- **Language:** Do you notice any specific figurative language or sound devices throughout the poem? (Sample response: Alliteration: "like," "lap," "lick;" "stop," "step;" personification: "lick," "stop," "feed itself;" simile: "neigh like Boanerges;" rhythm: unaccented-accented syllable pattern.)
- **Symbol:** What does the horse imagery represent? Why is the symbol of a horse used? How is the allusion to Boanerges a symbol? (Sample response: The horse is a symbol for the iron horse—a train. Boanerges was a vociferous disciple—loud and annoying—symbolic of the train.)
- **Tone:** What is Dickinson's attitude toward the train? What is the tone? (Sample response: Her tone is ambiguous—it is both positive and negative—she hates it but is also in awe of its power. At times her tone can also be unwelcoming and unapproving. Note how this is affected by her point of view and language.)
- **Conflict:** What is the significant conflict in the poem? (Sample response: Technology vs. nature.)
- **Theme:** What is the author's main message? (Sample response: Themes may relate to the the power of change, power of technology, or the intrusion of technology on nature.)

- **Mood:** Because this is a poem, it would be a stretch to be able to describe the mood based on the few lines that are given. It is suggested that this is not part of the poem analysis.

Step 3: Combined elements for complexity. Discuss how multiple elements interact to establish an overall interpretation of the poem.
- *How does Dickinson's use of language help develop our understanding of the character and the narrator's point of view?* She uses both positive ("docile," "omnipotent") and negative ("horrid," "Boanerges," "supercilious") connotations to show an ambiguous point of view—she loves and hates the train at the same time. The positive and negative connotations about the character help establish Dickinson's point of view.
- *How does the use of language help develop symbolism?* The horse imagery ("neigh," "feed itself at tanks," "stable") establishes the idea of "the iron horse." The *st-* alliteration helps create the sound of a train slowly stopping. The rhythm of the poem almost sounds like a train. The entire poem is a metaphor (horse compared to train) supported through similes (e.g., "neigh like Boanerges") and personification ("lick the valleys," "feed itself," "step").
- *How does setting help establish our understanding of the train's character? How does the setting help us understand the conflict?* The train can be considered as the main character, the "iron horse," who is proud and powerful, changing the landscape to fit its own needs. It pares a quarry to meet its own needs. The use of "shanties" in the setting implies how the train condescendingly looks down upon human things. The train "licks" the valleys up, revealing how it authoritatively takes layers off the landscape.
- *How does the tone and conflict establish the theme of the poem?* Dickinson's tone and attitude toward the new technology establish the conflict of nature versus technology. This clearly establishes the theme of the power and intrusion of technology on our lives.
- *If Dickinson were to change the theme to "overcoming obstacles," how would this affect how she describes the setting and character?* The character (the train) would be described more positively or even heroic ally. The setting would not showcase the train's domination; rather, it might be a hindrance to a train. Consider how the story "The Little Engine That Could" shows a contrasting theme (e.g., the setting poses an obstacle for the train instead of the train imposing on nature; rather than the train having "power" over the setting, the setting poses "power" over the train).

RHETORICAL ANALYSIS WHEEL INSTRUCTIONS

The Rhetorical Analysis Model is used to analyze how an author develops and supports an argument. Students examine how a writer achieves his or her purpose by analyzing how several elements work together to create an effective argument. This includes thinking about the rhetorical situation (e.g., purpose, context, audience), means of persuasion (e.g., ethos, logos, and pathos appeals), and rhetorical strategies (e.g., techniques, evidence, structure, etc.). The author develops a claim through the use of three rhetorical appeals: logos (reasoning), pathos (emotion), and ethos (credibility) in response to the situation. These rhetorical appeals are developed by point of view, specific strategies, techniques, and organization. The model allows students to see connections between multiple elements (e.g., credibility is influenced by point of view, specific techniques are used to evoke emotion, structure develops strong logos appeals, etc.).

Overview of Aristotle's Rhetorical Appeals

Aristotle's rhetoric includes logos, ethos, and pathos appeals. These appeals enhance a writer's ability to persuade an audience.
- **Logos:** How the author establishes good reasoning to make his message make sense. This includes major points, use of evidence, syllogisms, examples, facts, statistics, etc. Text focused.
- **Pathos:** How the author appeals to the audience's emotion. Audience focused.
- **Ethos:** How the author develops credibility and trust. Author focused.

Using the Rhetorical Analysis Wheel

The Rhetorical Analysis Wheel can be used to analyze how an author develops a claim through rhetorical appeals, techniques, and structure. Students also think through the point of view, assumptions, purpose, and implications of the document. It is meant to be interactive. The inner circle conceptually spins so that it interacts with elements on the outer circle.

The Rhetorical Analysis Wheel Guide (Appendix B) shows specific prompts to guide students in thinking through each separate element. The teacher may simply refer to the model during instruction or students may take notes on the Blank Rhetorical Analysis Wheel using arrows to show how elements relate. It is suggested that students first note the answers to each element separately on the graphic organizer, and then discuss how they influence each other. Consider making a poster of the Rhetorical Analysis Wheel Guide to refer to throughout the unit.

Appendix A

Students can make their own interactive paper-plate model of the wheel. Two different colored papers may be used for the inner and outer circles, secured with a brass paper fastener. Students may use the wheels as visuals in small groups.

Sample questions for rhetorical analysis. The following questions can be asked for analyzing argument. Note that complexity is added by combining elements.

- **Purpose:**
  - *What is the author's purpose?*

- **Context/Audience:**
  - *Who is the audience, and what is the historical situation?*
  - *What is the main problem in the historical context?*

- **Claim:**
  - *What is the main claim or message of the text?*

- **Techniques:**
  - *What specific techniques does the writer use to develop his or her claim? Here are some examples of specific techniques that may be asked:*
    - **Language:** Consider how specific word choice and style develop tone.
    - **Positive and negative connotations of words:** Consider how words evoke feelings.
    - **Personification:** Human qualities given to nonhuman objects/ideas.
    - **Simile:** A figure of speech that compares two unlike things using "like" or "as."
    - **Metaphor:** A direct comparison between two unlike things.
    - **Hyperbole:** An extreme exaggeration.
    - **Allusion:** A reference to a historical or Biblical work, person, or event. The writer assumes the reader can make connections between the allusion and text being read.
    - **Imagery:** Formation of mental images that appeal to the senses.
    - **Parallelism:** Using similar grammatical structures in order to emphasize related ideas.
    - **Repetition:** Repeating the same wording for emphasis, clarity, or emotional impact.
    - **Contrast:** A striking difference of ideas for effect.
    - **Rhetorical question:** A question asked by the writer, but not expected to be answered aloud. It evokes reflection.
    - **Liberty rhetoric:** Using patriotic appeals for freedom.
    - **War rhetoric:** Reasoning to convince war is necessary.

- **Syllogism:** A form of deductive logic—a conclusion drawn from two premises. Example: If x=y and y=z, then x=z. If citizens can vote and if women are citizens, then women should be allowed to vote.
- **Use of evidence, facts, statistics, examples, and counterclaims (strongly connects with logos):** Explicit support for the argument.

- **Point of View/Assumptions:**
  - *What is the writer's point of view toward the topic?*
  - *What assumptions does the writer make?*
  - *What is the writer's unstated premise or belief? What does the writer take for granted about the audience?*

- **Structure/Organization:**
  - *How does the writer organize ideas (e.g., problem-solution, point by point, chronologically, sequentially, compare/contrast)?*
  - *Where is the thesis? Why is it here?*
  - *Does the writer structure his or her message deductively or inductively?*

- **Logos (Focus on Text):**
  - *What reasoning is used to help the argument make sense? What are the main points?*
  - *Are statements easy to accept, or does the writer need to provide more evidence?*
  - *What research, facts, statistics, or expert opinions are used? Are these sufficient?*
  - **Logos/Structure**
    - *How does the structure of the document help the writer's argument make sense?*

  - **Logos/Point of View:**
    - *Does the writer assume that the audience already accepts a premise?*
    - *What do the writer's examples and facts (or lack of) reveal about his or her assumptions about the audience?*

  - **Logos/Techniques:**
    - *Which techniques are used to help the writer logically form his or her argument (e.g., syllogisms, comparisons, parallelisms, use of statistics, examples, etc.)?*

- **Logos/Context:**
  - *How do the problem, context, and audience influence the writer's approach in developing a logical argument? How does the historical context influence the way the writer organizes his or her reasoning?*

- **Pathos (Focus on Audience):**
  - *How does the writer appeal to the audience's emotions (guilt, fear, pride, etc.)?*
  - *What word connotations or imagery does the writer use to evoke emotion in the audience?*
  - *How do pathos appeals help the writer establish his or her claim?*
  - **Pathos/Point of View:**
    - *How does the writer's tone and point of view impact the desired emotional response?*
    - *How does the writer's bias influence the desired emotional response?*

  - **Pathos/Technique:**
    - *What techniques does the writer use to evoke emotion among the audience (e.g., repetition, liberty rhetoric, war rhetoric, similes, hyperbole, symbolism, rhetorical questions)?*

  - **Pathos/Structure:**
    - *Where does the writer place the emotional appeals? Why is this important? Do pathos appeals change throughout the text? How? Why? How does this enhance or take away from the argument?*

  - **Pathos/Context:**
    - *How does the historical situation/problem influence how the writer uses pathos appeals? How do pathos appeals help the writer accomplish his or her desired effect?*

- **Ethos (Focus on Writer):**
  - *Is the writer credible?*
  - *How does the writer establish trust?*
  - *Are sources credible?*
  - *Does the writer respect an opposing viewpoint?*
  - *Does the writer address counterclaims? How?*
  - *How do ethos appeals help the writer establish an effective argument?*
  - **Ethos/Technique:**
    - *What techniques does the writer use to establish credibility (e.g., uses reliable sources, discusses character/reputation, etc.)?*

- **Ethos/Point of View:**
  - *Does the writer's bias take away from his or her credibility?*
  - *Do the writer's assumptions about the opposing point of view reduce his or her credibility?*

- **Ethos/Structure:**
  - *Where in the document does the writer develop his or her credibility? Why is it significant he or she places his or her ethos appeals here?*
  - *Where does the writer address counterclaims? How does he or she address the counterclaim, and how does this enhance or reduce his or her credibility?*

- **Ethos/Context:**
  - *Why is it important for the writer to develop trust with this audience in this historical situation?*
  - *What must the writer consider about the audience when establishing his or her credibility?*

- **Implications:**
  - *What are the short- and long-term implications/consequences of this document?*

- **Evaluation:**
  - *How effective is the writer in developing his or her claim? To what extent is the purpose fulfilled?*
  - *Is there a balance of pathos, ethos, and logos appeals?*
  - *Is there too much bias or emotional manipulation? Is there adequate evidence to support the claim(s)? Is the evidence credible, rational, and organized logically?*

Students should consider the author's purpose (to entertain, inform, persuade, express) when determining how effective the argument is. For example, it may not be necessary to provide counterarguments if the purpose of the text is not to persuade. Students should also consider the balance of logos, ethos, and pathos appeals.

Example Rhetorical Analysis Lesson

Students should read the excerpt from Franklin D. Roosevelt's Second Inaugural Address available at http://www.historyonthenet.com/authentichistory/1930-1939/2-fdr/4-1936election/19370120_FDR_Second_Inaugural_Address.html.

Appendix A

Step 1: Text-dependent questions. Lead students through a close reading of the text for initial comprehension. You may also ask students to paraphrase sections of the text into their own words.
- According to Roosevelt, what brings an ever richer life to Americans?
- Why does Roosevelt personify Comfort, Opportunism, and Timidity? How are these "voices" considered distractions?
- What are some of the positive aspects of the current state of affairs?
- According to the text, why is prosperity dangerous?
- What is meant by "prosperity already tests the persistence of our progressive purpose"?
- Which one of Roosevelt's "I see" statements is most powerful?
- According to the text, how do we test our progress?
- What is Roosevelt's solution to the problems of tens of millions?
- What four words are most important to the text? Can you put these four words together in a sentence to summarize FDR's main message?

Step 2: Teach elements of rhetorical analysis. Teach students some basic principles of a rhetorical analysis:
- **Modes of Rhetoric (Logos, Pathos, Ethos):** Explain Aristotle's modes of rhetoric.
- **Techniques:** Students will consider how these appeals are developed through different techniques used by the author. Go over a few techniques with students. Note that language, positive and negative connotations, personification, repetition, and rhetorical questions are used.
- **Structure/Organization:** Students should consider where the appeals are placed within the documents and why they are there. They should also consider the overall structure of the document as it often supports the logos appeal (it helps the author's rationale "make sense" by putting ideas in this order). Why is it important that the points are placed structurally where they are? Throughout the analysis, the elements of logos, ethos, and pathos interact with structure, techniques and point of view.

Step 3: Rhetorical Analysis Wheel: Separate Elements. Lead students through completing relevant parts of the Rhetorical Analysis Wheel. Students do not need to write detailed explanations on the organizer, just notes. Focus first on the separate elements.
- **Purpose:**
  - *What is Roosevelt's purpose in delivering this message?* To persuade the American people to carry on toward progress by moving forward together.

Encounters With Archetypes

- **Message/Claim:**
  - *What is Roosevelt's main claim? What is the main idea he is proving?* America will carry on toward progress by addressing the concerns of all.

- **Point of View/Assumptions:**
  - *What is Roosevelt's point of view toward progress? What are his assumptions?* FDR believes Americans should cautiously handle prosperity; it can distract Americans from progressing because of the self-interest involved. He assumes that government involvement into the affairs of people is welcomed, justified, and of goodwill.

- **Structure:**
  - *What is the overall structure of the speech?* Problem-solution.

- **Techniques:**
  - *What are some techniques you notice within the speech?* Rhetorical questions, personification, etc.

- **Logos:**
  - *What are the main points? How does the author support his claim with evidence and facts? What are the main "reasons" that support the claim?* **Logos/Reasoning:** FDR notes that America has progressed, but not arrived, and the American people should be warned by the disasters of prosperity. He lists positive state of affairs, lists negative state of affairs, and explains a hopeful future via government involvement. He provides evidence of a negative state of affairs ("I see millions . . . ").

- **Pathos:**
  - *What emotion(s) does the author attempt to evoke in the audience (pathos)?* FDR appeals to a sense of sympathy ("I see millions . . . ") and pride ("If I know aught of the will of our people . . . ").

- **Ethos:**
  - *Is the author credible? How does the author establish trust? Is evidence credible?* FDR is speaking at his second inaugural address and acknowledges the progress made during his presidency. He also refers to the government as effective and competent to build trust. Evidence is not supported with specific credibility, and he is somewhat biased with his enthusiasm for a competent government addressing problems.

- **Implications:**
  - *What are the short- and long-term implications/consequences of this document?* This speech set the stage for many of FDR's initiatives. During his second term, Congress passed the Housing Act, laws were made to establish minimum wage (Fair Labor Standards Act), and more than 3.3 million jobs were developed through WPA (Works Progress Administration).

Step 4: Combined elements for complexity. Combine elements to develop more complex questions. Students may draw arrows on their wheels to show how elements relate (pathos + techniques, etc.).

- **Logos/Techniques:**
  - *What techniques are used to develop the reasoning in his argument?* He sets up the first point by asking a rhetorical question ("Shall we pause now and turn our back . . . "), uses personification to introduce the idea that we should be warned by the disasters of prosperity ("Comfort says . . . timidity says . . . "), addresses a counterclaim and acknowledges that we have progressed ("true, we have come far . . . "), and explains how progress today is more difficult in light of prosperity.

- **Logos/Structure:**
  - *How is the argument structured logically?* Problem-solution. It is also organized inductively. His main claim is that Americans will carry on by addressing the concerns of all. He provides evidence first and then makes this claim.

- **Pathos/Techniques:**
  - *What techniques are used to develop pathos appeals?* He uses repetition ("I see millions . . . ") to develop sympathy. He develops a sense of urgency with "at this very moment . . . " He uses loaded language ("meager," "indecent," "poverty," "denying work," "ill-housed," "ill-clad," "ill-nourished") for sympathy and pride ("goodwill," "effective government," "uncorrupted by cancers of injustice," "strong," "will to peace," "long-cherished ideals").

- **Pathos/Structure:**
  - *Where does he place pathos appeals (structure)? Why? Do they change? Why?* The pathos appeals are in line with the problem-solution logos structure. As he develops the problem, he evokes sympathy. As he develops the solution, he evokes pride.

- **Ethos/Techniques/Structure:**
  - *What techniques are used to establish ethos appeals, and why are they placed where they are?* He includes "we," and "us" throughout the speech to connect with the audience. As he uses "we," he establishes that he has been a part of the present gains. The "we" language shifts to "I"—revealing that the audience can really trust him because he himself sees the problems. He shifts again to "we" when connecting the audience to the goodwill of the nation.

- **Evaluation:**
  - *How effective is the author in supporting his claim? Is there a balance of pathos, ethos, and logos appeals? Is the claim fully supported?* Roosevelt is effective in supporting the claim that America will continue on toward progress by addressing the concerns of all. There is a balance of logos, ethos, and pathos appeals. FDR gives sufficient evidence of the problem with the repeated "I see" statements, though the credibility of this evidence is not specific, but general.

TEXT ANALYSIS WHEEL INSTRUCTIONS

The Text Analysis Wheel is used to help students analyze the development of a central idea. Similar to the Literary Analysis and Visual Analysis Wheels, students read an article or speech and complete the individual components of the wheel, including the author's points, with evidence, purpose, central idea, point of view/assumptions, structure, implications, and evaluation. Then students examine how the features of the text interact. An example from Franklin D. Roosevelt's Second Inaugural Address (available at http://www.historyonthenet.com/authentichistory/1930-1939/2-fdr/4-1936election/19370120_FDR_Second_Inaugural_Address.html) is used as an example to illustrate the features of the Text Analysis Wheel.

The following are simple and complex questions that could be used. The first question includes a simpler question, whereas the second question (when applicable) includes interactions between two different elements.

- **Purpose:**
  - *What is President Roosevelt's purpose in delivering this message?* To persuade the American people to carry on toward progress by moving forward together.

- **Central Idea:**
  - *What is Roosevelt's central idea (main message)?* We will carry on toward progress by addressing the concerns of all.

- **Point of View/Assumptions:**
  - *What is Roosevelt's point of view toward progress? What are his assumptions?* Roosevelt believes Americans should cautiously handle prosperity; it can distract Americans from progressing because of the self-interest involved. He assumes that government involvement into the affairs of people is welcomed, justified, and of goodwill.

- **Point 1/Evidence:**
  - *What is one important point Roosevelt makes to develop his central idea?* Point 1: Americans should be warned by the disasters of prosperity. Evidence: "Comfort says, 'tarry a while.' Opportunism . . . To hold progress today, however, is more difficult . . . ."
  - *How does this point develop his central idea?* This explains the state of affairs—the nation has made great progress and experienced prosperity, but prosperity can also present a problem. He asks the nation to consider the nature of progress.
  - *What techniques are used to develop this point?* He personifies comfort, opportunism, and timidity to explain that the nation is at a place of decision in the face of prosperity. He describes symptoms of prosperity with negative word connotations ("dulled conscience, irresponsibility . . . ").
  - *Why is it important that the author discusses this point at this particular part of the speech (structure)?* This allows him to introduce the problem of prosperity. This sets him up to explain to the audience that not everyone is reaping the benefits of prosperity, which is important in developing his central idea.

- **Point 2/Evidence:**
  - *What is another important point Roosevelt uses to develop his central idea?* Point 2: He explains a negative state of affairs. Evidence: "I see millions . . . ill-housed, ill-clad, ill-nourished."
  - *How does this point develop the central idea?* It explains the problem of poverty, that the concerns of all citizens are not addressed even within a time of prosperous progress.
  - *What techniques are used to develop his point?* He uses both repetition ("I see millions") and loaded language ("meager," "indecent," "poverty," "denying work," "ill-housed," "ill-clad," "ill-nourished") to develop sympathy (pathos appeal).
  - *Why is it important that the author discusses this point at this particular part of the speech (structure)?* At this part of the speech, he is developing the problem before he offers a solution. As he develops the problem, he evokes sympathy.

- **Point 3/Evidence:**
  - *What is another important point Roosevelt uses to develop his central idea?* Point 3: Roosevelt explains a hopeful future via government involvement. Evidence: "But it is not in despair I paint you that picture . . . government is competent. . . ."
  - *How does this point develop the central idea?* It explains how the nation can address the concerns of all of its citizens, even those in poverty.
  - *What techniques are used to develop his point? How does this technique develop his point?* He revisits the personified comfort, opportunism, and timidity to remind the audience about the problem of prosperity within his solution for more government involvement. He uses positive word connotations when referring to the government and the American people ("men and women of good will," "warm hearts of dedication," "competent," "effective"). He refers to the government as effective and competent to build trust (ethos appeal).
  - *Why is this point where it is in the document (structure)? How does it help develop the central idea?* This point includes his closing where he offers a solution for the American people—come together with the government to address the problems of both comfortable prosperity and poverty.

- **Structure:**
  - *What is the overall structure of the document?* Problem-solution.

- **Implications:**
  - *What are implications/consequences of this document?* This speech set the stage for many of Roosevelt's initiatives. During his second term, Congress passed the Housing Act, laws were made to establish minimum wage (Fair Labor Standards Act), and more than 3.3 million jobs were developed through WPA (Works Progress Administration).

- **Evaluation:**
  - *How effective is the author in using sufficient, relevant evidence to develop a central idea?* Roosevelt is somewhat effective in supporting the central idea that America will continue on toward progress by addressing the concerns of all. He speaks of the problem of progress and prosperity in general terms, but allows the audience to consider the problem through the present context. He provides a sufficient amount of evidence for stating the problems of poverty through the repetition of "I see" statements, and he effectively explains how the government and the American people can work together to address the concerns of all.

VISUAL ANALYSIS WHEEL INSTRUCTIONS

The Visual Analysis Model is used to guide students through analyzing how an artist develops a main idea in art. Students analyze specific techniques, organization, and the artist's point of view toward the idea. Additionally, students examine prominent images and symbolism, the author's background, and emotions portrayed and evoked in the art. The model allows students to see the connection between multiple concepts (e.g., images are organized intentionally to create the main idea, point of view is influenced by the artist's background, specific techniques are used to evoke emotion, etc.).

Using the Visual Analysis Wheel

The Visual Analysis Wheel can be used to guide students through an in-depth analysis of art or visual media. It is meant to be interactive. The inner circle conceptually spins so that it interacts with elements on the outer circle.

The Visual Analysis Wheel Guide (Appendix B) shows specific prompts to guide students in thinking through each separate element. The teacher may simply refer to the model during instruction, or students may take notes on the Blank Visual Analysis Wheel using arrows to show how the elements relate. It is suggested that students first note the answers to each concept separately on the graphic organizer, and then discuss how they influence each other.

Students can make their own interactive paper-plate model of the wheel. Two different colored papers may be used for the inner and outer circles, secured with a brass paper fastener. Students may use the wheels as visuals in small groups.

Sample questions for visual analysis. The following questions can be asked for analyzing art. Note that complexity is added by combining different elements.

- **Purpose:**
  - *What is the purpose of the art?*

- **Context:**
  - *What year was this art created? What artistic movements may have influenced this work? What type of art is this? What historical events were happening at the time this was made? Is there a specific audience for which the art was created?*

- **Main Idea + Message:**
  - *What is the main idea of this art? What is the message of the art?*

Encounters With Archetypes

- **Techniques:**
  - What specific techniques does the artist use? (Consider color, shape, brushstroke, patterns, contrast.)

- **Point of View + Assumptions:**
  - What is the artist's point of view toward the topic?
  - What assumptions does the artist make?
  - What is the artist's unstated premise or belief? What does the artist take for granted about the audience?

- **Structure:**
  - How does the artist organize ideas?
  - What is the central part of the painting?
  - Where is your eye drawn first? Why?

- **Images/Symbols:**
  - What are the main images?
  - Do they symbolize a deeper meaning? How?

- **Images + Structure:**
  - Why does the artist intentionally place the objects where they are?

- **Images + Point of View + Assumptions:**
  - What do the artist's images reveal about his or her point of view/assumptions about the topic displayed?

- **Images + Techniques:**
  - What specific techniques does the artist use to create the main images of the art?

- **Images + Purpose/Context:**
  - How does the historical context influence the artist's choice of images in his or her art?
  - How does the audience for which this is intended influence the artist's choice of images?

- **Emotions:**
  - What emotions does this art evoke in you?
  - What emotions does this art reveal/portray?

- **Emotions + Point of View/Assumptions:**
  - *How does the artist's point of view toward the topic influence your emotional reaction to the art?*

- **Emotions + Technique:**
  - *What techniques does the artist use to portray and evoke emotion from his or her art?*

- **Emotions + Structure:**
  - *Are some parts of the art more emotionally powerful than others? How did the artist organize his or her painting to evoke or portray emotion?*

- **Emotions + Purpose/Context:**
  - *How does the historical situation influence how the artist expresses or evokes emotion?*

- **Artist Background:**
  - *What do you know about the artist's personal life? Who influenced his or her work? How did his or her work influence others?*

- **Artist Background + Technique:**
  - *What techniques does the artist use that are unique to his or her style?*

- **Artist Background + Point of View/Assumptions:**
  - *How does the artist's background influence his or her point of view/assumptions about the topic?*

- **Artist Background + Structure:**
  - *Does the artist's background influence the way he or she organizes his or her art?*

- **Artist Background + Purpose/Context:**
  - *How is the artist influenced by the historical context of his or her time? How does the artist influence the historical context of his or her time?*

- **Implications:**
  - *What are the short- and long-term consequences of this art?*
  - *What are the implications for you after viewing this art?*

- **Evaluation:**
  - *Do you like this art? Why or why not? Use specific elements from the wheel in your answer.*
  - *What does this art make you think? Would you hang this in your home? Why or why not?*
  - *What elements of this art are most important to consider and why?*

Example Visual Analysis Lesson

Students view the lithograph "Relativity" by M. C. Escher (available online). Do not reveal the title.

Step 1: Close-viewing questions. Lead students through an initial viewing of the art.

- What detail of this art is interesting to you? (Ask every student; short response.)
- How many staircases are there? (Sample response: Seven; some overlap.)
- How many sources of gravity are in this picture? (Sample response: Three.)
- What behaviors do you see of the people?
- What is the focal point of the picture? Justify your answer.
- How does Escher produce "dual effects" on this painting? (Sample response: The ceiling is also a floor.) Note that even though two people may be on the same staircase, they exist in two separate dimensions. Do they know of each other's existence? (Sample response: One is going up, one is going down, but they are going in the same direction.)
- Round-robin: If you had to give the lithograph a title, what title would you give it? (Ask every student; short response.)
- Share with your neighbor why you chose this title (or if time permits, elicit this as a whole group).
- Share the real title of the lithograph, "Relativity." Why do you think Escher gave it this title?

Step 2: Visual Analysis Wheel, separate elements. Lead students through completing relevant parts of the Visual Analysis Wheel during discussion. Focus first on the separate elements.

- **Purpose/Context:**
  - *What is the context of this art?* Lithograph printed in 1953.
  - *What do you think Escher's purpose/motive was in creating this?* To express an idea of reality. (*Note*: Students may not be able to determine this until after discussing the art to some extent.)

Appendix A

- **Point of View/Assumptions:**
  - *What is Escher's point of view toward reality?* Escher is revealing that there are multiple experiences and perceptions of reality. People perceive reality differently.

- **Images:**
  - *What do you believe are the most prominent images in the picture? Why? How might they be symbols for something deeper?* Staircases = journey in life; featureless people = unaware people, emotionless; windows to outside = ways to get out of isolation.

- **Emotions:**
  - *What emotions does this evoke in you? What emotions are revealed?* The featureless people reveal a lack of emotion, indicating that people are coming and going in life in an emotionless state.

- **Artist Background:**
  - *What do you know about the artist's background? How is the artist influenced by the historical context of his time?* M. C. Escher (1898–1972) was a famous 20th-century Dutch artist who is known for developing impossible structures within his art. He made more than 448 lithographs (original prints) and woodcarvings, and more than 2,000 drawings (M. C. Escher Foundation, 2017). Escher also wrote many poems and essays, and he studied architecture, although he never graduated from high school. He used many mathematical aspects in his works. Most of Escher's works involve his own fascination with the concept of reality. His works showing paradoxes, tessellations, and impossible objects have had an influence on graphic art, psychology, philosophy, and logic.

- **Main Idea:**
  - *What is Escher conveying about life in this painting? What is Escher's main idea?* Each person has his or her own view of reality and may be unaware of others' realities.

- **Implications:**
  - *What are the implications of this art on you the viewer?*

Encounters With Archetypes

- **Evaluation:**
  - *Do you like this art? Would you hang it in your home? Does it make you think? Was the artist successful in presenting his ideas? Justify your answers with evidence.*

Step 3: Combined elements for complexity. Combine elements to develop more complex questions. Students may draw arrows on their wheels to show how elements relate (images + techniques, etc.).

- **Images + Techniques:**
  - *What techniques does Escher use to enhance images?* The people are all identical and featureless. There are three sources of gravity and seven staircases. The outside world is park-like. Some appear to be climbing upside down, but according to their gravity, they are climbing the staircase normally. Parts of the picture look two-dimensional, and other parts look three-dimensional. He includes paradoxes (two people standing on the same staircase in separate realities). The basements add a surreal effect.

- **Images + Structure:**
  - *How does Escher intentionally place the objects in the painting to reveal meaning?* He purposefully draws two people standing on the same step (top center); they coexist, yet they are in different gravity worlds. *What does this reveal about life?* We are preoccupied with our own journeys; we do not acknowledge others' points of view.

- **Artist Background + Technique:**
  - *What techniques does Escher use that are unique to his style?* Escher creates impossible realities within this work (three gravity worlds existing as one). He is known for creating paradoxes in his art.

- **Emotions + Structure + Technique:**
  - *How did the artist organize his art to portray or evoke emotion? What techniques were used to evoke or portray emotion?* It is interesting that the staircase structure is an upside-down triangle. Perhaps this is to give a more chaotic feel to the picture. Those within the staircases are "lost" in a world of coming and going, living life unaware beyond their own self-centered world. His technique of painting featureless people portrays a lack of emotion. The lack of emotion interplays with a main idea that the people are not aware of each other's existence, particularly in the other gravity worlds.

Appendix B

Blank Models and Guides

Encounters With Archetypes

BLANK LITERARY ANALYSIS WHEEL

Directions: Draw arrows across elements to show connections.

Text: _____

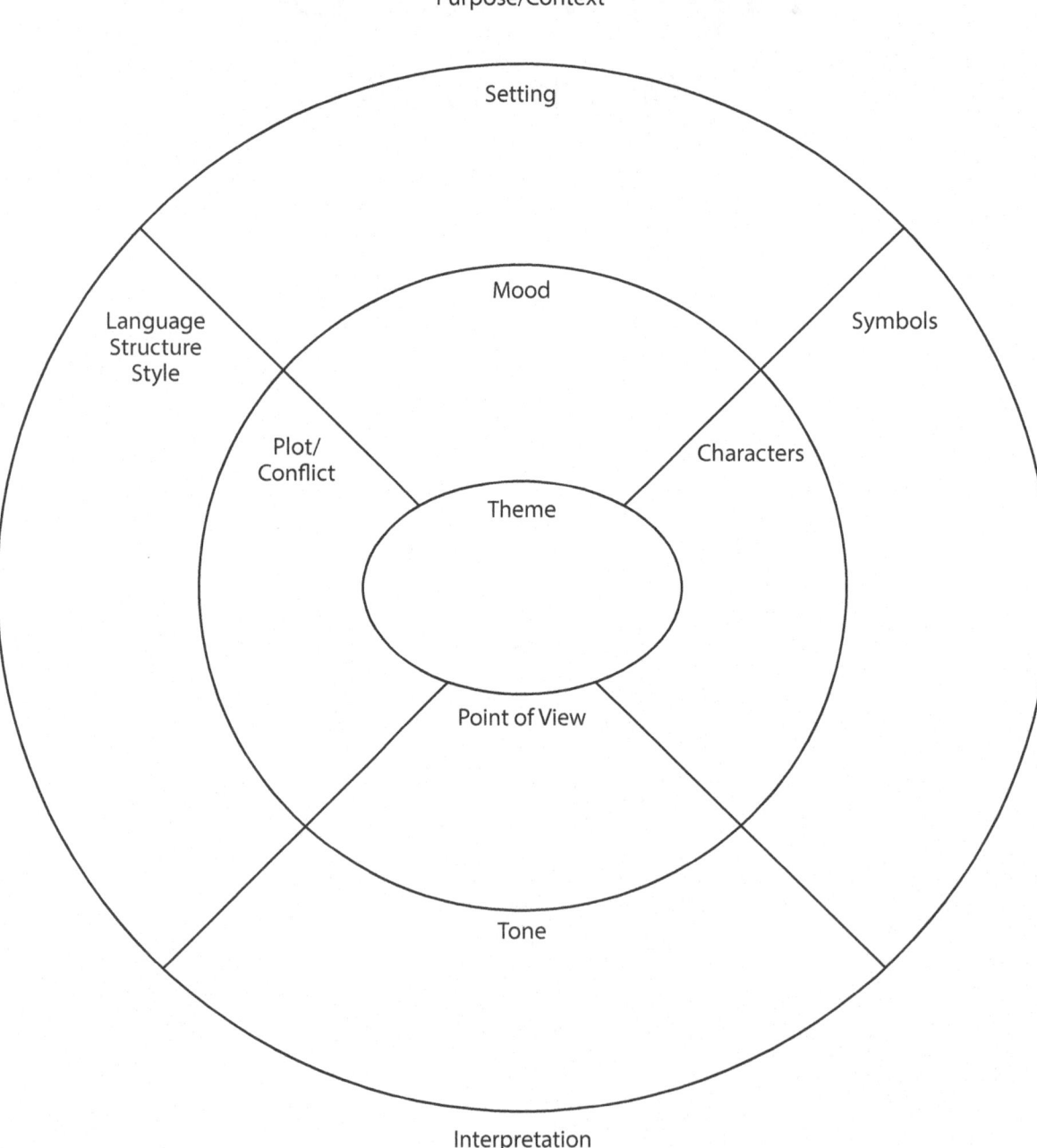

Created by Tamra Stambaugh, Ph.D., & Emily Mofield, Ed.D., 2015.

232

Appendix B

LITERARY ANALYSIS WHEEL GUIDE

Text: _____

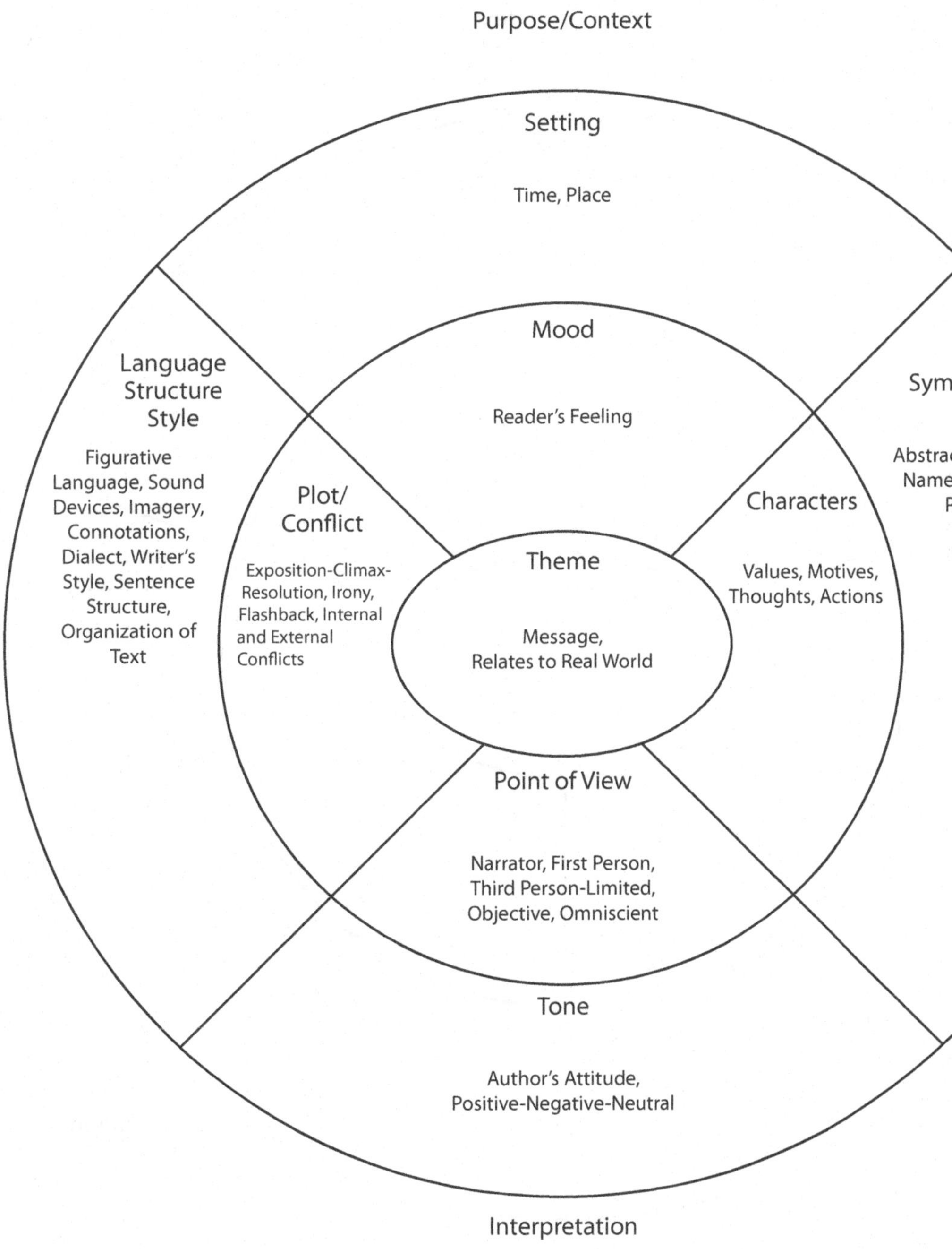

Purpose/Context

Setting
Time, Place

Language Structure Style
Figurative Language, Sound Devices, Imagery, Connotations, Dialect, Writer's Style, Sentence Structure, Organization of Text

Mood
Reader's Feeling

Symbols
Abstract Meaning, Names, Objects, Places

Plot/Conflict
Exposition-Climax-Resolution, Irony, Flashback, Internal and External Conflicts

Theme
Message, Relates to Real World

Characters
Values, Motives, Thoughts, Actions

Point of View
Narrator, First Person, Third Person-Limited, Objective, Omniscient

Tone
Author's Attitude, Positive-Negative-Neutral

Interpretation

Created by Tamra Stambaugh, Ph.D., & Emily Mofield, Ed.D., 2015.

Encounters With Archetypes

BLANK RHETORICAL ANALYSIS WHEEL

Directions: Draw arrows across elements to show connections.

Text: _____

Purpose/Context

Point of View

Logos

Techniques

Pathos   Claim   Ethos

Structure/Organization

Implications

Evaluation

Created by Emily Mofield, Ed.D., & Tamra Stambaugh, Ph.D., 2015.

Appendix B

RHETORICAL ANALYSIS WHEEL GUIDE

Text: _____

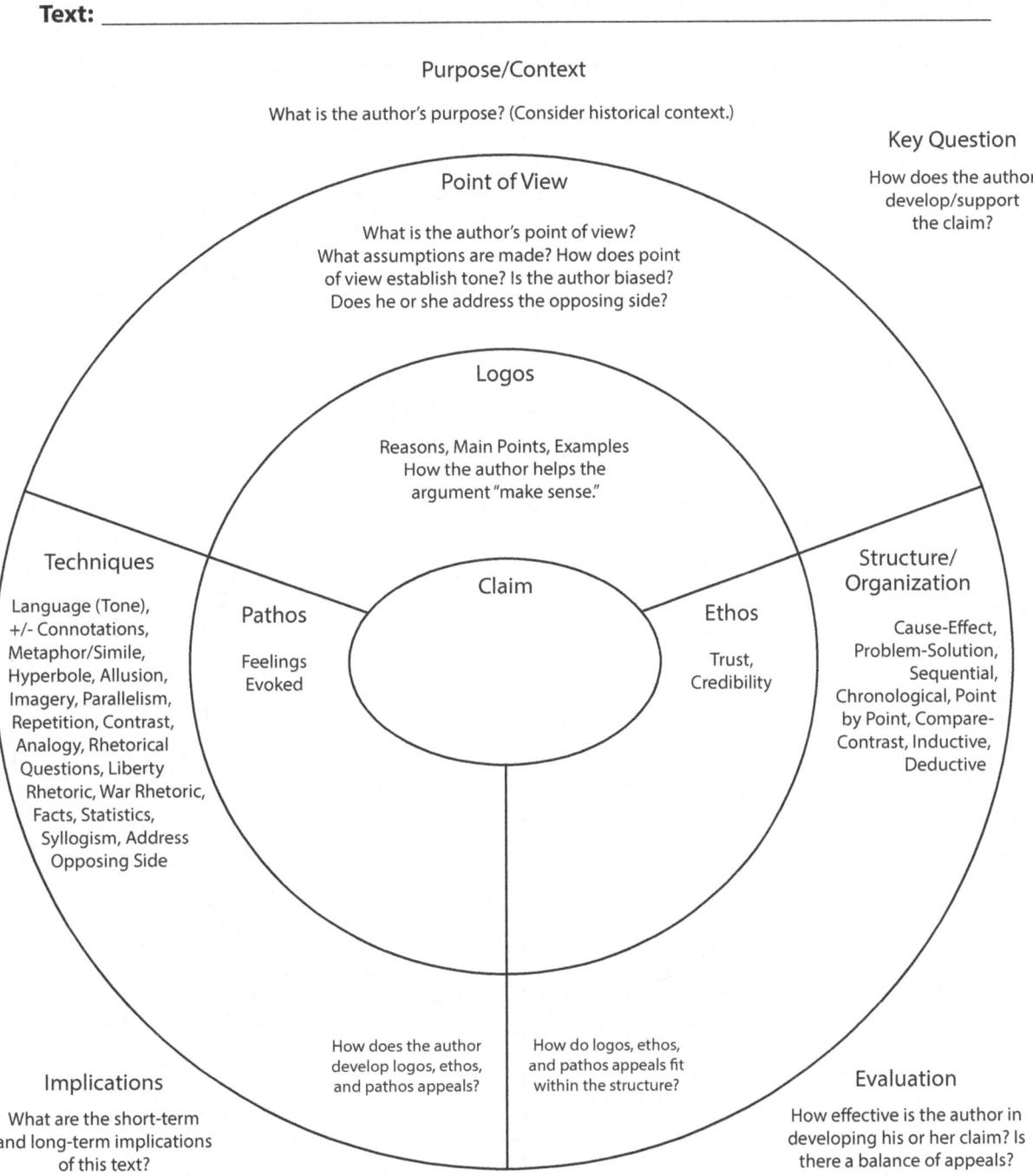

Created by Emily Mofield, Ed.D., & Tamra Stambaugh, Ph.D., 2015.

Created by Tamra Stambaugh, Ph.D., & Emily Mofield, Ed.D., 2017.

Encounters With Archetypes

BLANK TEXT ANALYSIS WHEEL

Directions: Draw arrows across elements to show connections.

Text: _____

Purpose/Context

Point of View

Point #2

Evidence

Techniques

Central Idea

Structure/Organization

Point #1

Point #3

Evidence

Evidence

Implications

Evaluation

Created by Emily Mofield, Ed.D., & Tamra Stambaugh, Ph.D., 2015.

Appendix B

TEXT ANALYSIS WHEEL GUIDE

Text: _____

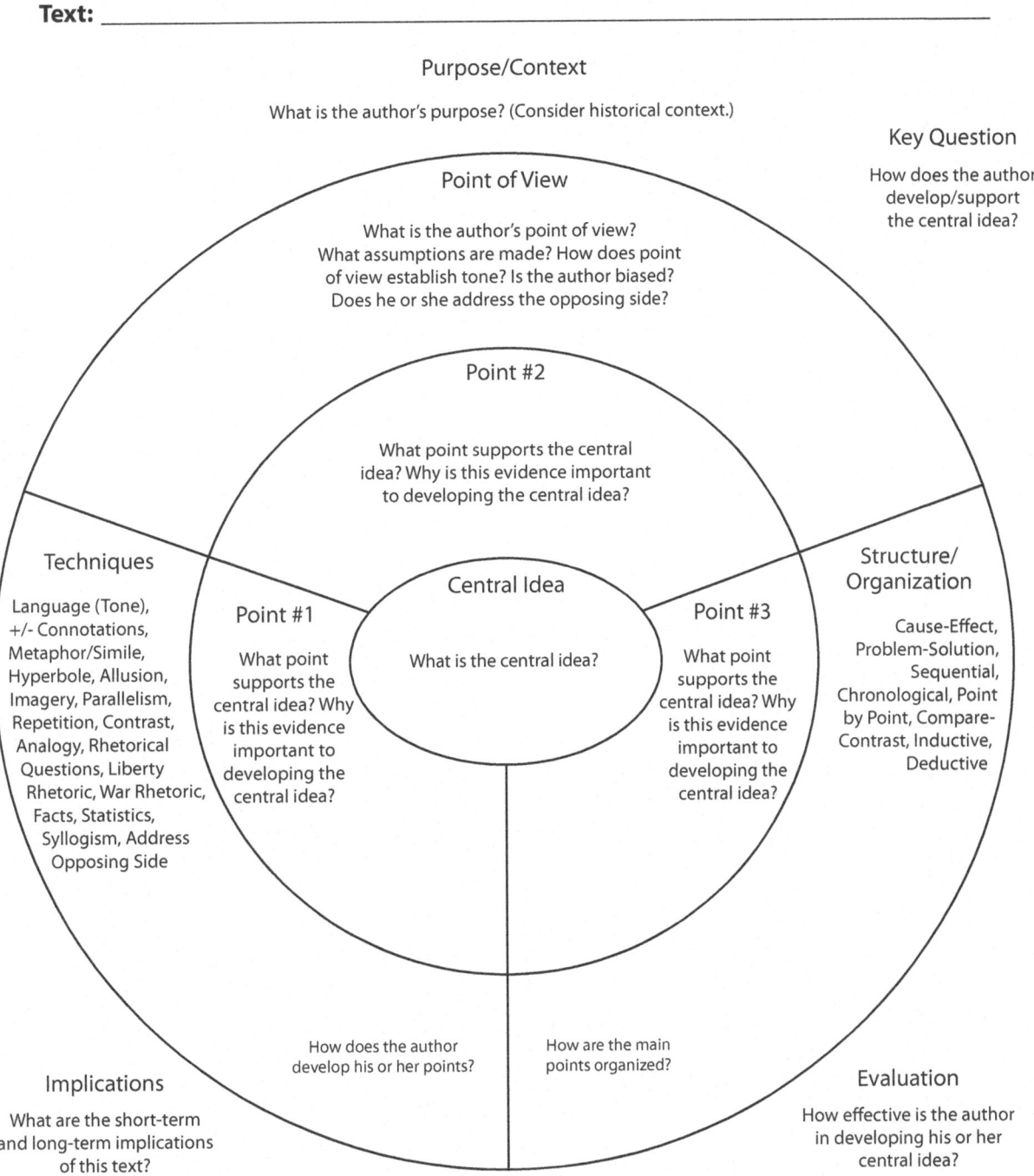

Created by Emily Mofield, Ed.D., & Tamra Stambaugh, Ph.D., 2015.

Encounters With Archetypes

BLANK VISUAL ANALYSIS WHEEL

Directions: Draw arrows across elements to show connections.

Art Piece: _____

- Purpose/Context
- Point of View
- Images
- Techniques
- Emotions
- Main Idea
- Artist Background
- Structure/Organization
- Implications
- Evaluation

Created by Tamra Stambaugh, Ph.D., & Emily Mofield, Ed.D., 2015.

Appendix B

VISUAL ANALYSIS WHEEL GUIDE

Art Piece: _____

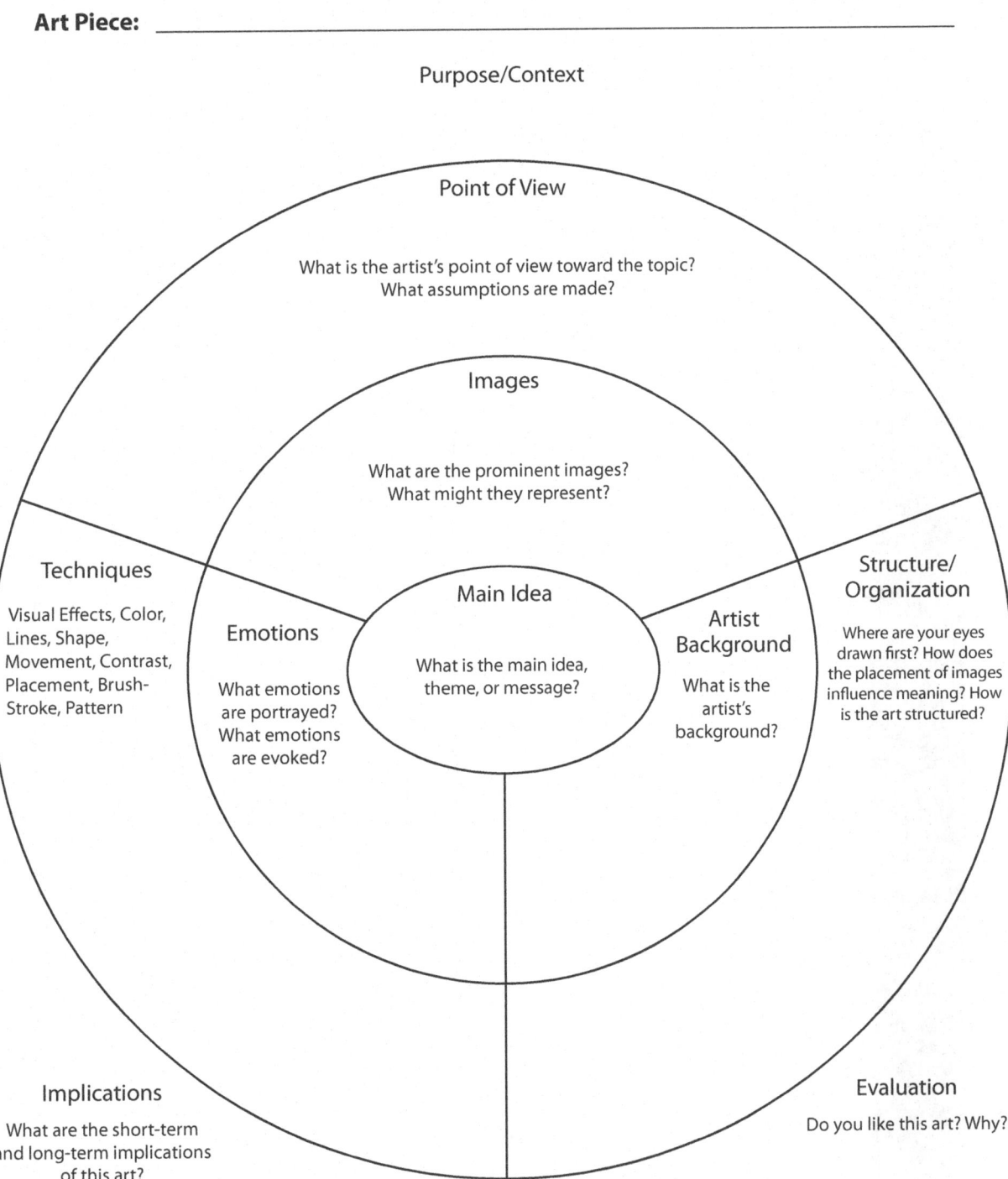

Created by Tamra Stambaugh, Ph.D., & Emily Mofield, Ed.D., 2015.

Encounters With Archetypes

CONCEPT ORGANIZER

Directions: How does each topic exemplify each generalization? What new generalization can you make?
1. Encounters allow for reflection and change.
2. Encounters allow for prediction.
3. Encounters can result in positive or negative outcomes.
4. Encounters may result in threats and opportunities.

	Connection to Other Concept	
Connection to Encounters Generalizations (1, 2, 3, 4)		
Lesson Topic		

Appendix B

REASONING ABOUT A SITUATION OR EVENT

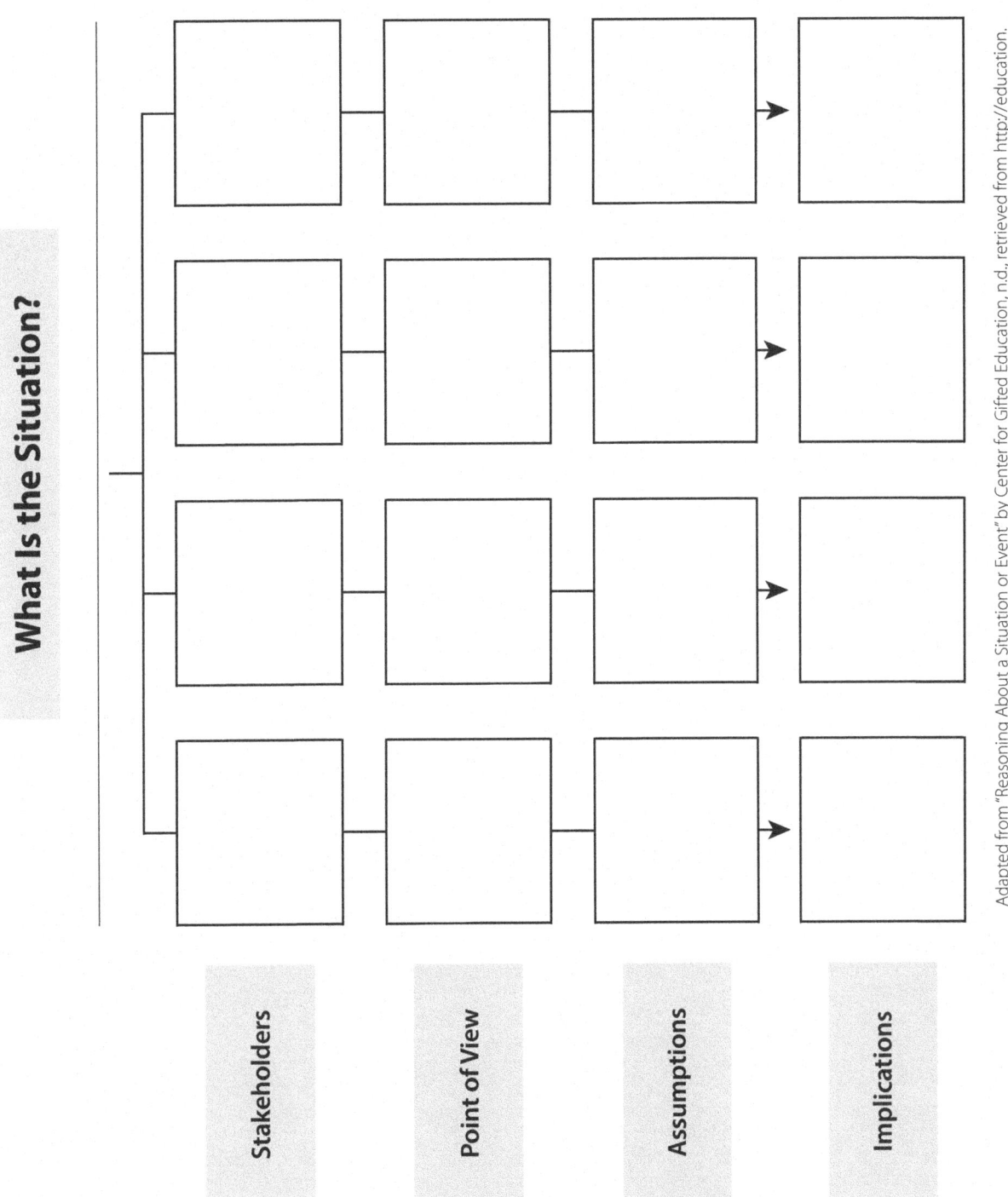

Appendix C
Rubrics

RUBRIC 1: PRODUCT RUBRIC

Name: _____ Date: _____ Lesson: _____

	Unacceptable/Needs Improvement	Fair	Acceptable	Excellent
Completion	Not turned in or late.	Missing key pieces.	Completed but lacks thought and professionalism.	Satisfactorily meets all requirements and expectations of the task.
Content/ Concept	Limited or vague connection.	Little connection from lesson content is made to the ideas of encounters.	Accurately relates lesson content ideas of encounters to assignment.	Insightfully relates the ideas of encounters to assignment.
Thinking	Limited or vague evidence.	Reasoning is inaccurate; lacks originality, logical conclusions, or substantial claims.	Demonstrates some evidence of higher level thinking (creativity, evaluation, or analysis).	Demonstrates substantial evidence of higher level thinking (creativity, analysis, or evaluation with evidence).
Student-Developed Criteria				

Comments:

RUBRIC 2: CULMINATING PROJECT RUBRIC

Name: _____ Date: _____

	Unacceptable/Needs Improvement	Fair	Acceptable	Excellent
Completion	Not turned in or late.	Missing key pieces	Completed but lacks thought and professionalism.	Satisfactorily meets all requirements and expectations of the task.
Evidence	Limited or no evidence.	Little support or elaboration to support ideas and generalizations.	Gives support/elaboration to support ideas.	Gives meaningful support/elaboration to support ideas and generalizations.
Concept	Limited or vague connection.	Little connection from unit content is made to the big idea encounters.	Accurately relates ideas of encounters to assignment.	Insightfully relates the big idea of encounters to assignment.
Content	Limited or no content application.	Vague connections are made to content.	Some connections to content are made with some evidence.	Synthesizes content across lessons with substantial support and evidence.
Process	Limited or vague evidence.	Reasoning is inaccurate; lacks originality, logical conclusions, or substantial claims.	Demonstrates some evidence of higher level thinking (creativity, evaluation, or analysis).	Provides insightful evidence to support higher level thinking (creativity, evaluation, or analysis) in developing complex conclusions.
Student-Developed Criteria				

Comments:

About the Authors

Tamra Stambaugh, Ph.D., is an associate research professor in special education and executive director of Programs for Talented Youth at Vanderbilt University. Stambaugh conducts research in gifted education with a focus on students living in rural settings, students of poverty, and curriculum and instructional interventions that promote gifted student learning. She is a frequent keynote speaker at national and international conferences and the coauthor/editor of several books and book chapters focused on curriculum and instructional development and differentiation, gifted students from low-income households, and gifted students from rural backgrounds. Stambaugh is the recipient of several awards, including the Margaret The Lady Thatcher Medallion for scholarship, service, and character from the William & Mary School of Education; the Doctoral Student Award, Early Leader Award, and multiple curriculum awards from the National Association for Gifted Children; the Legacy Book Award for best scholarly book in 2015 from the Texas Association for the Gifted and Talented; the Jo Patterson Service Award and Curriculum Award from the Tennessee Association for Gifted Children; and the Higher Education Award from the Ohio Association for Gifted Children.

Emily Mofield, Ed.D., is an assistant professor in the College of Education at Lipscomb University. She has taught and led gifted programs for 15 years and currently serves as the NAGC Chair for Curriculum Studies. She regularly presents professional development on effective instruction and differentiation for advanced learners. She is a National Board Certified Teacher in Language Arts and has been recognized as the Tennessee Association for Gifted Children Teacher of the Year. Three of her units coauthored with Tamra Stambaugh have been awarded the National Association for Gifted Children's Curriculum Award. She has written several research publications on the social-emotional needs of gifted students and is the corecipient (with Megan Parker Peters) of the NAGC Hollingworth Award for her research on growth mindset, perfectionism, and underachievement.

Eric Fecht, Ed.D., is an educational consultant for Vanderbilt Programs for Talented Youth. He supports a number of programs and special projects, including the Reading Academy at Vanderbilt. He taught elementary and middle school in Baltimore, MD, before helping develop gifted and talented programs in public schools in Abu Dhabi, U.A.E. He regularly consults with teachers who work with low-income gifted students and is involved in research related to serving low-income gifted students, relevancy in middle grade literacy, and coaching teachers of gifted students.

Kim Knauss is a gifted education middle school teacher for grades 6–8 for the Shelby County, TN, school system. She holds a B.A. in English and an M.Ed in secondary education. In 2006, Ms. Knauss transitioned into education as a middle school ELA teacher. As a mother of two sons, both of whom were identified as gifted and talented, she explored the field of gifted and talented education with emphasis on training and professional development. As an educator, she has dedicated herself to the development of the whole student with a focus on cultivating a love of learning. Before working as an educator, Ms. Knauss owned her own technical writing business. She specialized in the design and development of standard operating procedures, training materials, and business communication for Fortune 500 companies that include Procter & Gamble and Medtronic.

Common Core State Standards Alignment

Activities	Common Core State Standards
Lesson 1	RL.6.6 Explain how an author develops the point of view of the narrator or speaker in a text.
	RL.7.1 Cite several pieces of textual evidence to support analysis of what the text says explicitly as well as inferences drawn from the text.
	RL.7.3 Analyze how particular elements of a story or drama interact (e.g., how setting shapes the characters or plot).
	RL.8.2 Determine a theme or central idea of a text and analyze its development over the course of the text, including its relationship to the characters, setting, and plot; provide an objective summary of the text.
	RL.8.3 Analyze how particular lines of dialogue or incidents in a story or drama propel the action, reveal aspects of a character, or provoke a decision.
	W.7.10 Write routinely over extended time frames (time for research, reflection, and revision) and shorter time frames (a single sitting or a day or two) for a range of discipline-specific tasks, purposes, and audiences.
	SL.6.1 Engage effectively in a range of collaborative discussions (one-on-one, in groups, and teacher-led) with diverse partners on grade 6 topics, texts, and issues, building on others' ideas and expressing their own clearly.
	SL.7.2 Analyze the main ideas and supporting details presented in diverse media and formats (e.g., visually, quantitatively, orally) and explain how the ideas clarify a topic, text, or issue under study.

Activities	Common Core State Standards
Lesson 2	RL.7.1 Cite several pieces of textual evidence to support analysis of what the text says explicitly as well as inferences drawn from the text.
	RL.8.9 Analyze how a modern work of fiction draws on themes, patterns of events, or character types from myths, traditional stories, or religious works such as the Bible, including describing how the material is rendered new.
	RI.6.9 Compare and contrast one author's presentation of events with that of another (e.g., a memoir written by and a biography on the same person).
	W.7.10 Write routinely over extended time frames (time for research, reflection, and revision) and shorter time frames (a single sitting or a day or two) for a range of discipline-specific tasks, purposes, and audiences.
	SL.6.1 Engage effectively in a range of collaborative discussions (one-on-one, in groups, and teacher-led) with diverse partners on grade 6 topics, texts, and issues, building on others' ideas and expressing their own clearly.
Lesson 3	RL.6.6 Explain how an author develops the point of view of the narrator or speaker in a text.
	RL.7.1 Cite several pieces of textual evidence to support analysis of what the text says explicitly as well as inferences drawn from the text.
	RL.7.3 Analyze how particular elements of a story or drama interact (e.g., how setting shapes the characters or plot).
	RL.8.2 Determine a theme or central idea of a text and analyze its development over the course of the text, including its relationship to the characters, setting, and plot; provide an objective summary of the text.
	RL.8.3 Analyze how particular lines of dialogue or incidents in a story or drama propel the action, reveal aspects of a character, or provoke a decision.
	W.6.1 Write arguments to support claims with clear reasons and relevant evidence.
	W.7.10 Write routinely over extended time frames (time for research, reflection, and revision) and shorter time frames (a single sitting or a day or two) for a range of discipline-specific tasks, purposes, and audiences.
	SL.6.1 Engage effectively in a range of collaborative discussions (one-on-one, in groups, and teacher-led) with diverse partners on grade 6 topics, texts, and issues, building on others' ideas and expressing their own clearly.

Activities	Common Core State Standards
Lesson 4	RL.6.6 Explain how an author develops the point of view of the narrator or speaker in a text.
	RL.7.1 Cite several pieces of textual evidence to support analysis of what the text says explicitly as well as inferences drawn from the text.
	RL.7.3 Analyze how particular elements of a story or drama interact (e.g., how setting shapes the characters or plot).
	RL.8.2 Determine a theme or central idea of a text and analyze its development over the course of the text, including its relationship to the characters, setting, and plot; provide an objective summary of the text.
	RI.5.3 Explain the relationships or interactions between two or more individuals, events, ideas, or concepts in a historical, scientific, or technical text based on specific information in the text.
	W.6.1 Write arguments to support claims with clear reasons and relevant evidence.
	SL.6.1 Engage effectively in a range of collaborative discussions (one-on-one, in groups, and teacher-led) with diverse partners on grade 6 topics, texts, and issues, building on others' ideas and expressing their own clearly.
Lesson 5	RI.5.3 Explain the relationships or interactions between two or more individuals, events, ideas, or concepts in a historical, scientific, or technical text based on specific information in the text.
	RI.6.9 Compare and contrast one author's presentation of events with that of another (e.g., a memoir written by and a biography on the same person).
	RI.7.1 Cite several pieces of textual evidence to support analysis of what the text says explicitly as well as inferences drawn from the text.
	RI.7.2 Determine two or more central ideas in a text and analyze their development over the course of the text; provide an objective summary of the text.
	RI.7.5 Analyze the structure an author uses to organize a text, including how the major sections contribute to the whole and to the development of the ideas.
	W.6.1 Write arguments to support claims with clear reasons and relevant evidence.
	W.7.10 Write routinely over extended time frames (time for research, reflection, and revision) and shorter time frames (a single sitting or a day or two) for a range of discipline-specific tasks, purposes, and audiences.

Activities	Common Core State Standards
Lesson 5, *continued*	SL.6.1 Engage effectively in a range of collaborative discussions (one-on-one, in groups, and teacher-led) with diverse partners on grade 6 topics, texts, and issues, building on others' ideas and expressing their own clearly.
Lesson 6	RL.6.6 Explain how an author develops the point of view of the narrator or speaker in a text.
	RL.7.1 Cite several pieces of textual evidence to support analysis of what the text says explicitly as well as inferences drawn from the text.
	RL.7.3 Analyze how particular elements of a story or drama interact (e.g., how setting shapes the characters or plot).
	RL.8.2 Determine a theme or central idea of a text and analyze its development over the course of the text, including its relationship to the characters, setting, and plot; provide an objective summary of the text.
	RL.8.3 Analyze how particular lines of dialogue or incidents in a story or drama propel the action, reveal aspects of a character, or provoke a decision.
	W.6.1 Write arguments to support claims with clear reasons and relevant evidence.
	W.7.10 Write routinely over extended time frames (time for research, reflection, and revision) and shorter time frames (a single sitting or a day or two) for a range of discipline-specific tasks, purposes, and audiences.
	SL.6.1 Engage effectively in a range of collaborative discussions (one-on-one, in groups, and teacher-led) with diverse partners on grade 6 topics, texts, and issues, building on others' ideas and expressing their own clearly.
Lesson 7	RL.6.6 Explain how an author develops the point of view of the narrator or speaker in a text.
	RL.7.1 Cite several pieces of textual evidence to support analysis of what the text says explicitly as well as inferences drawn from the text.
	RL.7.3 Analyze how particular elements of a story or drama interact (e.g., how setting shapes the characters or plot).
	RL.8.2 Determine a theme or central idea of a text and analyze its development over the course of the text, including its relationship to the characters, setting, and plot; provide an objective summary of the text.

Activities	Common Core State Standards
Lesson 7, *continued*	W.6.1 Write arguments to support claims with clear reasons and relevant evidence.
	W.7.10 Write routinely over extended time frames (time for research, reflection, and revision) and shorter time frames (a single sitting or a day or two) for a range of discipline-specific tasks, purposes, and audiences.
	SL.6.1 Engage effectively in a range of collaborative discussions (one-on-one, in groups, and teacher-led) with diverse partners on grade 6 topics, texts, and issues, building on others' ideas and expressing their own clearly.
Lesson 8	RL.6.6 Explain how an author develops the point of view of the narrator or speaker in a text.
	RL.7.1 Cite several pieces of textual evidence to support analysis of what the text says explicitly as well as inferences drawn from the text.
	RL.7.3 Analyze how particular elements of a story or drama interact (e.g., how setting shapes the characters or plot).
	RL.8.2 Determine a theme or central idea of a text and analyze its development over the course of the text, including its relationship to the characters, setting, and plot; provide an objective summary of the text.
	RI.7.4 Determine the meaning of words and phrases as they are used in a text, including figurative, connotative, and technical meanings; analyze the impact of a specific word choice on meaning and tone.
	W.6.1 Write arguments to support claims with clear reasons and relevant evidence.
	SL.6.1 Engage effectively in a range of collaborative discussions (one-on-one, in groups, and teacher-led) with diverse partners on grade 6 topics, texts, and issues, building on others' ideas and expressing their own clearly.
Lesson 9	RL.8.3 Analyze how particular lines of dialogue or incidents in a story or drama propel the action, reveal aspects of a character, or provoke a decision.
	W.7.10 Write routinely over extended time frames (time for research, reflection, and revision) and shorter time frames (a single sitting or a day or two) for a range of discipline-specific tasks, purposes, and audiences.

Activities	Common Core State Standards
Lesson 9, *continued*	SL.6.1 Engage effectively in a range of collaborative discussions (one-on-one, in groups, and teacher-led) with diverse partners on grade 6 topics, texts, and issues, building on others' ideas and expressing their own clearly.
Lesson 10	W.6.1 Write arguments to support claims with clear reasons and relevant evidence.
Lesson 10	W.7.10 Write routinely over extended time frames (time for research, reflection, and revision) and shorter time frames (a single sitting or a day or two) for a range of discipline-specific tasks, purposes, and audiences.
Lesson 10	SL.6.1 Engage effectively in a range of collaborative discussions (one-on-one, in groups, and teacher-led) with diverse partners on grade 6 topics, texts, and issues, building on others' ideas and expressing their own clearly.
Lesson 11	W.7.3 Write narratives to develop real or imagined experiences or events using effective technique, relevant descriptive details, and well-structured event sequences.
Lesson 11	W.7.4 Produce clear and coherent writing in which the development, organization, and style are appropriate to task, purpose, and audience.
Lesson 11	SL.6.1 Engage effectively in a range of collaborative discussions (one-on-one, in groups, and teacher-led) with diverse partners on grade 6 topics, texts, and issues, building on others' ideas and expressing their own clearly.